LIVING WITH THE
Environment
IN THE PINE RIVERS SHIRE

John Bowden

for Pine Rivers Shire Council

PINE RIVERS

Published by the Pine Rivers Shire Council

PINE RIVERS

Requests for this book should be made to:

Pine Rivers Shire Council
PO Box 5070
Strathpine Q 4500
Australia

Phone: (07) 3205 0691
Fax: (07) 3881 3204

Written and illustrated by John Bowden
With thanks to Jim McEvoy and the Environmental Services Branch, Pine Rivers Shire Council

Photographs courtesy of Pine Rivers Shire Council (PRSC), Department of Environment and Heritage (DEH), Queensland Museum (QM), Brisbane Forest Park (BFP), Richard McGuire(RM), Kate Honnef (KH), John Bowden (JB) and Jim McEvoy (JM).

Designed by Russell Morris and Amanda Duson, Community Support Unit, Pine Rivers Shire Council

Published by the Pine Rivers Shire Council

First Printed 1999

Cover photo of the Platypus courtesy of Department of Environment and Heritage
Inside front cover photo of the native Red Passion Flower, John Bowden
Back cover photo of the Powerful Owl courtesy of Richard McGuire

ISBN 0-9586 337-0-3

Printing: Fergies, Brisbane

PREFACE

Pine Rivers Shire is one of the fastest growing local authorities in Queensland. With this growth has come a passionate desire to protect and enhance the Shire's natural environment, its character and heritage.

Our residents, of all ages, have an increasing interest in the natural habitat around their homes and in the nearby parks and forests and we find that there is an ever-increasing demand for information relating to the flora, fauna and heritage of the many diverse districts in the Shire.

In response, the Council has employed John Bowden, a long time Pine Rivers Shire resident, teacher and environmentalist, to prepare this book as one of the many steps Council has taken to form a co-operative partnership with the community to care for our environmental future.

John has done a wonderful job in producing *"Living with the Environment in the Pine Rivers Shire"* and has worked closely with our environmental-focused community groups, such as the Wildlife Preservation Society, the Society for Growing Australian Plants, Waterwatch, the North & South Pine Integrated Catchment Association and the Dayboro Landholders Conservation Group. Many other organisations and residents have unselfishly given their time to contribute to the contents of the book. Their involvement has been much appreciated.

I would like to make specific mention of Councillor Brian Burke whose inspiration it was to produce this book. Councillor Burke's own efforts to protect the lifestyle of the Samford Valley in particular have set an example which has been a guiding force in responsible and sensitive development throughout the Shire over the past twenty-five years. The members of the Pine Rivers Shire Council have also given this project their unreserved support.

Y. A. Chapman

Yvonne Chapman
Mayor
Pine Rivers Shire

CONTENTS

LIVING WITH THE ENVIRONMENT IN PINE RIVERS SHIRE

PART ONE - OUR EARLY HISTORY

PART TWO - FROM NOW ON

CONTENTS

LIVING WITH THE ENVIRONMENT IN PINE RIVERS SHIRE

CONTENTS

PART THREE - UNTIL NOW

CONTENTS

APPENDICES

FOREWORD

Pine Rivers Shire Council is to be commended for this excellent publication which is timely, comprehensive and informative.

In a time when we are constantly assailed with figures about the destruction of our environment a book such as this telling individuals what they can do in their garden or rural subdivision is of enormous value. Never has the old cliche "Think globally, act locally," been more apposite. Our community is looking for answers with *"Living with the Environment"* arriving at the right time.

Few books today have five pages of Contents and so many sections, but John Bowden and the Council needed no padding to reach its size. Every line is packed with information, sometimes several facts to a sentence, and it has to be so when the width of the book's coverage is considered. From the environmental history of Gondwana, the Aborigines and early European settlement to advice on slope-binding, fire-retardant plants and a host of environmental problems, it is all here.

As well as being a good read, *Living with the Environment* is a font of wisdom and information. There has long been a need for a comprehensive list of animal "problems" and potential solutions as is now found in this publication. Final detailed chapters covering the right plant in the right place are as comprehensive as those in any local publication I have seen. Practical tips about encouraging native animals will mean a better life for some of our wildlife.

Living with the Environment has so many parts able to be used all over south-east Queensland that I am confident it will have far wider readership than originally anticipated by its authors.

With more publications like this we could feel increasingly confident about the future of our environment. Pine Rivers Shire will be a better place because of those who conceived, designed, funded and wrote *Living with the Environment.*

Pat Comben
Former Qld
Environment Minister

Mountain Stream - Terrors Creek, Dayboro (PRSC)

PART ONE

OUR EARLY

History

CHAPTER

The First Australians

Aborigines have been in Australia for at least 40 thousand years. They may well have been here for 60 thousand or even 120 thousand years (T. Flannery, 1994 p. 153). It is likely that the first people migrated from south-east Asia during one or more times of low sea level during ice ages. At these times the distance across the deep water separating the islands on the Asian crustal plate from those of the Australian plate would have been as little as 50 to 100 kilometres. Having crossed these narrow deep stretches people could have walked to the Australian mainland. Traditional belief is that Aborigines have always been here - since the Dreamtime.

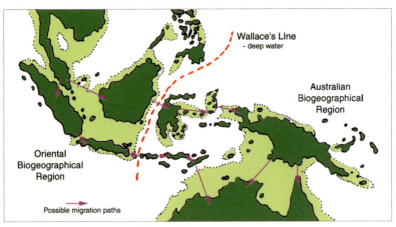

Migration of the first Australians

A different world

The new arrivals found a land very different from that left behind. The old world animals, such as buffalo, deer, elephants, dogs, tigers, monkeys and apes, were not to be found here. Instead, there were marsupials, monotremes and giant flightless birds. Many animal species which lived in Australia at this time are now extinct. As happened in many other countries, the arrival of humans heralded the extinction of the 'mega-fauna'. Giant kangaroos, wombats and emus, and the bullock-sized diprotodons were among those that died out as a result of Aboriginal hunting pressures and a drying climate. These largest animals needed great amounts of food and, being uncommon, were most vulnerable. The terrifying, eight-metre-long monitor lizard, Megalania, was wiped out because, like its living relatives the goannas, it probably layed eggs in decaying leaf litter and did not protect them. Aborigines would have relished these and their young as food. It is likely that the species was deliberately targetted for extermination (R. Neil, pers com 1994). Megalania, together with a giant python, may be the origin of myths and paintings of serpents and bunyips (N. Butler, pers com, 1996).

When people first arrived, it is very likely that most animals, not having had any contact with humans, would have had no fear of them. Hunting entailed simply walking up to animals and killing them as they stood there (T. Flannery, 1994, Chap. 17). Eventually however, after animals learned that humans had to be avoided, successful hunting required experience, patience, endurance and often considerable skills.

Many of the plants too were very different. Centuries of experiment and innovation increased the number of species that could be used as food and revealed the preparation necessary to render poisonous plants edible. Species with medicinal properties, those with the best fibres for string and rope and those suitable for making weapons, baskets, carrying vessels and other useful implements became part of everyday knowledge (See G. Blainey, 1982).

Impact and change

The greatest Aboriginal impact on the Australian environment resulted from the use of fire. Before Aborigines arrived, widespread fires, caused by lightning strikes, would have occurred very infrequently. Until then, vast areas of eastern and northern Australia were covered by rainforests (T. Flannery, 1994, p. 224). The soil fertility, the drainage, slope, aspect, proximity to the sea and so on, determined the type of rainforest in each region, but most were probably depauperate, drought-resistant 'dry-vine-scrubs'. The moisture transpired by these forests would have influenced the climate, making it relatively humid with higher rainfall (T. Flannery, 1994, p. 234). Charcoal fragments and a change in the frequency and types of pollen in continental shelf and lake deposits give an indication of the time of arrival of Aborigines and their impact. Fire-tolerant and fire-dependent species such as the eucalypts and wattles, now typical of the Australian landscape, replaced previous plant communities. Widespread erosion would have occurred, leading to deposition of silt in streams and protected coastal areas. This increase in alluvial deposits encouraged growth of greater areas of mangroves (T. Flannery, 1994, p. 227). In turn, there would have been higher populations of fish, molluscs and crustaceans. Eventually new balances would have been reached.

Adapting to a different environment

Because of the extremely capricious nature of the Australian climate, influenced by the El Nino Southern Oscillation and typified by long periods of drought and unpredictable flooding rains, Aborigines never took up farming. Instead, they managed their country by use of fire. After hundreds of generations of experience and familiarity with the use and effects of fire, they developed a fire regime of frequent, cool fires. Fires, burnt at the right seasons and at the best time of day, did not need to be put out (J. Flood, 1993). The result was a mosaic of habitats in various stages of recovery. Hot fires, resulting from natural causes, deliberately lit or because of human miscalculation, could not burn far. They added to the mosaic and encouraged further diversity of habitat. The unburnt and regrown areas provided cover and breeding sites for ground-dwelling mammals, reptiles and birds. Recently burnt patches provided green food for animals, stimulating many to breed. These green areas attracted feeding animals, allowing close approach for easier spearing, netting or trapping. Because of the possibility of close approach to prey, and the forested and woodland nature of the country, local Aborigines did not use spear-throwers (C. Campbell Petrie, 1904, p. 102). The types of animals and plants encouraged by this fire regime were those most sought after as food - small to medium mammals, herbaceous plants and others stimulated by fire to grow, flower and fruit. The several hours needed each day to procure all their needs allowed Aborigines time for leisure; and time to attend to cultural, social and spiritual pursuits.

Samford 'bora' ring - a ceremonial place

Dohles Rocks midden - a camping place

Social adaptation

In coastal areas, in times of past sea level change, social stability of groups and inter-clan relationships must have been severely tested. Territories, greatly expanded during times of lowered sea level during ice ages, were inexorably consumed by the rising sea as interglacial periods approached. Within a lifetime, coastal people could have seen thousands of hectares of their hunting grounds covered as the sea rose. They had to move inland, forcing other groups to do likewise. However, people of Aboriginal groups have extensive links that connect them to others far away - links that would greatly lessen the impact of such destabilising events. They developed relationships with members of neighbouring groups and groups farther away - trading links, marriage and totemic links. Some of the most important bonding customs, developed over tens of thousands of years, were the extended visits to other territories for feasts and the sharing of abundant resources, and culture. The interchange of information, stories, dances and songs, the trading of weapons, other manufactured goods and raw materials, and the taking and giving of brides helped to promote goodwill. These customs forged connections that could be called upon in times of drought and other hardships. Survival of groups within their own territories was aided by the establishment of refuge areas, food taboos applied according to age, sex or totem, and population control measures. Coevolution of these social adaptations with the environment helped Aboriginal societies to survive the most severe of natural disasters.

A new predator

About four thousand years ago the dingo was brought to Australia, probably by visiting traders seeking sea slugs on the northern coast. Dingos occur throughout most of south-east Asia. The Aborigines adopted it as a companion and hunting aid but it soon became feral. This efficient hunter no doubt had a great impact on populations of many prey species.

Two animals that could not compete with the dingo and were forced into extinction on the mainland were the Thylacine or 'Tasmanian tiger' (*Thylacinus cynocephalus*) and the Tasmanian devil (*Sarcophilus harrisii*), both of which became extinct (except in Tasmania) about 3000 years ago. These large carnivores once hunted in the forests and woodlands of the Pine Rivers valley. Their survival in Tasmania was possible because the dingo could not cross Bass Strait, which formed again about ten thousand years ago at the end of the last ice age.

Dingo - arrived in Australia about
4000 years ago

Tasmanian devil - now extinct on
mainland Australia

Aborigines of Pine Rivers Valley

In the Pine Rivers area, at the time of arrival of Europeans, there were dialects of probably three Aboriginal languages spoken within the Shire boundaries. The 'North Pine Clan' spoke a dialect of Yugerabul; to the west the Gurumgnar people spoke a dialect of Wakka; and to the east and north, the Undambi dialect was of the Kabi (Gubi) language. These three groups had much social interaction. They shared in bunya feasts at the Blackall Range and Bunya Mountains, and there were feasts of fish, dugong, turtle and other sea foods at the coast and on the islands of Moreton Bay. There are ceremonial rings at Samford, Samsonvale, Petrie and Kippa Ring where these groups met for combined rituals. Because 'bora' rings are very often near the perimeters of territories, the siting of these local ones may give some indication as to boundaries. As the 'Brisbane blacks' died out, the victims of disease, alcoholism and 'dispersal', they were replaced by refugees from outer regions. These desperate people moved to escape persecution and starvation when white squatters took over their best hunting grounds. They were no longer allowed to burn their country and often were prevented from passing through their hunting grounds, now appropriated for grazing land. Relocation of people from various tribal lands makes for confusion about the old boundaries, especially if writings and utterances of later authorities are not compared with those of earliest observers.

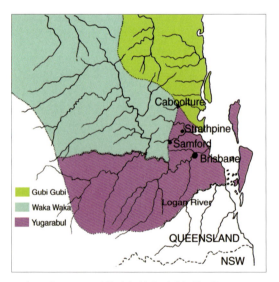

Approximate extent of Aboriginal 'tribes' of the Pine Rivers area

Canoeing - North Pine River (PRSC)

CHAPTER **2**

The Coming of the Whites

Ex-convicts

The first white people to set foot on land that is now part of the Pine Rivers Shire were Pamphlett, Parsons and Finnegan, ticket-of-leave ex-convicts who had become lost during a storm at sea off Sydney. They thought that they had been blown south and so sailed north in an attempt to reach Sydney. They were in fact blown to the north and on April 15, 1823 were shipwrecked on Moreton Island. The island Aborigines cared for them and gave them a canoe so as to reach Stradbroke Island. Here they constructed a dugout canoe and used this to cross to the mainland, landing near Ormiston on June 5. Unable to cross the Brisbane River they journeyed upstream to Oxley Creek where they found some canoes. After returning downstream they followed the coast northward to the Redcliffe Peninsula.

In November 1823, Pamphlett and Finnegan were rescued by John Oxley, on the 'Mermaid', at Bribie Island where they had been living with the Joonoobarrie clan (J. Lergessner, 1993). Parsons, who at the time was further north, near Noosa, was not picked up until the following year. Finnegan spoke of a large river (the Brisbane) they had found earlier that year and guided Oxley by mistake to the Pine River. As a result Oxley called it the 'Deception River'. They travelled upstream and landed at Oxleys Inlet, now commemorated by the John Oxley Reserve. Aborigines were 'in great numbers' and Oxley was impressed by 'a great many very fine cypresses (Hoop Pine)' and 'good soil'. He also reported a 'weir' across the river, probably a fish trap.

John Oxley Reserve and Oxleys Inlet - time has brought change

Convicts

In September the following year, accompanied by botanist and explorer, Alan Cunningham, Oxley returned to the Pine River and cut Hoop Pine logs for 'pine spars'. He had travelled from 'Red Cliff', the penal colony newly established by Lieutenant Miller. By the end of the year the Redcliffe settlement was abandoned because of mosquitoes, a shortage of suitable water, and troublesome Aborigines. Soldiers guarding convicts who were cutting firewood (near Yebri Creek) shot and killed an Aborigine who had taken an axe. This, understandably, led to retaliatory actions by the original inhabitants. In 1825 the penal colony was re-established at Brisbane. The Aborigines began to refer to 'Red Cliff' as 'Humpybong', meaning dead houses.

This was not the last that the local Aborigines saw of white people. Convicts, such as John Graham, David Bracewell and James Davis, who escaped from Brisbane, travelled through this area on their way north and lived for many years with the Aborigines. It is likely that others were killed, though many were returned to the 'Mi-an-jin' (Brisbane) penal colony for rewards - and possibly in the hope that the British would go away, as they had from Humpybong.

Missionaries

In 1837, a German Mission was established at Zions Hill, Nundah. Several journeys were made to the north as part of the missionary work and to establish a mission out-station on Stony Creek (near Burpengary). They crossed the South Pine River near Cashs Crossing. The mission failed but many of the mission group stayed to become some of the earliest free settlers.

Squatters

In 1840, the Archer brothers established Durundur Station (near Woodford). This was outside the 50 mile (80 kilometre) limit from the Moreton Bay settlement required by colonial regulations. Others had taken up selections outside the Pine Rivers' boundaries at Kilcoy and Mt Brisbane. The 50 miles restriction was lifted in 1842. This allowed free settlement closer to Brisbane. In the same year the Archers blazed the first European 'road' through the Pine Rivers district to Brisbane. It went via the German Station (Nundah), Eaglefarm and Breakfast Creek. On the return trip they travelled along what is now known as Old North Road. Going through Brisbane saved the squatters the long inland journey down to Maitland. It is likely that the original path followed by Old North Road is that used by Aborigines for thousands of years on their way north and south to attend festivals (J. Steele 1978).

Old North Road - one of the oldest sections
of road reserve in Queensland still in the original condition

Squatters, Settlers and Aborigines

Captain Griffin, in 1843, selected a vast area of land north of the North Pine River, known as 'Whiteside'. The following year, William Joyner 'took up' the land between the North and South Pine Rivers, which he called 'Samsonvale'. Sheep were the first animals brought in to graze the luxuriant woodlands created by the burning practices of the Aborigines. However, the relatively high rainfall, especially during the hotter months, caused footrot; and spear grass ruined fleeces and killed some sheep. Cattle were much more suited to the environment. Aborigines resented the loss of their lands and found it necessary to hunt the new grazing animals which competed with their traditional food - animals such as kangaroos, wallabies and bandicoots. Shooting and poisoning of Aborigines, and spearing and clubbing of white shepherds and settlers were the outcome, and the beginnings of further conflict.

Surveying of lands outside of Brisbane began in 1842. This and changes to the Land Acts enabled others to acquire smaller portions of land. For many of the first squatters this was a chance to obtain legal possession of at least some of their originally vast land holdings.

Resistance from Aboriginal clans continued. For a time, enthusiasm to take up land in some areas was greatly diminished by the reporting of the success of attacks on personnel, stock and possessions. In 1858 Tom Petrie was able to acquire ten square miles of Whiteside from Mrs Griffin because 'it was unsafe for anyone to go down there' and 'they could do nothing with cattle on account of the blacks' (C. Campbell Petrie, 1904, p. 180). Tom Petrie succeeded at 'Murrumba' (meaning good) because he had the blessing, help and protection of Dalaipi , 'head man of the North Pine tribe', and his son Dal-ngang.

Would Tom Petrie recognise "Murrumba" as it is today?

With the influx of white people came diseases to which Aborigines had had no previous exposure, and therefore no immunity. Measles, influenza, tuberculosis, small pox and venereal diseases were for them often fatal. The increased intake of processed foods such as flour and sugar did not assist their resistance to infectious diseases. Loss of their lands and the collapse of tribal custom and law led to despair and alcoholism. For people who, in their original state, were rarely sick, recovered quickly from even severe injuries, who remained active well into old age and for whom obesity was unknown, this was a calamitous change that took place in just one or two generations. The stationing of the native police at Sandgate in 1852 led to the dispersal of many of the last camps where Aborigines still lived, at least partly, a traditional life style. The destruction of the 'Pine River camp' in 1858 (E. Fisher, 1992, p. 46) is one of many such incidents which led ultimately to the removal of nearly all Aborigines to 'reserves', such as those at Stradbroke, Bribie, Durundur and Barambah (Cherbourg).

3

Environmental Effects of European Settlement

Timber

One of the earliest European interests in the country of South-east Queensland, apart from grazing, was in timber. The most valuable tree species were targeted first. Red cedar (*Toona australis*) was sought out, not only as a valuable export but for local building. Because it was at first extremely common its uses included the construction of house walls, floors, ceilings, and frames, even roof shingles, as well as joinery and furniture. Today red cedar is rare and, because of attacks by tip-borers, is not suited to monoculture in forestry plots. Other species which had a similar history of over-exploitation leading to rarity include white beech, silky oak, rosewood, crow's ash, deep yellowwood, yellowwood and hoop pine.

Hoop Pine

When he explored the Pine River, John Oxley showed great interest in hoop pines as timber for masts. His interest was followed by that of others seeking supplies of the species for its exceptional quality as a general building timber. One of the first surveyors of the district, Robert Dixon, in 1842 named the North Pine the 'Eden' River (J. Steele, 1975 p. 268), an indication of the great beauty of the riverine forests and their numerous emergent hoop pines. Many early settlers of the Pine Valley turned to timber cutting instead of agriculture (D. Dorman & D. Cryle, 1992, p. 108). Natural stands of mature hoop pines are now rare in the Pine Shire but they are still evident in our landscapes and more are being planted. Similarly, the once common giant red cedars, white beech and silky oaks have all but disappeared from our forests, as they have from other parts of eastern Australia. The historical, economic, ecological and aesthetic value of the hoop pine to the Pine Rivers is commemorated in the Shire Council logo.

Hoop pine

The Pine Rivers Shire logo

Scrub

When the large, first land holdings were subdivided, and even before this, rainforest ('scrub') was targeted for clearing. The belief was that here soil was richest. This was true in some cases, such as on alluvial flats of creeks and rivers, and in places where the parent rocks are dark and volcanic, such as those found at Mt Glorious, Mt Mee and near Dayboro. In many places though, rainforest existed on much less-fertile soils, such as those derived from shaly rocks and sandstone. This is because in some areas rainforests advanced out from the fertile areas. Other sites had not been subject to fire. Once cleared and used for crops however, leaching by rainwater soon proved the true infertility of many 'scrub' soils. The rainforests had only existed there because of the efficient re-cycling of nutrients in soil built and maintained by the rainforests themselves. What is more, rainforests were usually easier to clear and keep clear than open forests, where stumps and logs took years to rot and where, even after burning, there was persistent regrowth of eucalypts and wattles. A system called 'driving' was used to clear heavy rainforest. A large tree, the 'driver', was crashed down upon a series of others partly cut through (W. Francis, 1981, p. 10). Stumps and logs rotted away in a few years. Burning of the fallen rubble near the forest also killed the fire-sensitive trees, and many older trees died after exposure of their trunks to sunlight (W. Francis, 1981, p. 10).

Rainforests on flood plains of streams were first to go, and then those on plateaux made accessible by the first primitive roads. Clearing of forests allowed the first dairy farms to be established. With closer settlement, most land suitable for agriculture became cultivation for corn, fodder, small crops and, on the flats, sugar cane. Later, clearing of hillsides for more grazing land and to grow bananas, pineapples, pawpaws and other fruits, exposed slopes to water erosion and slope failure.

The result of clearing steep slopes

Rainforest Remnants

In the Pine Rivers area practically all of the lowland rainforest is gone. One remnant of particular importance is Bell's Scrub at Lawnton. It is situated on the flood-plain of the North Pine River on an island created by gravel extraction, and is on private land. Though only a few hectares in area and degraded by invasive exotic weeds, it has a rich diversity of native species, some rare. It serves as a reminder of the original richness and beauty of the North and South Pine River flats. Bell's Scrub is a source of invaluable propagation material for rehabilitation plantings of catchments and habitat within and outside the Shire. Many species of small trees, shrubs, vines and smaller plants have potential for use in home gardens and street planting. The owners are eager for the protection, rehabilitation and preservation of this valuable remnant.

Bell's Scrub - an invaluable lowland rainforest remnant

The almost continuous riverine forests, that in previous times clothed one or both banks of streams of the Pine Rivers' catchment, are now fragmented. A few important remnants of closed riverine forest survive, such as in John Oxley Reserve, Gold's Scrub at Samsonvale, and Neilsen's Scrub at Brendale.

Neilsen's Scrub

On the mountains of the D'Aguilar Range, we have some lush areas of sub-tropical rainforest. These are mostly associated with rich soils derived from Tertiary basalt flows, and moist, nutrient-rich alluvial valleys, especially on the southern and eastern slopes of the ranges. Larger forests are protected in national parks, others are in State Forests and some are on private property. Boombana and Maiala National Parks are popular places where our magnificent rainforests may be enjoyed and studied.

Maiala National Park

Hardwood

Timber trees of open forest and woodland were also much sought after by early and later colonists. Some of the best hardwood timbers in the world occur in eastern Australia. Ironbark was cut for fence posts, house stumps, poles, sleepers and timber. Up until just after the second world war, most homes used wood-burning stoves for cooking and heating. The dairy industry also used large quantities of wood for fuel. Ironbark, because it burns with a persistent high heat and splits readily, was considered the premier firewood. In areas close to settlement it was becoming increasingly scarce. Since the increased use of electric and gas stoves, and the decline of the dairying industry, many areas that were almost treeless fifty years ago have regenerated so well that they are now regarded by some people as original habitat. Other hardwood species cut for their timber include tallowwood, rose gum, blue gum, grey gum, spotted gum, bloodwood, blackbutt and brushbox.

There were many sawmills in the Pine Rivers area. Timber, as well as being one of the first industries of the district, supplied settlers with the raw materials for constructing their first slab huts, then later, for more substantial dwellings. Sale of timber also provided a means of affording the upgrade of cattle herds and machinery.

Ringbarking and clearing

Not only rainforest areas were cleared to make way for grazing and cultivation. Open forests and woodlands were often ringbarked and almost totally cleared. The mistaken belief was that this was sound land management. The initial good growth of grass was not sustained after the nutrients from leaf decay were removed by grazing, leaching and erosion. It was often a requirement of land settlement that clearing be done; and, until quite recently, the expense of ringbarking and clearing was tax deductible for rural land owners. Much valuable timber was therefore wasted, land degraded and wildlife habitat needlessly destroyed.

Often, to make available the maximum amount of land for cultivation, trees were cleared to the very edges of streams. Stock also grazed the undergrowth on banks, and the emergent plants. Erosion and scouring of levees and flood plains, and the collapse of stream banks were the results.

The waste in past land clearing

The result of clearing stream-bank vegetation

Lowlands

Historically, in south-east Queensland, lowland ecosystems have been held in very low esteem. They were considered expendable; and this general assessment of their worth did not change until fairly recently. Even now, some people still mistakenly believe mangroves, salt marsh flats, marine couch grasslands, swamp she-oak woodlands, melaleuca wetlands, and other lowland habitats to be virtually useless.

Lowland habitats have a beauty of their own

Mangroves in rural areas provided supplementary grazing for cattle. In residential areas they were often cleared to improve the sea view. Because they were thought to be smelly, mosquito-breeding, worthless mudflats they often became unofficial or public rubbish dumps. Some mangrove species provided good timber for the making of boat keels. To maintain a supply of this resource, laws were passed to protect them. However, the laws were very seldom, if ever, enforced.

Reclamation projects and old dump sites in mangrove areas now provide space for sports fields and golf courses. The latest land uses that pose a danger to mangrove areas are canal developments and marinas. In the Pine Rivers Shire we are lucky that our coastal mangroves escaped most of the misuse that others of their kind suffered in nearby local government areas. They are now protected here because Hays Inlet is a declared fish-habitat reserve.

The major importance of mangroves lies in their production. Leaves, twigs, fruit, wood and other plant products fall to the mud below and begin the food webs that continue with bacteria and other microscopic organisms. Immense numbers of crustaceans (such as crabs, yabbies, shrimps and prawns), molluscs (snails, slugs, whelks, oysters and other bivalves) and worms are part of the food chains that support many other animals (such as fish, birds, and the beautiful Australian water rat). Most of the fish, crabs and prawns caught by our commercial fisheries in Moreton Bay depend on mangroves for their existence. The nutrients that come from the breakdown of plant and animal products in mangrove habitats also wash to nearby environments - to sandy and muddy flats, tidal streams and seagrass beds, where other acquatic plant and animal communities flourish. There is historical evidence that dugong once fed on seagrass flats at the mouth of the Pine River (T. Petrie, 1904 p.66).

Mangroves help protect shorelines and tidal stream banks from erosion. They support endemic species such as mangrove honeyeaters, mangrove warblers (gerygones) and mangrove kingfishers. As well, they are places of unique beauty. Mangroves, in the past, have had a reputation as breeding grounds for mosquitoes and biting midges. Studies have shown however that it is the clearing and alteration of mangrove habitats that favour the breeding of these pests.

Because mangroves germinate and grow where deposition is occurring, litter and other wastes that are washed or thrown into stormwater drains, streams and the sea, are moved by tides to collect among the mangrove roots.

Melaleuca (swamp paperbark) wetland, in south-east Queensland, has suffered clearing more than any other plant community, even rainforest. Clearing and draining provided land, firstly for grazing and then industrial and residential developments. Casuarina (swamp she-oak) woodland was similarly affected. The she-oak supplied good firewood, especially for pioneer bakers' ovens.

Paperbark woodlands and forests occur where freshwater accumulates during periods of high rainfall. Melaleuca wetlands are very productive ecosystems. Swamp paperbark flowers from February to July, producing copious amounts of nectar and pollen and providing a balanced diet for numerous species of honeyeaters, lorikeets and fruit bats. Insects attracted to the flowers become food for insectivorous birds (whistlers, fantails and flycatchers). The ephemeral ponds of melaleuca wetlands are important breeding sites for native frogs and waterbirds. Because wetlands dry up in times of drought they have great capacity to absorb water and mitigate the effects of floods.

In the Pine Rivers Shire, much melaleuca woodland and nearby eucalypt woodland were cleared to plant exotic pine for timber and paper production.

Because the sediments underlying many coastal lowlands were deposited in times of higher sea levels, they can contain high levels of acid sulfides. (See pages 42 & 43) This can result in environmental problems when lowland sediments are disturbed during development. This is another reason why we should not have further developments on our lowlands.

Pine Plantations

When it became apparent that supplies of timber, especially softwoods, would become scarce in Queensland and elsewhere in Australia, reafforestation projects began. In the Pine Rivers Shire, exotic pine forests were established to provide for our future paper-making and building needs. The most commonly planted species was slash pine *(Pinus elliotii)*. Unfortunately most of those plantations replaced natural open forests and woodlands; and slash pine proved to be an invasive species, becoming established well outside the areas of planting. The plantations did however provide habitat for kangaroos, and food for cockatoos.

Slash pine

Changed habitats - gains and losses

Some native animals have benefited by the clearing of bushland along the coast. Magpies, which prefer open cleared areas, are now much more common. They have even modified their nest-building techniques to include the use of various types of wire. Masked lapwings (spur-winged plovers) have also benefited by creation of wider expanses with low grass. Galahs and crested pigeons, once considered inland birds (J. Leach, 1915, p. 18), moved to coastal regions where forests were cleared and grassland established. They are now two of the most common local species.

Many forest and woodland fauna did not benefit when land was cleared. Gliders, possums, phascogales, quolls, insectivorous bats and many birds need trees, not only for shelter and breeding sites but for food as well. Many of these animals eat insects. They kept in check populations of beetles, bugs, moths, scale insects, leaf hoppers and phasmids (stick insects) that feed on the leaves, bark and other parts of trees. The burning down and removal of the old and dead trees with hollows also affected the survival of these animals higher up the food chains, allowing hordes of insects to infest the surviving trees.

Crested pigeon

Galah

Masked lapwing

Some birds which have benefited from clearing

Another modification to the landscape undertaken to increase the amount of land available for grazing and cultivation was the drainage and filling of lagoons and swamps. This had the bonus of decreasing mosquito breeding habitat, but it also destroyed the living places of many other aquatic animals, such as frogs, freshwater fish and waterfowl. The building of farm dams was, for some species, a recompense.

Pied Geese

A bird that once occurred in the Pine Rivers district in large numbers was the pied (magpie) goose. At the time of first white settlement of Australia, they were in huge flocks along the east coast as far south as Victoria. The destruction of their breeding and feeding grounds caused them to become rare in southern Queensland and extinct further south. With protection, they now appear to be recovering and moving back into and breeding in areas of south-east Queensland.

The pied goose - a victim of habitat loss

A damaged environment

The almost total clearing of some areas had harmful effects, not only on the remaining trees but often on the land itself. During hot summers, stock gather for shade around remnant isolated trees, compacting the soil and adding to nutrient levels. These factors, especially when combined with activities of leaf-eating beetles and phasmids, as well as root fungi, cause dieback in trees, and eventual death.

After vegetation is removed, the water table (the level to which rocks and soil are saturated by ground water) rises. In some areas this may bring dissolved salts nearer to the surface and within reach of roots, killing the plants. If this land is irrigated, the chance of salination increases. Such land can thus become less productive, or even useless, and take years and great expense to rehabilitate.

Dieback causes loss of remnant trees

Clearing may cause the water table and salt levels to rise

As has happened in other parts of Australia, much of the land cleared for agriculture and dairying in the Pine Rivers Shire was marginal or unsuitable for these purposes. Some blocks were too small to be viable and were later added to neighbouring properties. Land that had been good wildlife habitat is now degraded and almost invariably infested with exotic weeds.

Weed infestation on cleared land

Domestic stock

With white settlement came large numbers of domestic stock. These caused great changes to the environment. The hard hoofs, and the feeding habits of sheep, cattle and horses were new factors. Native grasses, herbaceous plants and seedlings were not adapted to the trampling, compaction and low grazing by these new animals.

Introduced pasture grasses, without their natural disease and parasitic organisms, and adapted to grazing by the imported stock, replaced their native counterparts, especially the most nutritious ones such as kangaroo grass. The changed fire regime, now of very hot fires that burnt large areas, caused the decline of many plants and encouraged the spread of some species such as native blady grass. Native animals dependent on the natural understorey vegetation for food and shelter were severely disadvantaged. Some, such as native rodents, had their burrows collapsed by the heavy, hoofed animals. The grass shelters of bandicoots and bettongs (rat-kangaroos), and the shelter and feeding places of grass birds, fairy wrens and cisticolas were destroyed. Grazing stock ate off grass and herbaceous plant seed heads, the food of quail, finches, and parrots. Burning-off in springtime, to encourage new growth, coincided with the time when most animals had eggs or young.

Kangaroo grass

Brown quail

Double-barred finch

Kangaroo grass, now becoming rare, is food and habitat for animals

Overstocking, especially during times of drought, had severe impacts; some plants became rare, some locally extinct, some totally so. Tracks to and from watering and feeding places became the foci of gully erosion. Loss of ground-cover, due to artificially high stock numbers, culminated in sheet erosion and deflation by water and wind. Erosion, in turn, led to silting of streams and coastal inlets.

Erosion due to overstocking

Grazed and ungrazed

Some negative aspects of grazing

Dingos

The only local native animal that posed a real threat to grazing stock was the dingo. Sheep were particularly vulnerable. Calves, and older cattle weakened by drought, were also preyed upon. The war that was waged upon the dingo from earliest times continues to this day. It was not until the poison '1080' was used that the survival of the dingo as a sub-species was threatened. Lowered dingo numbers leads to increases in inter-breeding with domestic dogs. While the dingo may sometimes have an impact upon stock numbers, as the top predator it also has an important role in the maintenance of biological balance. It is one of the few controls on the numbers of kangaroos, wallabies, feral cats, hares, foxes, and pigs. The loss of the dingo from our terrestrial ecosystems could produce problems much worse than those it causes. The use of '1080' bait is a major environmental problem. Like all poisons, it is not selective and may cause considerable loss of native birds, reptiles and mammals.

Dingo baits do not only kill dingos

Agriculture

Early farming techniques, such as ploughing steep slopes and cultivating without regard to contours, too often resulted in sheet erosion and gullying, causing severe loss of valuable, irreplaceable soil. Unpredictable and unseasonal downpours caused flooding that exacerbated this problem. After cultivation of the land, extended dry spells and non-arrival of predicted rains frequently allowed wind to carry away precious top-soil. Many long-used farming practices were not, and are not, suitable to the Australian environment. Yield decline, salination, loss of nutrients and waterway pollution are some of the problems which need to be reversed if we are to have a sustainable agricultural system. New systems need to be developed that will synchronise with natural ecosystems and that are attuned to local environments.

Downstream effects

With increased erosion, greater amounts of mud and silt were deposited in tidal streams and along protected coastlines, favouring the development of mangroves - especially with the sea level rising. On the positive side, it may have increased populations of crustaceans and fish. Light penetration, however, is lowered in more turbid water, resulting in less growth of underwater plants and less food for animals that feed on them. This situation is even more complicated by the greater nutrient load in water, caused by the increased use of fertilisers since the second world war.

Also, higher human population has increased the levels of nitrates and phosphates added to streams from sewage treatment works. This can cause excessive growth of water plants. Death of older plants and parts of plants then leads to such high populations of bacteria that oxygen is depleted, causing death to almost all other life in the water. This process is called eutrophication.

The result of excess nutrient in streams

A lot of dung

The dung of cattle and many other imported animals posed another problem. The droppings of our native animals, even of the largest kangaroos, are very small compared with the size of a cow 'pat'. Dung beetles roll dung into balls, lay their eggs in them and bury them. Australian dung beetles cannot handle these large clumps and so dung dried out and accumulated unprocessed in fields, preventing for years the return of nutrients to the soil. Another problem is that while dung is still fresh and in large pieces, it is a breeding place for flies. Also, in times of drought, accumulated dung near streams and along gullies was washed into ponds, pools and farm dams by isolated storms. With not enough rain to cause stream flow, water became polluted. Since world war two, many species of dung beetle from other countries, where cattle, horses, pigs, dogs etc are part of the natural environment, have been released in Australia. These beetles now promote the rapid recycling of nutrients, and at the same time greatly decrease populations of some fly species.

Introduced dung beetles help to recycle nutrients

CHAPTER

4

Urbanisation

The most profound changes that have occurred to the natural environment since European settlement are those associated with increasing human population. Surveying and subdivision of land has produced a complex crisscross pattern, mostly in straight lines, of fences, pathways and properties. The resulting rural and urban layout is not based closely on the topographical features of the country, and bears even less relationship to the shapes and boundaries of the original natural communities. Over the years each subsequent change has seen an increase in the number of blocks of land and a decrease in block size. To maintain the growing human population, more roads, streets and service easements have been needed.

Wildlife corridor - also a buffer, a screen, shade and wind break

Islands of bush in suburbia

Habitats and corridors

Decrease in habitat size creates numerous problems for wildlife. The smaller the habitat the greater the circumference to area ratio. This means that the 'edge effect' is greater - invasive species and predators from outside have relatively greater opportunity to enter at more points; and all parts of the habitat are closer to the outside and more accessible. For some species, smaller habitat can mean narrower protective buffer zones. This can result in less protection from abiotic environmental factors such as wind, sunlight, frost and temperature variation. Shape of smaller habitats becomes critical, elongate and irregular shapes being more susceptible to invasive species than circular ones. Tracks, trails, wash-outs and fire breaks that cut into or across a habitat become points and paths of invasion and degradation.

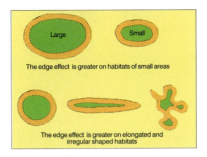

Large   Small

The edge effect is greater on habitats of small areas

The edge effect is greater on elongated and irregular shaped habitats

Habitat isolation

Bigger animals, such as kangaroos, wallabies and emus need bigger habitats. Their populations are therefore smaller. The loss by accident, predation, disease, or starvation during droughts, of just a few individuals, is particularly disastrous for small populations. When habitat size is diminishing, bigger animals are therefore the first to be lost. With an absence of corridors, in an isolated habitat, there is no possibility of recolonisation for some animals except by human intervention. Restoration of corridors may be another alternative.

Many animals, such as birds, require territories of a minimum size. If a remnant is too small it will not support these species.

Another problem faced by organisms confined to smaller habitats is that of gene flow. For most animals and plants there is a minimum population size below which inbreeding occurs to such an extent that there can be a loss of genetic variability. Slight environmental changes may then lead to the loss of the entire population. Inbreeding may also result in infertility of the offspring; or it can result in greater incidence of characteristics not conducive to survival.

Hazards of urbanisation

Many natural habitats become isolated when connecting corridors are cut or destroyed, for example when roads are built. Roads are also widened to accommodate increased traffic flow which itself makes them extremely risky for wildlife to cross. Ironically, verges of some older roads, especially those in rural areas, are sites where threatened plants and animals may still survive. The plants along these road verges, like the vegetation on some stream banks, have been, and continue to be, important corridors along which animals move. Corridors also provide roosting and nesting sites for birds which then forage during the day in our surburban backyards.

Hazardous wildlife-crossing

Last refuge for some species

Particularly just after winter, lizards and snakes come out to bask on the warm surfaces of streets, roads and highways. Many become road-kills. Their remains, and insects struck by traffic, attract carnivorous birds - hawks and butcherbirds during the day, owls and frogmouths at night. Crested pigeons and pale-headed rosellas, attracted to roadsides by spilt grain and seeds of roadside plants, fly into passing vehicles. At night, bandicoots, possums, koalas, wallabies and kangaroos, dashing from one roadside to the other or blinded by vehicle lights, also become victims. On rainy nights during warm weather, where roads cross frog habitats and corridors, many native frogs are killed. They mostly hop high enough to be struck by cars, unlike cane toads, which hop low and are only killed by direct hits by car tyres.

| Striped marsh frog | Striped rocket frog | Green treefrog |

Frogs commonly killed on the road

| Bearded dragon | Blue-tongued skink | Carpet python |

Common road-kill reptiles

| Grey butcherbird | Boobook owl | Whistling kite |

Birds commonly struck by cars when feeding on road-kills

Brown bandicoot   Swamp wallaby   Squirrel glider

Mammals which commonly become road-kills

One of the animals occurring commonly in suitable habitat in the Pine Rivers Shire is the **koala**. In the wild, koalas are not the cuddly, good-natured creatures depicted in story books and tourist brochures. The males especially are not social animals. They spend most of their adult lives as solitary individuals, pairing briefly to mate. The female takes care of the one young only until independence at the age of about eighteen months, when it is driven out of the territory. This is the period in the young koala's life when it is most at risk because it is forced to cross roads and to travel longer distances along the ground in search of its own habitat.

Koala - victim of dogs and cars

Roads are not the only dangerous places for wildlife in an urban setting. More houses and streets mean new hazards. Possums, fruit bats and pythons electrocute themselves on high voltage wires; and birds, migrating or hunting at night, fly into them. Ducks crash onto shiny roof tops at night, mistaking them for pond surfaces. In the daytime bush birds fly into reflective windows and doors.

Man-made structures - hazards for wildlife

Once a small creek with vegetation and habitat

Poor planning from earliest times has seen suburban development on flood-prone low areas. Clearing of forests, less grass cover in rural and open-space areas, and greater expanses under roadways, parking lots and house roofs have caused greater rates of run-off during rain. Places that previously were above flood levels were now susceptible. Programs implemented to alleviate flooding have involved straightening of stream channels, concreting of beds and banks of streams and removal of in-stream and near-stream vegetation. These measures have destroyed the natural beauty of many creeks, as well as their value as wildlife corridors and as habitat for aquatic invertebrates, native fish, frogs, aquatic reptiles and water birds.

Winners and Losers

Not all species of native animals are losers in suburbia. Most people are very aware of the large numbers of **Toressian crows** now resident in cities and towns. Crows are especially common where there are suitable trees for nesting and roosting. In Queensland, up until 1972, crows were not protected. A bounty was paid by some local shires for the heads of crows. This was because crows eat crops such as watermelons, pawpaws and corn; and eggs. It was common then for most boys to own an air-rifle, and for most teenage boys and adults to have at least a .22 rifle. These guns were carried and used almost anywhere, and crows were often the targets. Crows seemed to be able to recognise a .303, as distinct from a 'pea rifle' (.22), an air-rifle or a shanghai; and to know the range of each. It is sad that many people hate crows for their persistent cawing, particularly at very early hours of the day. If we understood the reasons for their high populations we would be much more tolerant of these very intelligent and beautiful birds. Yes, they do eat little birds and birds' eggs; but this they have always done. If it was not for crows, which do a magnificent job of eating food scraps and carrion (flesh of dead animals), we would have many more disease-carrying flies, cockroaches, rats and mice. Crows are also important predators of insects that defoliate our eucalypts. They have also learned to eat cane toads safely by pecking the underneath.

In districts where crows are in large numbers, the raucous calls of the **channel-billed cuckoo** can be heard in spring and summer. They lay their eggs in the nests of crows. The young channel-bills, as soon as they hatch, move around backwards in the nest, shoving out all crow eggs and young. One or two huge channel-billed young are raised by the crows instead of their own.

Torressian crow - has adapted successfully to suburban living

(JB)

Channel-billed cuckoo - eggs are hatched and young raised by crows

(DEH)

Chemicals

With more people come more homes and gardens. People want to protect their lawns, garden beds, vegetable patches, shrubberies and fruit trees from weeds, nematode worms, insects, slugs and snails. They endeavour to rid their homes of spiders, ants, silverfish and cockroaches. The number of dogs, cats and other pets increases and so parasites need to be controlled. As well, urban growth brings greater demands for sporting fields, golf courses and swimming pools. All these developments bring more reasons to use chemicals - fertiliser, weedicide, insecticide, fungicide, and other potential pollutants.

The problems that can arise when chemicals are used excessively and without caution became apparent after World War 2. DDT was used to control flies, mosquitoes, other insect pests of gardens and farms, and cattle ticks. Unfortunately, many non-target species and natural predators, such as hatchet wasps, spiders, skinks and birds, also died. The decrease in numbers of natural predators made continued use of the poison seem even more necessary. Pests quickly developed resistance to DDT, and effective control required stronger concentrations of the chemical. By a process called **biological magnification**, animals further up the food chains received higher doses of DDT. These higher order consumers began to show the symptoms of poisoning. Kookaburras, tawny frogmouths, hawks and owls were often found paralysed. DDT also caused soft egg shells in these birds, and behavioural changes that affected their breeding success. Another problem was that DDT has a very long half-life value - it takes an extremely long time to decompose into harmless compounds. Eventually, use of DDT was banned; and other related chemicals were used. Because of similar problems they too were banned. Chemicals which break down very quickly (biodegradable ones) are now being used, and with more care, so that there is less effect on non-target species and less chance of chemicals contaminating surface and underground water systems.

Tawny frogmouth

Kookaburra

Magpie lark

Birds at the end of food chains - killed by concentrated doses of pesticides

Termites are a group of insects that cause concern. Traditionally, potent and long-lasting chemicals have been used under concrete slabs and around posts and poles to protect homes and other structures. Leaching and washing of chemicals into ground water and streams has resulted in the banning or strict control of many compounds. However, there are demands that the use of these chemicals should continue. Alternative methods of termite control are available.

Termite damage

Subterranean termite mound

Arboreal termite mound

Termites, often called 'white ants', are not ants nor are they white. They are related to cockroaches. Australia has almost 400 species of them. Australians are paranoid about termites but most species eat grass, leaf litter and rotting timber - only a few local kinds are harmful to sound timber in buildings. Termites are social insects and colonies may contain millions of individuals. They play an important role in the recycling of nutrients, contained in plant matter, that would otherwise be unavailable to other organisms. Their winged forms (alates) fly from the colonies in thousands, often at the approach of summer storms, becoming food for insectivorous birds, bats and skinks. Kingfishers dig holes for nesting in arboreal termite mounds.

Mound of grass-eating termite

Kingfisher nesting

Willie wagtail

Termites are of great importance to the natural environment

Beautiful, innocent victims

The plants we use in our gardens have animals that feed on them - their roots, stems, leaves, bark and so on. Some plants may be affected, from time to time, more than others. The animals that feed on plants nearly always have animals that prey upon them; and all plants and animals have parasites and disease organisms that affect them. A food-web is thus built up for any community of organisms. This is normal. But some of us (maybe most of us) want an unnatural system where the plants in our lawns and gardens are not part of this natural system. Why do we not want trees, shrubs and smaller plants with leaves missing here and there; or leaves with chewed edges? The grubs, caterpillars, nymphs and adult insects that feed on our plants are, in turn, food for animals such as other insects, spiders, frogs, reptiles, birds and bats. When we use chemicals to kill our garden pests we kill other things as well - the butterflies, bees, honeyeaters, silver-eyes, willy-wagtails, green treefrogs, blue-tongued lizards, and so on.

What is so terrible about having patches of brown in the lawn? Is this not infinitely better than applying a poisonous fungicide to stop 'dollar spot', or spraying insecticide to kill the lawn grubs. If left alone, harmless hatchet wasps will get rid of most lawn grubs, and many of the rest will be eaten by ground feeding birds. Isn't it much more interesting to have a healthy family of friendly, trusting magpie larks than a sterile, monotonous lawn? What of the health of our own families? In dry weather, what is wrong with having a lawn that is mostly brown? This is natural, especially in Australia. The lawn will recover when it rains again; and without the addition of any artificial fertilisers or expensive treated water.

Water Pollution

Like all living things, we need water. With increasing population and urbanisation more and more people have to be supplied with water - for drinking, cooking, bathing, washing, cleaning, and for our gardens. In modern towns and cities, less use is made of rainwater from household tanks. Instead, water is piped to houses from reservoirs that

Brendale water treatment plant

receive water from streams and dams. This water has to be filtered to remove suspended particles, and chlorine gas is added to kill harmful organisms such as bacteria. These treatments are expensive. Treated water is used, not only for our personal uses, but for watering the lawn, the garden and washing the car; and to transport our body wastes through septic or sewage systems. During some of our uses of expensive treated water, we also add other substances - soaps, water softeners, cleansers, detergents and disinfectants. From septic systems these substances enter and contaminate the ground water which subsequently flows to streams or the sea. When passed through sewerage systems the break-down products of these chemicals usually enter streams or coastal waters.

Soap has a very short half-life - about two days. This means that it takes this time for one half of any amount of soap to biodegrade - to break down when exposed to natural processes. Detergents are made from petroleum and take much longer to degrade. 'Hard' detergents have a half-life of about 16 days and 'soft' detergents much less. The newer (but expensive) ones degrade almost as quickly as soap. Detergents, however, contain phosphates to make them foam more readily and, when degraded, release the phosphates. These are not readily removed by sewage treatment and usually enter streams or the sea, where they can cause green algal blooms and eutrophication (see pages 32 & 33). New processes are being developed to remove phosphates from sewage. It is possible to treat sewage so that the water is suitable for drinking, but this is very expensive.

At the Brendale Water Treatment Plant, the water from the treated sewage is used to water playing fields. This is a way of making use of the nutrients to promote growth of grass and shade-trees, as well as being an alternative to the use of expensive town water. Similar procedures could be used to provide irrigation water and fertilisation for agricultural land.

Another major source of pollution of water is industrial waste. (See pages 139 & 140).

Acid sulfates

Some chemicals that occur naturally, under changed conditions can become harmful to the natural environment. This is so with acid sulfates. The last 2 million years has been a time of glaciation. Ice ages have alternated with times of higher temperatures when polar ice melted, causing the sea level to rise and cover coastal regions periodically - sometimes up to 4 metres higher than the present sea level. Mud, built up along the coast during interglacial periods and rich in organic compounds, has high levels of sulfate from sea water. This reacts with iron oxide in the mud and forms iron sulfide. While this compound remains covered in sediment, especially water-logged sediment lacking in oxygen, the environment is not adversely affected. If however, the iron sulfide is uncovered and exposed to air, it forms sulfate ions which, in water, produce sulfuric acid. Sulfuric acid, even in low concentrations, is fatal to most organisms.

Coastal disturbance may release acid sulfates

In our coastal lowlands and river flats, there are sediments containing iron sulfide. This remains dormant while covered. Exposure occurs naturally during erosion of the coast and lowland stream banks, but here the formation of acid sulfates is gradual and the acid is harmlessly diluted and dispersed by water flow. This is not the case however, when we dig deep drainage canals across lowlands containing sulfides, or expose large areas of these sediments during extraction operations. Water polluted by acid sulfate has a characteristic blue colour and may be so acid as to be devoid of life. Careful surveys need to be done so that we do not interfere with environments containing potentially hazardous levels of sulfide.

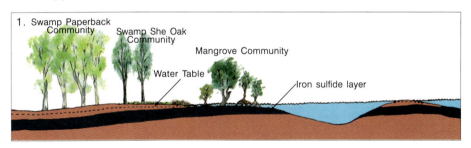

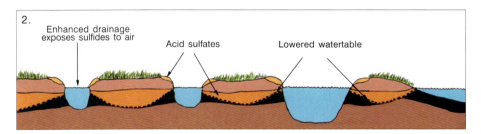

Formation of acid sulfates in mined or drained sediments

Feral animals and plants

A great number of animals and plants brought to Australia from overseas have become feral. Many introductions have been deliberate, some accidental. Some of the organisms that are now part of our environment have had little or no apparent harmful effects. Some introduced as biological controls have been particularly beneficial. Many however have had, and continue to have, disastrous consequences for our natural environment, our gardens and primary production.

Introduced weeds

New settlers came to Australia with a knowledge of plants from elsewhere; and ideas from afar as to 'beauty' of landscape. They grew fodder crops, cash crops and plants to supplement their own food supply. They put in trees and shrubs for shade and as avenues, and used many plants as ornamentals. Species came from all around the world; but not much attention was given to Australian native plants. The 'hostile', 'untidy bush' had to be cleared, the landscape remoulded and some 'colour' added to this brown country. Many plants escaped into the bush to become environmental weeds. Of course, people then had no inkling of the damage that some plants would eventually cause to the natural environment. Today though, we have no excuse, except perhaps ignorance or indifference, when we continue to plant many of the very same species or worse ones. As a result we now have a long and increasing list of invasive, choking weeds.

Many introductions, intended to beautify home gardens, are now weeds:

Lantana	Creeping lantana	Groundsel	Indian hawthorn
Ochna	Mother of millions	Singapore daisy	Broad-leaf pepper
Mother-in-law's tongue	Balsam	Periwinkle	Easter cassia

Do not use these plants

Crofton weed (JB)

Mist flower (JB)

Morning glory (PRSC)

Madiera vine (JB)

Cat's claw creeper (DEH)

Moth vine (JB)

Japanese honeysuckle (JB)

Black-eyed Susan (JB)

Japanese sunflower (JB)

Wandering Jew (JB)

Purple wandering Jew (PRSC)

Yukka (JB)

Cyperus involucratus (PRSC)

Canna lily (JB)

Blue Billy-goat weed (JB)

Asparagus 'fern' (PRSC)

Climbing asparagus (JB)

Mile-a-minute (JB)

Balloon vine (JB)

Fishbone fern (JB)

Golden fern (JB)

Spanish 'moss' (PRSC)

Originally garden plants - now serious weeds.
Do not use these plants

Plants that are extremely easy to grow and which multiply rapidly in gardens are often thinned-out and the excess disposed of. Uncaring or unknowing people often throw these plants into bushland areas. These become the start of infestations that are sometimes virtually impossible to eradicate.

Some plants were cultured as hedge rows. Their prickly stems and/or close growth were intended to deter stock and act as fences. Some are planted as garden hedges. Many are now invasive weeds:

| Murraya (mock orange) | Boxthorn | Privet | Prickly pear |

'Hedge row' plants - now bushland weeds

Some of the plants brought here for their fruit are also invading the bush. A few, such as bush lemons and peaches, may not have much effect and remain uncommon. Others however are proliferating:

| Persimmon | Passionfruit | Guava |

Fruit trees and vines - some are now bushland weeds

Of tree species planted for shade and avenue trees, or intended for timber and forestry plots, many are now serious bushland weeds. Some, such as the beautiful but disastrous camphor laurel, were planted around homesteads and school grounds very early in white settlement and have been declared as having 'heritage value'. Thus protected, these trees now act as seed sources to infest bushland. Because of the beauty, large size and number of camphor laurels growing in some 'natural' areas (often to the exclusion of almost all other species), local authorities are reluctant to remove them. Well-meaning but uninformed residents object, regarding these trees as natural bushland.

| Camphor laurel | Golden rain tree | Jacaranda | Chinese elm |
| African tulip | Queen palm | Cockscomb coral | Weeping willow |

Pencil willow

Introduced trees that invade the bush, decrease biodiversity and change the character of bushland

Many aquatic plants, introduced as ornaments for garden pools have become major weeds of our waterways and wetlands:

| Water hyacinth | Salvinia | Parrots feathers (Myriophyllum aquaticum) |

Exotic water plants - now major weeds

Many species of plants have been introduced into Australia to improve pastures. Some of these are legumes. Although useful as stock fodder, many of them are now bushland weeds.

Phasey bean   Siratro   Vicia

Desmodium   Leucaena

Some invasive weeds of the pea family

One of the most destructive climbing and scrambling plants, introduced for pasture improvement, is glycine vine (*Neonotonia wightii*). It produces many seeds and develops roots wherever stems touch the ground. It smothers shrubs and trees, bending and breaking stems. It is very common along streams of the Pine Rivers Valley and is spreading rapidly.

Glycine vine smothering vegetation along the South Pine River, Samford

Numerous species of grass have been introduced to Australia for pasture improvement. Many of these are now essential food for grazing stock, but in natural areas they are invasive weeds, taking over from local native grasses.

Green panic   Johnson grass   Rhodes grass   Paspalum

Pigeon grass   Paragrass   Red Natal grass

Fodder plants may also be serious invasive weeds in natural areas

A great number of plants now in Australia were not brought here intentionally. No one in their right mind would even think of bringing some of these. They came here as seeds in packing, or attached to clothing and animals' fur, in fodder for animals during shipping, in potting soil, and in many other accidental ways.

Scotch thistle   Flat weed   Stinking Roger   Green cestrum

Weed plants unintentionally introduced

Two plants which arrived in Australia last century are the 'red cotton bush' and the 'balloon cotton bush', probably in cargoes from America. Soon after these two plants arrived, the 'wanderer butterfly' was first recorded in Australia. It had flown from its American homeland across the Pacific Ocean to Australia. It has made this journey for probably hundreds of thousands of years; but now it was able to establish because there was food for its caterpillars - the cotton bushes.

Red cotton bush

Balloon cotton bush

Wanderer butterfly

The Wanderer Butterfly could not establish in Australia until after its caterpillars' food, the cotton bushes, had arrived here.

Not all invasive weeds are from overseas. Some plants from tropical Australia, grown locally in gardens and as street trees, have escaped into bushland:

Eucalyptus torelliana

Weeping fig

Alexandra palm

Umbrella tree

Water lettuce

Plants from northern Australia - now invading local natural areas

Feral animals

As in most parts of Australia, feral cats occur in all natural areas of Pine Rivers. They live on our native birds, small mammals, reptiles and frogs. Foxes are similarly destructive of our wildlife. Foxes are very common even in many suburban areas, and people only become aware of this when foxes raid the hen house, or the dog's food disappears. Feral pigs are also numerous in forestry reserves and national parks, such as at Mt Glorious, where diggings indicate their presence. They destroy palm trees and other plants by eating new shoots, fleshy stems, tubers or roots. They also feed on fruit and seeds of rainforest trees. Brown hares destroy regrowth of native plants.

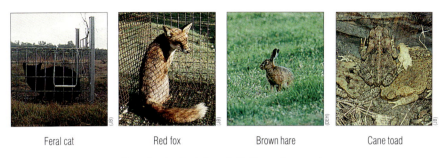

| Feral cat | Red fox | Brown hare | Cane toad |

Some feral animals harmful to the environment

Introduced birds compete with native species for food, nesting sites and space. Sparrows and feral rock pigeons occur mostly in suburban areas, unlike starlings that also inhabit the bush. Spotted turtle-doves are continuing to move out into bushland areas, apparently at the expense of the native and once-common, bar-shouldered dove. Common mynahs, often confused with the native noisy miner, arrived in the Pine Rivers Shire only a few years ago, and are destined to become much more common. They are aggressive nesters, taking over whole trees where nesting hollows are found, chasing away native birds and infesting nest sites with bird lice.

Cane toads, by the very numbers of their tadpoles and adults, deprive native frogs of space, food and shelter. Adults also eat small animals. Many frog-eating native animals are now rare or locally extinct in places where once they were common. This is because they do not distinguish between the poisonous cane toad and native frogs, their natural food. Red-bellied black snakes, goannas, and possibly brush-tailed phascogales, are some species affected. One animal, the common keelback snake, has probably benefited by the introduction of cane toads. It eats, without ill-effect, great numbers of small toads, as well as the tadpoles of cane toads.

The common, harmless keelback snake eats cane toads without ill-effect

Frogs

The number and variety of frogs found in a region is a good indicator of the health of the natural environment. Throughout the world, certain groups of frogs have declined in the last twenty years or so, especially frogs from mountain rainforests. One such frog from south-east Queensland is the southern dayfrog, which may now be extinct. We do not know the reason for their demise. For other species, loss of breeding ponds and swamps and competition from cane toads has led to declines in populations. The green-striped frog and salmon-striped frog are species whose numbers are decreasing. On the other hand, striped marsh frog numbers are very high, probably because they are tolerent of slightly polluted water.

On the D'Aguilar Range, the southern day frog (*Taudactylas diurnus,* also called Mt Glorious torrent frog) was common until the seventies. They have not been sighted for some twenty years Recently however, another rare frog, the marsupial frog (*Assa darlingtoni*), has been found at Mt Glorious.

Southern dayfrog   Australian marsupial frog

Rare frogs of the D'Aguilar Range

Local native fish

South-east Queensland has many beautiful, small native freshwater fish. These include rainbows, blue-eyes, gudgeons, smelties, hardyheads and glass perch. They have all decreased in range and numbers since the release and establishment of exotic aquarium fish, such as swordtails and 'mosquitofish'. These imported fish bear live young; and they out-breed our small native species, destroying eggs, young and adults. Larger introduced fish, such as goldfish and tilapia, are also increasing their range at the expense of native fish such as spangled perch. The large eastern cod is no longer found in most south-east Queensland river systems where it once existed. Dynamite and gelignite, used by settlers early this century to remove tree stumps from paddocks before ploughing, were also used to kill cod. This is one factor that led to their decline.

Pacific blue-eye   Purple-spotted gudgeon

Some small native fish of the Pine Rivers, suitable for aquaria and ponds

In Lake Samsonvale there are huge numbers of the imported fish, tilapia. They can tolerate brackish water and have recently spread from the North Pine into the South Pine River. Tilapia are declared noxious under the Fisheries Act and so may not be kept. The spread of tilapia at the expense of our native fish is an example of what can occur when exotic fish are released into ponds and streams or flushed down storm-water drains and toilets. Unwanted exotic fish should be destroyed humanely by putting them in plastic bags and freezing.

Swordtail   Mosquitofish   Tilapia

Some imported fish, now displacing native species in the Pine Rivers system

To supply water for the increasing numbers of people in south-east Queensland, and to mitigate the effects of floods, many major dams have been built. Some organisms have benefitted greatly by this large increase in habitats, while the habitats of others have been destroyed. Dewfish and bony bream numbers are very high in large dams. Sea mullet, which spend part of their life-cycle in fresh water streams, are prevented by dam walls from migrating upstream. Below dams, the water flowing from outlets is cold for kilometres downstream. Many native fish and their food species cannot live here and others need warm water in which to breed.

Dewfish - large numbers occur in Pine Rivers dams   Sea mullet - prevented from upstream migration by dams

Dam construction benefits some fish species, but not all

PART TWO

FROM NOW

On

CHAPTER **5**

Our Homes Our Habitats

We spend a major part of our lives at home. This is our habitat. Home may be a house that we own or rent, a flat or a room. We may live on rural land, on acreage or on a smaller block. Whatever our circumstances we would all prefer our homes and their surroundings to be pleasant and healthy places for ourselves, our families and friends. We can have this and at the same time retain the natural environment for our native plants and animals. Let us look at the ways of achieving this.

Plants

Reasons for planting and/or preserving trees, shrubs and other plants include:

Aesthetic | Plants are things of beauty.

Conservation | We can help provide habitat and food for animals. We can also help conserve plant species that may be rare or endangered. A neighbourhood policy of planting local Australian native plants on footpaths and in our gardens can recreate habitat and corridors, even in and through the most developed urban, industrial and rural environments.

Environmental | We can make our surroundings more pleasant by use of plants. They provide shade, screens, windbreaks, and condition the air.

Economic\material | Plants may be used for production of timber, fruit, honey, flowers. Plants may be used to add value to properties.

Australian native plants

Why should we plant Australian plants, especially local native plants? Some reasons are:

- Encouragement and preservation of native animals - Native animals depend on native plants to obtain a reliable supply of suitable food and habitat. By planting a wide variety of local native species we can provide a range of micro-habitats which favour and protect our native animals. Literally thousands of minute and larger invertebrate animals live on or in the leaves, bark, wood and roots of Australian plants. These are food for larger animals such as our native birds and marsupials. Introduced plants are dispersed when birds and fruit-bats eat the fruit, but they do not provide for the great variety of other organisms that natives do.

- <u>All-year-round natural beauty of foliage, flowers and form</u> - A selection of local native plants will provide a changing scene throughout the year, of flowers and coloured new growth, a wide range of leaf-shapes, and natural informal vistas.

- <u>Ease of care</u> - Suitably chosen and sited native plants will not require much maintenance after the initial planting and watering-in. A light pruning after flowering may be beneficial for some species.

- <u>Saving of water</u> - Many native plants are adapted to dry conditions and drought and, after establishment, do not require watering.

- <u>Philosophical</u> - Australian plants maintain the unique landscape character of Australia. We can take pride in the beauty of our own country, its very special and different natural scenery, plants and animals.

Plants as air conditioners

Plants are the great air conditioners of the world; and they operate for free. Plants improve air quality and remove impurities such as airborne dust, smoke, soot, fumes, pollen, spores and odours by:

Dilution

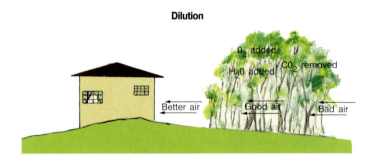

O_2 added
H_2O added
CO_2 removed
Better air
Good air
Bad air

Filtration & washing

Moist and pubescent leaves trap particles
Deposits washed off by rain
Clean air
Air with suspended particles (dust, etc)

Slowing and precipitation

Precipitation of particles

Slower clean air

Moving polluted air

Masking

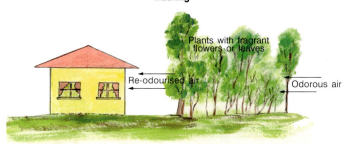

Plants with fragrant flowers or leaves

Re-odourised air

Odorous air

Humidifying

H₂O   Transpiration   H₂O

Slower moist air

H₂O

Dry air

Stabilisation of temperatures

Air - cooled in hot weather - warmed in cold weather

Air - hot in hot weather - cold in cold weather

Trees and the suburban environment

<u>Some facts</u> (see 'Australian Plants', Vol 6, No.49, pp 206 - 209):

* Green belts 50 to 100 m wide reduced summer temperatures by not less than 3.5°C.

* Air in a city centre had 6 to 18 times the dust content of a treed 4 hectare park.

* In its 80 years of life a large tree (15m wide by 45m high) has taken up and transformed the total carbon content of 80 thousand one-family homes - or the volume of 3 homes per day. This tree, per hour, produces 1712g of oxygen and removes 2352g of carbon dioxide.

* A moderate sized tree, standing alone in the open loses 300 to 400 litres per day of transpired water. A forest of small trees transpires as much as 1300 tonnes of water per hectare per day.

Plants and wind turbulence

Solid structures such as houses and some fences cause turbulence. This can create drafts, cause drying out of soils and result in damage during high winds.

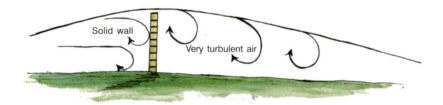

Solid walls create turbulence

Wind breaks of shrubs and trees can help to decrease turbulence and resulting draughts that cause drying out of the garden. They can also help to prevent damage during strong winds.

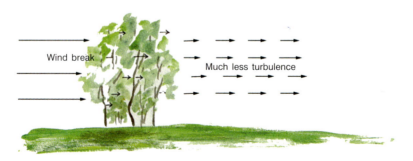

Wind-breaks and turbulence

Plants and wind speed

Wind-breaks of trees and shrubs allow some air to pass through, but at much reduced speed. They also affect the speed of the wind on each side and above the wind break. It has been found (for example in Darwin, during cyclone Tracey) that older, well-vegetated suburbs fare much better during severe storms than do newly developed ones where protective trees and larger shrubs have not yet had time to become established. This is in spite of some house damage caused by falling trees and branches.

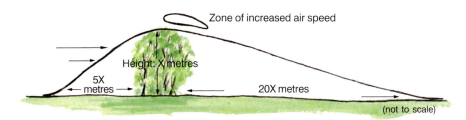

Zone of increased air speed

Height: X metres

5X metres

20X metres

(not to scale)

Effect of windbreaks on wind speed (Side elevation)

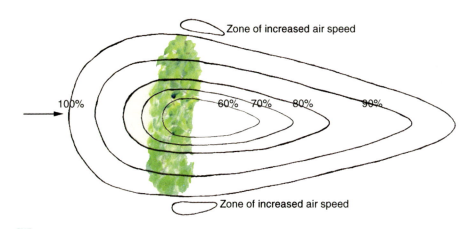

Zone of increased air speed

100%   60% 70% 80%   90%

Zone of increased air speed

Effect on windbreaks on wind speed (Plan view)

Sunlight and the home environment

The angle of the sun's rays and their direction, at particular times of the day, change with the seasons. This influences the amount of radiation that is absorbed as heat. It also determines the amount and direction of shadow that is cast at any time during daylight.

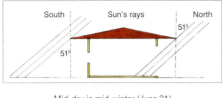

Mid-day in mid-winter (June 21)

Mid-day in mid-summer (Dec 21)

Angle of the sun's rays in Brisbane (North of Brisbane, angles are less, and to the south more)

The angle and direction of the sun's rays determine whether or not various locations around a house will receive sunlight, and the intensity and duration of sunlight during the year. These factors determine when and if the sun shines in through windows, onto verandahs and patios, and if walls and rooms become warmer or cooler through the day. It also influences what plants grow best around the house. Where the shade cast by plants will fall during the day or the seasons is also affected by the change in the position of the sun and the inclination of sun rays.

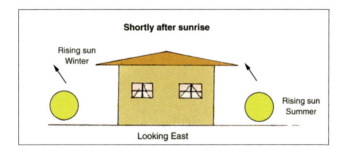

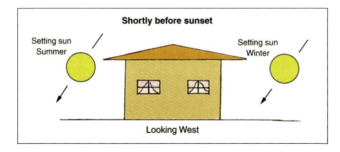

The positions of the rising and setting sun, seasonally (Southern Hemisphere)

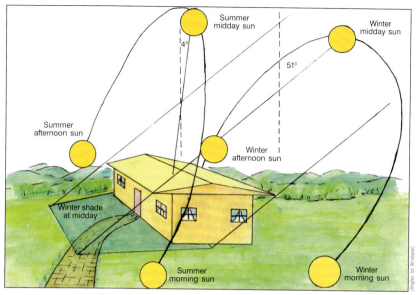

Aspect and the sun's rays (Southern Hemisphere)

In the diagram labels: Summer midday sun, 4°, Winter midday sun, 51°, Summer afternoon sun, Winter afternoon sun, Winter shade at midday, Summer morning sun, Winter morning sun, (Angles for Brisbane)

In our part of the world, the ideal aspect environmentally, for a house, is towards the north; and it should be elongate east-west. However, little regard to these criteria is taken during the design and building of most of our homes. The factors which usually dictate the direction a house faces are the location and orientation of the street. Thus, not everyone has a house which benefits by having features such as open glassed areas, windows, verandahs, and solid walls, facing the optimum directions. However, we can all exercise at least some control over where to plant trees and shrubs to benefit from the shade they cast and the sunlight they may allow in at particular times of the year. Before building, retention of appropriate shrubs and trees in appropriate places can aid in control of the seasonal temperatures within the house. (See pages 161 & 162 for ways of saving energy).

Use of plants for best of sunlight and shade

In general, for maximum sunlight during winter and shade during the summer, the following scheme for plantings or retentions can be applied.

To the north of the house:

Close to the house - tall, sparse-foliaged, bare-trunked trees (These allow winter sunlight to shine in and warm the house; and they provide some shade above the roof in summer). Deciduous trees are also an option. Australia has few trees deciduous in winter, but there are some lovely ones. Try these instead of Jacaranda and Poinsiana: - red cedar, white cedar, bat's wing coral, koda, peanut tree, flame tree and silky oak.

<u>Further from the house</u> - low to medium shrubs and trees. (These should be low enough for their shade not to reach the house in winter.)

To the south of the house:
The trees and shrubs on this side of the house cast their shade away from the house at all times except mornings and afternoons during summer. Here is the best place then to establish the most shady and shade-tolerant species, such as those from rainforests. Consideration though may be necessary for close neighbours to the south who will have their winter sun blocked if tall trees are allowed to develop. However, there are many excellent large shrubs and small trees of local rainforests which are suitable for this situation. (See plant list on pages 181 to 190)

On the southern side, close to the house it is best to forget about growing the usual lawn grasses because this is the shady side. Native grasses of rainforests, such as oplismenus and ottochloa (see page 182), and native violet, are good substitutes.

To the east of the house:
In winter we want the morning sun to shine upon and into the house for warmth; and in summer the hot (and early) sun to be screened or filtered out. To achieve this, plants to the south of the eastern side (that is, to the right as we face east) should be taller and more dense and shady. Towards the north of the eastern side (to the left as we face east), shrubs should be lower.

To the west of the house:
Because the sun sets north of west in winter and south of west in summer (opposite to sunrise in the east), our planting and retention scheme will be opposite to that for the east. This will give us afternoon winter sunlight until sundown, and in summer block out the hot sun of the long afternoons. Therefore it is best to plant or retain taller, dense and shady trees and shrubs to the south of the western side (ie to the left when looking west). Shrubs to the north of west (to the right, looking west) should be lower.

Shade

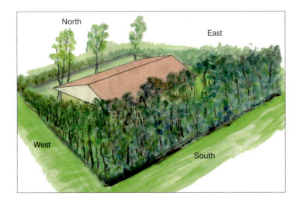

Planting and plant-retention for optimum control of sunlight

In Queensland we have the highest incidence of skin cancer in the world. Trees in gardens provide shade and therefore protection from harmful ultra-violet rays of sunlight. Outdoor living areas, barbecues and seating can be located near trees to receive shade during times of greatest UV risk (10 am to 3 pm) and to be in sunlight when it is cooler and there is less risk of skin damage.

Through Breezes

During our hot weather, houses can be much more pleasant places in which to live if the positioning of windows and doorways allows the flow of cooling breezes. House design should take into account the direction of prevailing winds.

Some other factors to consider

Of course, there are many more factors to be taken into account when considering where to plant and retain shrubs and trees for light and shade for optimum benefit in controlling the home environment. For example, we need to think about the **size of the house block**, the proximity and height of **neighbouring houses**, location and size of plants in neighbouring blocks, **slope** of the land, aspect and orientation of the block, and the aspect of our house if already built. If the house is on a concrete slab, we have to think more seriously about the effect of the **roots** of nearby trees. Similarly, location of water **pipes**, drainage pipes, **overhead wires**, car tracks and swimming pool will need to be considered.

A sample layout for plants - and some factors to consider

CHAPTER 6

Encouraging Native Animals

The kinds of animals that we can attract into suburban gardens include a great variety of birds, small mammals, reptiles, amphibians and invertebrates. To do this we need to provide **food, water, shelter**, and, for animals which are unable to move easily to and from other habitats, **breeding places**. If many neighbouring gardens can combine to create a larger area of habitat, the number of species and their populations can be increased. Permanent, easily-accessed drinking water will greatly enhance a habitat for birds. It should be in the open so birds can see the approach of cats and dogs but close enough to shelter to allow a quick escape to places where cats and dogs find the going tough.

Artificial feeding

Many people are tempted to provide food for birds that visit their gardens. Lorikeets, and honeyeaters are often fed honey mixtures. Magpies, butcherbirds and kookaburras are given mince and meat pieces. Seed mixtures are put out for finches, parrots and pigeons. If these treats are provided occasionally in very small amounts there is probably little harm done. If however native animals become dependent upon handouts, artificially high populations can result. Other species of animals may be driven away. Cockatoos may be attracted and, sitting around during the day, destroy house fittings. Another problem caused by feeding of artificial foods is that the nutrition of the animals is upset, leading to their ill-health. Care must be taken not to encourage pest species (particularly sparrows, spotted turtle-doves and feral pigeons) attracted by the food. For healthy and long-term high populations of friendly and trusting native animals in home gardens it is best to provide suitable habitats of native plants.

The 'English' garden

The imported concept, the English (or European) garden, with lawns, flower beds, formal hedges and non-native standard shrubs and trees, is not conducive to attracting many native animals. The opposite is true. This style of garden greatly discourages the majority of native animals and distinctly disadvantages them in competition with exotic species. In the most carefully planned cities (such as Canberra) and parts of cities, where these types of gardens and parks prevail, imported pest bird species (sparrows, starlings, feral pigeons, spotted turtle-doves and common mynahs) are by far the most common birds. As well, to set up and maintain these parks and gardens, it is necessary to use fertilisers, insecticides, fungicides, weedicides, abundant water and intensive labour. All this to install centres from which an ever-increasing list of newly-imported plant species and long-established exotics can make forays into the surrounding bushland. What planning? In the next quarter of a century, will native flora and fauna still exist in our sprawling new suburbs if we continue, with a total lack of ecological understanding, to change the

Australian landscape? Will our present fetish for overseas garden designs and exotic plants, and our apparent biological cringe, continue to decrease our natural bio-diversity?

Combining native and exotic plants

It is possible to combine exotic and native plants in gardens. This can improve an otherwise totally artificial ecosystem, the European-type garden, and attract more native animals; and may even decrease the need for watering and chemicals. We should not use plants known to be invasive. However, the most environmentally sound way to go is to create a genuine

The 'English' garden - not very attractive to many native animals

Australian garden of local native plants and forget about using any chemicals at all. If any plant specimen is not doing well, let it die, or replace it. Leave the insects that are attacking plants for predatory insects, spiders, birds, lizards and frogs; or pick them off by hand.

| Assassin bug | Praying mantis | Dragonfly | Hatchet wasp |

Some insects helpful for controlling garden pests - but destroyed by insecticides

| Golden orb-weaver | Garden orb-weaver | Tent spider | St Andrew's cross spider |

Some common garden spiders helpful for controlling garden pests - but destroyed by insecticides

Garden Structure

We should think about the structure of the garden we wish to establish. Do we want a closed forest (rainforest), an open forest with shrubby understorey, an open woodland, heathland or a combination of these structures?

Rainforest structure

Open-forest with shrubby understorey structure

Heathland structure

Woodland structure

Overall structures of gardens

We can include some of each of these structures, especially if the garden is big enough. In new estates there may already be established native trees left by the developer, and these can be incorporated into our desired structure. Invasive exotic trees, such as camphor laurel, are best removed and replaced with local native species. If the house and garden are already established with exotics, to make the garden more environmentally friendly, it is best to take some or all of these out one by one over time, the most invasive ones first. (See pages 237 to 247.)

Woodland has open grassed areas and trees. If we create a woodland in our garden we will encourage animals that prefer this habitat. Generally, in most suburban areas, animals that feed on the ground in the open have plenty of habitat. There is no shortage of mown playing fields, parks, road verges, footpaths and lawns; so magpies, noisy miners, butcher birds, crows, galahs, masked lapwings, grass skinks, bearded dragons and cane toads are very common. Many open-space birds are aggressive towards other species and chase them out of nearby habitats. Animals that need shrubby and grassy areas to seek food, to shelter and to find breeding places can be encouraged if we provide habitat where they can find protection. We should also decrease the number and extent of open areas of mown grass. By growing shrubs, grass clumps and scrambling plants amongst the trees we can convert a woodland into an **open forest with a shrubby understorey**. In doing this we will greatly increase the variety of birds and other animals that will live in or visit our gardens. We will then enjoy resident and visiting fairy-wrens, small honeyeaters, warblers (gerygones), pardalotes, whistlers, blue-tongued and pink-tongued skinks and many more, especially if there are adjacent patches of natural bushland; or neighbours nearby who have an understanding of and love for our Australian environment.

Heath-land habitat consists of low shrubs and scrambling plants, mostly a metre or less tall. This is the ideal replacement for lawns and, once established, requires practically no maintenance. Almost the entire yard can be converted to this kind of habitat, with walking paths allowing access. The many flowering heath species attract nectar and pollen feeding birds, as well as insects which, in turn, are food for insectivorous birds, reptiles and frogs.

Rainforest will attract possums, especially the less-common ringtails. Ringtailed possums need dense leaves of trees and vines in which to build their nests (dreys). Fruit-eating birds such as figbirds, orioles, Lewin's honeyeaters and fruit-pigeons will visit. So will insect-feeding spangled drongos, monarchs and robins. The shrubby margins will invite eastern whipbirds; and the leaf litter and mulch on the forest floor is where noisy pittas, logrunners and scrubwrens may search for food.

| Superb fruit-dove | Yellow robin | Ring-tail possum |

Some fauna attracted to rainforest gardens

Planting a rainforest

There is no need to look any further afield than South-east Queensland for plants suitable for creating a rainforest patch. The Pine Rivers valley is especially rich in species. There are also some beautiful plants endemic to nearby parts of South-east Queensland and some rare and endangered native plants that are eminently suitable for garden culture. For small gardens it is probably best to avoid the many available rainforest trees that will ultimately become huge. Instead, select small trees, shrubs and understorey species. (See pages 181 to 190 for a list of plants for small gardens.)

The southern side of the garden is generally the place for a rainforest, but other considerations may mean that the rainforest is more appropriate elsewhere - for example in a gully area, or next to a sound-barrier fence or where it will block out an unwanted view.

We do not need to (and should not) use large amounts of water to create and maintain a rainforest patch. The answer to the need for water is in the use of **mulch**. Use organic mulch such as pine chips, bark chips, wood chips, wood-shavings, bush mulch, macadamia shells, sugar bagasse, etc in the greatest quantity possible - the deeper the better. In dry well-drained areas, especially those facing west, mulch should be no less than 15 cm deep. Newspaper, cardboard, hessian and any biodegradable bags, cloth and blanket material, used as a underlay for the mulch, will kill and discourage grass and weeds. These materials soon break down and help enrich the soil. Place a collar of thick cardboard around the stem of new plants to keep the mulch away. Grass clippings and garden prunings can be added to the mulch but care must be taken not to introduce invasives such as the exotic wandering Jew. Do not use organic mulches or cardboard or paper underlay near the house. This will encourage subterranian termites.

The best time to start planting a rainforest in South-east Queensland is after the hottest part of summer. The worst time is in late winter and spring when we have our driest months. Regardless of the time of year, and especially if we have to plant in less than optimum times, we should wait until just after good soaking rain, when soil moisture is high. This will give new plants a better start without the need to use constant artificial watering. Unless there are now very hot and/or windy conditions, the deep mulch and its underlay will most likely keep the roots of young plants cool and moist until the next rains. Water plants only if they look stressed, and then late in the evening.

To provide protection for newly-planted rainforest species, plant hardy quick-to-establish **pioneer species** first. Some pioneers can be planted, initially in large numbers, and then cut back periodically or culled out when the other trees and shrubs develop. Macaranga is an excellent plant for this and gives a leafy rainforest effect very quickly. Plant it and similar pioneer species every few metres (not equally spaced or in lines) and cut them back before they are large. Eventually, remove all except for one or two specimens of each pioneer species. Leave the prunings to rot away into the mulch. (See list of rainforest species noted as pioneers - Pi), (pages 181 to 204). Some young rainforest plants are sensitive to sunlight and wind.These are best put in after the pioneer and hardy species have formed a canopy.

When trees are a few metres tall, plant some **vines**. Use the less vigorous ones in small gardens. On the rainforest floor, when there is sufficient shade created by the canopy, establish **ferns**, **lilies** and **trailing plants**. Later, attach **epiphytes** such as staghorns, crows-nests and orchids to stems of trees and shrubs. Do not use bromeliaeds (such as Spanish moss) or other plants from overseas which have potential to become invasive weeds. Avoid also rainforest plants from elsewhere in Australia, such as Queensland umbrella trees and Alexandra palms (these are serious invasive weeds of local bushland), unless they are known to be non-invasive. We will be proud of our beautiful and authentic natural rainforest, recreated by using only local plants, rare and endangered species from elsewhere in South-east Queensland, and some non-invasive species from farther north in Queensland, or northern New South Wales.

Open-forest and understorey plants

Understorey species can be planted at the same time as open-forest trees and shrubs. This will eventually become an open forest with a shrubby understorey. Or, understorey plants can be planted among already existing trees to transform a woodland to open forest. The plan here is to produce several layers of vegetation - trees, large shrubs, small shrubs, ground covers, clumps of mat rush, dianellas, grasses, and climbers. This structure will provide for the greatest range of native animals. Some birds such as little lorikeets, flycatchers and weebills prefer to feed in the upper tree canopy. Some such as brown honeyeaters and shrike-thrushes prefer the middle canopy of taller shrubs. Others such as fairy-wrens, whipbirds and scrubwrens inhabit the low shrub layer. Treecreepers search up and down the trunks and branches of trees for food. On the ground there are ample cover and hiding places for brown bandicoots, skinks and frogs, especially if the surface is strewn with sticks and logs. Logs, root-balls and hollows should not be taken from bushland areas - wildlife species need them here as well. When developers are flattening bush for new housing estates, ask for root balls of trees, logs and tree hollows to be set aside for delivery to the garden. They are destined otherwise for burning. A lot of shrubs and heath plants are spiky or prickly and these should be liberally mixed in with the softer foliage plants to make it safer for native animals and discourage cats and dogs.

Shrubberies and heath-land plantings should be set out in sweeping curves and provide corridors from one part of the garden to the others, or hopefully, from one garden to the neighbours'. To plant a heath-land, simply use plants that grow to a height of one and a half metres or less in an area that receives plenty of sunlight. (See pages 206 to 212.)

When planting to create open forest, woodland or heath-land, to keep out grass and other unwanted plants, **organic mulch** can be used on an **underlay** of newspaper, about eight sheets thick. Here the mulch does not have to be very deep - about 5 centimetres. **Inorganic mulches** of river rocks and coarse gravels can also be used, especially if we wish to create the impression of a dry stream or gravel bank. These materials are the by-products of the extraction of sand and gravel and thus can be made useful again for wildlife. For mulching of gardens close to houses, materials such as pebbles and river rocks, underlain with plastic weed mesh, do not attract termites.

There is no need to have borders between lawned and mulched areas except where gravel or small rocks are likely to spill out onto the lawn. Borders that look natural can be made from logs (pruned branches and stems from culled plants do nicely), sleepers and large river rocks. Concrete mowing edges help keep out lawn grasses. **Tracks and trails** through forest, shrubbery and heath-land can be made of mulch of a different colour or texture. These should be planned out at the start. To discourage traffic through planted areas, mulches that are uncomfortable to walk on, such as macadamia shells, may be used.

Seedlings of **invasive plants** will appear in amongst the trees and shrubs we retain or plant. Identify these and pull them out. A few of the common ones to look out for are camphor laurel, Chinese elm, broad-leaf pepper, Brazilian cherry, ochna, umbrella tree, golden raintree, privet, asparagus 'ferns' and lantana. Some local native species may also appear. Leave these where they are if in suitable positions or, if not, transplant them. We can also pot them and swap for other desirable native plants.

Colourful flower gardens and annuals - using native plants

Some people love their flower beds and borders planted with annuals, their pruned and shaped flowering shrubs and, with each season, a new variety of colour and form. They appreciate the hard work involved and feel the need to be attentive to the garden each day. A completely native garden does not mean forgoing colourful flowers. It is possible to have garden beds and borders planted entirely with native annuals (or short-live perennials used as annuals) and formal flowering shrubs. We can plant, prune, shape and modify these all we like to create seasonally changing and spectacular displays. What is best though is that we can do this and not use one exotic potentially-invasive weed - no periwinkles, no Singapore daisies, no busy-lizzies, no petunias, salvias and no wandering Jew. There are many spectacular Australian plants now in use and many more just waiting to be used in gardens. At the moment some are difficult to grow successfully, almost impossible, but the secrets are being revealed by people willing to be pioneers in this field.

Many native plant species have a range of colours. Lovely **colour forms** are being discovered and introduced into gardens. Exciting new **cultivars** are being developed by **selection and cross-breeding**. Many of these are hardier than their naturally-occurring parent forms.

South-east Queensland has warm to hot, humid weather, from late spring until early autumn. Many beautiful Australian plants are not adapted to these conditions. Some plants from elsewhere in Australia, that in the past have proved unreliable, are being **grafted** onto hardy root-stock, cross-bred with local natives or selected to enable them to do well in our conditions. Many purists who grow native plants would not use some of these non-local plants. However, none of them is ever likely to become an invasive weed; and they do not look out of place in an Australian setting, as most imported plants do. Like the majority of native plants they are also very attractive to native fauna.

Neighbourly co-operation

Many people are not aware of the great beauty of native plants and the benefits of growing them. They obtain most of their information and ideas on what to plant from television programs and radio talk-back gardening shows. On these, 'experts' mostly from southern states and elsewhere, recommend and promote foreign plants almost exclusively. As well, they` tell us what chemicals to apply if as much as a chewed leaf appears on a shrub or in the lawn. If we make suggestions to the neighbours that they are establishing an incongruous assemblage of garish exotic weeds, we will not make friends and influence them towards becoming more environmentally aware. We have to be more subtle. It is best to **set a good example** for the neighbours to emulate. When our first project is under way and we have beautiful flowers, charming plant forms, colourful new leaf growth, inviting vistas, and visiting bird life, we then invite the neighbours. If we grow plants from seeds and cuttings we always have more than we need. Give some of these to our neighbours, with information about positioning and care.

CHAPTER **6**

Getting the knowledge

It takes years of experience to become an expert in native plants, but we can learn a lot in a very short time. It is exciting to learn about our country. We never stop learning, and there is so much to learn. Help is close at hand. Join the local branch of the **Society for Growing Australian Plants**. This gives us access to expert knowledge, free seeds and plants; and we will visit beautiful gardens full of natural plant and animal life.

Of course, once we have a native garden, or at least a garden with many native plants, we are going to see more animals - mammals, birds, lizards, frogs, insects and so on. We will need to know more about many (or all) of these new friends. To learn about them, or help other people learn, we can do no better than to join our local branch of the **Wildlife Preservation Society.**

Lawns

Lawns have an important place in the home garden and play an important role in our lifestyle. Outdoor living places where we can gather, play, eat and entertain are typically areas of lawn. Especially in yards close to natural bushland, lawns, strategically placed, can be an important part of protection during bushfires.

Ecologically though, lawns, in Australia, are artificial creations. Left alone a lawn soon develops into an unruly (but more natural) grassland with sedges and herbaceous plants. Under natural conditions and with time, except in arid regions, grassland becomes dotted with shrubs, tree-saplings and low climbers. Left to natural succession and not heavily grazed, the result is an open forest with a grassy and shrubby understory. Fire converts this to woodland - trees separated by areas of grass; and this immediately begins to revert to forest.

The desire of Australians to have extensive lawns probably derives partly from our European heritage. A country estate with open woodlands where grazing herbivores kept grass to a verdant carpet was a mark of success - something to admire and strive to achieve. A need for order, control and symmetry seems also to originate from our disciplined feudal past. Coupled with these factors is the fear of bushfires.

For some people though, lawns become an obsession. The whole or most of the yard has to be lawn - a monoculture of bright green, of uniform low height and without a blemish. To achieve this there has to be (once again) a continuing input of fertilisers, weedicides, insecticides, fungicides, copious amounts of water and much hard work. The labour that we are willing to expend (or pay for others to do) to tend our lawns is our own business, but the addition of chemicals to the environment should be everyone's concern. As well as having detrimental effects in situ, chemicals added to lawns find their way, via surface run-off and ground water, to streams, wetlands, bays and oceans. Waste of expensive treated water, paid for by the public, is another by-product of the cult of the 'perfect' lawn. The chemical industries that manufacture these products promote the idea that lawns are beautiful, that they should be extensive, and should be of a golf-green or bowling-green nature.

Lawns - not good habitat

Many lawns could be made smaller or replaced by paved areas, pebble gardens, rockeries or heathland gardens.

The larger the lawn the more need there is to use a motor mower. The many hundreds of thousands of mower engines that rev up each week day and every weekend throughout cities and towns consume huge amounts of fuel, converting it into greenhouse gases. As well, they add significantly to sound pollution. Many of us, especially those on acreage blocks, during the warmer months of the year become slaves to our lawns, spending hours pushing or riding our power mowers. All this to create an unnatural environment that is foreign and uninviting (even dangerous) for many native species, one that is attractive to aggressive birds of open spaces, and one that is particularly suited to exotic pest species.

Australian magpie

Pied currawong

Noisy miner

Some aggressive native birds of lawns and open spaces

Common mynah

House sparrow

Spotted turtle-dove

Some introduced birds - pests of lawns and open spaces

New 'bushland' blocks

Some of us are lucky (very lucky) enough, when we acquire our new block of land, to still have the original small under-storey plants. On small blocks this is unlikely to happen because the developer usually 'selectively' clears the whole development. The trees are bulldozed and the ground ripped so that the only plants left are a few tall spindly trees and saplings, many with injured root systems. The majority of the remaining trees are then removed to allow for building of the house. If any small gems do happen to survive the 'development' phase they are invariably crushed by the builders' boots and machinery, or covered by brickies' loam, concrete spills and carpenters' rubble.

An unfriendly place for native plants and animals

When we buy our block of land to build our new home, we should select carefully the site for the house. We may be able to save original trees, shrubs or smaller plants. We should also inform the builder of our concern for the well-being of the plants we wish to retain and protect. A clause in the building contract that imposes fines for damaging these may help a lot. We should supervise, as much as possible, the coming and going of delivery vehicles and the day-to-day activities on the building site. Builders should be aware of measures that they can take to ensure that soil is not washed off the site before and during the building phase. See pages 101 to 104 for best practice advice to developers and builders.

Our chances are better with larger blocks. The concept of acreage blocks was initiated by planners to allow for housing development in bushland areas without threatening the conservation of natural habitats and corridors between areas of non-urban bushland. Acreage caters for people who wish to live in rural or natural settings away from more closely inhabited residential areas. However, many of us on acreage blocks have not maintained the natural environment and the diverse range of native plant species that we might. By mowing and clearing and 'cleaning up' we probably exterminated many delightful and delicate plants, such as native pansies, love flowers, ground orchids, bush peas, rice flowers, flag irises, fringe lilies, blue bells, koala bells and bearded heaths.

| Fringe lily | Flag iris | Ladies tresses orchid | Love flower | Hyacinth orchid |

Just a few bushland gems lost with 'selective' clearing

By creating extensive lawns and using fertilisers we probably exterminated dormant plants that normally come up and flower in their season. We thereby, unknowingly, decreased the natural beauty, the botanical interest and value of our bushland as native habitat. More of us, no doubt, would retain these precious, interesting and beautiful plants if we knew they existed. Others of us would do so if we had an understanding of our newly acquired bushland and its opportunities and possibilities for natural landscaping; and if there were more good examples for us to emulate. Some among us would give almost anything to be able to grow and enjoy a

An example of poor environmental landscaping

range of the exquisite small plants that grace our local natural bushland. Many of these lovely bushland plants are almost impossible to acquire, yet people unwittingly wipe them out and replace them with introduced plants - plants with garish colours that jar the subdued beauty of our native landscapes.

Ponds

Garden ponds are not only attractive features in gardens, they can be important for wildlife. They are a source of **drinking and bathing water** for birds and other animals. They also provide **breeding places** for insects with aquatic larvae, such as dragonflies, damselflies, caddisflies and mayflies. Water bugs and beetles also find their homes here. As well, they are habitat for frogs and native fish. Bigger ponds in larger gardens can also attract tortoises, water skinks, water dragons, kingfishers, ducks and wading birds.

Ponds, bog gardens and other water features should be located in sites where they could be expected to occur - in the lower places, in gullies and depressions. When sited here, reeds, rushes and sedges look part of the ambient topography. Waterfalls and ponds somehow do not look as natural when perched on the top of a rockery.

The best aspect for a pond is in partial sunlight. If the position is too sunny, growth of algae will be excessive. Also, warm water is less able to dissolve oxygen. Be careful not to locate the pond near neighbours' bedrooms. The calls of some frog species can be annoying for people who do not appreciate sounds of the natural world.

Usually, the first frogs to breed in garden ponds are striped marsh frogs. This species is the least fussy of our local native frogs. It produces eggs dotted in a foam mass that floats on the top of the water. Later, species such as graceful treefrogs and green treefrogs may lay their eggs. Cane toads will also use the pond. They should be caught when the males' calls (like an idling motor) are heard, and killed by putting them in the freezer in plastic bags. Use a sieve to remove the long strands of grey transparent slime containing the small black eggs from the water. Toad tadpoles are small and black and swim in dense groups, often in shallow water. Native frog tadpoles usually swim alone and the dark-coloured ones are not as black. Catch toad tadpoles by using a fine net or sieve.

A pond can be made of concrete or moulded fibre glass, or much cheaper ones can be constructed by digging a cavity and lining it with heavy-duty polythene plastic. Used doubled, this gives a good seal. PVC or butyl rubber are longer lasting but are more expensive. In stony soils it is necessary to dig about 5 centimetres deeper and wider so that a sand covering of the hole can protect the liner. To estimate the dimensions of the plastic needed, add twice the depth of the pond to the length; and also the breadth; and allow a metre at each end and each breadth for the plastic to extend beyond the pond edges. A depth of 60 centimetres to a metre is needed for water-lilies. Use a spirit level to ensure that the tops of the banks are level. It is safe to plant plastic and fibre glass pools with local native aquatic plants as soon as construction is finished.

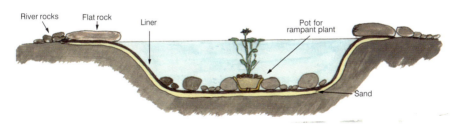

A simple and inexpensive way to construct a garden pond

The plastic that extends out around the pool should be covered by large flat river rocks and sand, and some flat rocks should overhang the pool as protection for native fish. Wading birds such as egrets and herons visit ponds to feed on fish, frogs and insects. A few other rocks can be placed within the pool itself. To prevent mosquitoes breeding in the pond, native fish should be introduced. Blue-eyes are especially suitable because they will destroy mosquito larvae but do not attack tadpoles.

The concrete used for ponds should have water-proofing compound added at mixing. The sides and bottom should be left rough. Add a thin soil-covering over the concrete surface on the sides and bottom while it is still wet and wash it off after drying. This will help to give a natural look and to assist plant attachment. Allow a period of at least ten days for the curing process before filling the pool with water. Leave this to stand a few days and then empty it. Repeat this procedure two more times.

Before the final filling for new concrete pools, and the initial filling for fibre and plastic lined pools, spread a layer of soil over the bottom to a depth of about 5 centimetres, then sand (another 5 centimetres) and, on top of these, some smooth pebble gravel. Add the water slowly so as not to stir up the soil layer and, if water is chlorinated, allow it to stand for at least 5 days. It should now be safe for planting and the addition of fish.

Where young children are likely to frequent, it might be advisable for their safety to cover ponds by use of weldmesh. To support wide expanses of covering mesh, rocks or metal supports can be used.

A garden pond

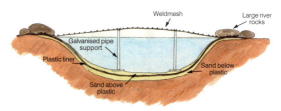

Support for wide expanses of mesh cover

Bog garden construction

A bog garden

A bog garden can be built attached to the pond, or separate from it. Here we can grow interesting native bog plants.The sand, gravel and organic mulch will be cool and moist for frogs to find shelter and refuge. Frogs that burrow into sand and fine gravel include the ornate burrowing frog and the scarlet-sided pobblebonk. Some frogs that hide under leaf litter are the beeping froglet, sandy gungan and great brown broodfrog. Those that shelter in cracks and crevices between rocks and pebbles include the naked treefrog and bleating treefrog. Finding shelter and refuge in clumps of grass and in grass litter are the striped marshfrog and spotted marshfrog.

Plants for ponds and bog gardens

To provide food and shelter for tadpoles, fish and other aquatic animals, it will be necessary to establish plants in the pond. Use local aquatic plants. Many imported plants and a few from northern Australia are some of our worst waterway weeds. Species to avoid include, water hyacinth (*Eichornia crassipes*), salvinia (*S. molesta*) and water lettuce (*Pistia stratiotes*). Some plants will need to be controlled by growing them in submerged containers that can be taken up occasionally for trimming back excess growth. Some plants may need a depth of one metre for good growth, but 60 cm is generally sufficient.

| Bulrushes | Sedges | Native waterlilies | 'Common reed' | 'Nardoo' |

Some emergent plants

Duckweed   Azolla

Some native floating plants

Ceratophyllum   Hydrilla   Potamogeton

Some native submerged plants

| Koala bells | Star goodenia | Frogsmouth | Water primrose | Purple violet |

Some native bog plants

| Mat rush | Pimelia | Thyme honey-myrtle | Swamp grasstree | Wallum bottlebrush |

Some small plants (< 2 m) for areas near ponds and bog gardens, and for heathlands

Nest Boxes for native animals

Few very **old hollow trees** are left standing after clearing for grazing in rural areas and for urban development. Almost all are removed or severely pruned in public parkland. This is because falling branches pose a threat to the safely of domestic animals and people. In bushland, hot fires often cause old trees to fall and sometimes to burn away entirely. It is these trees containing hollows that provide breeding places and micro-habitats for many animals to shelter.

Animals that use tree hollows include the following:

- <u>Birds:</u> parrots (such as cockatoos, rosellas, king parrots and lorikeets); kingfishers (including kookaburras); dollar birds; wood swallows; tree martins; tree creepers; owls; nightjars; kestrels; some ducks.

- <u>Mammals:</u> insectivorous bats; native rats; brush-tail possums; gliders; phascogales.

- <u>Reptiles:</u> some skinks; lace monitors; tree snakes.

- <u>Frogs:</u> green treefrog, graceful treefrog, emerald-spotted treefrog, laughing treefrog, bleating treefrog; naked treefrog.

Cutting down trees and collecting fallen logs from the bush are not the solutions to providing hollows in gardens. **Logs in the bush** are vital resources needed by wild animals. When land is being cleared for development, many hollow trees are burnt. Most developers are quite happy to allow the taking of hollow logs when land is being cleared, if permission is sought and if people do not put themselves in danger. It is best not to buy hollow logs from landscape and garden supply outlets and so encourage their removal from the bush, unless an assurance can be given that they are only taken from land destined for clearing.

Nest boxes can be obtained from suppliers or can be home-made. These are specially designed to suit the needs of particular species of animals. Boxes are as attractive to wild animals as natural hollows, and can be attached to trees, walls of houses and poles. Whenever possible trees with natural hollows should be retained. Artificial nesting facilities should not be installed simply as an excuse to remove old trees.

Because the environmental factor that limits populations of many animals is the availability of tree hollows, when we put up artificial facilities animals soon move in. Observations of their use of nest boxes can provide much interest and enjoyment. Care must be taken to ensure unwanted species do not take over boxes intended for native animals. This is why it is best to put them at a height that can be reached by home extension ladders. Feral honey bees are a common problem and, unless we have the proper equipment and knowledge to remove these, it is best to invite the services of a beekeeper. Some bee enthusiasts will pay to take a good bee colony. Other species that should be evicted include house sparrows, common starlings, feral pigeons and common mynahs. Any eggs of these pests should be smashed and their young destroyed. A puff of lice powder may be needed to kill infestations after birds have finished nesting. This is available from pet shops.

The availability of nesting hollows may not be the limiting factor for populations of some species. Supply of food, or other requirements, may be the crucial determinants of numbers. If this is so, then these species will not benefit from extra nesting sites.

Making nest boxes

Nest boxes can be easily made. Use **hardwood** so that the box does not rot away in a few years. Similarly, use **galvanised nails**. Wood that is too thin will allow the inside to become too hot or cold when outside temperatures change. A ladder of wood or weldmesh should be attached inside below the entrance hole. Place the box on a pole, the side of the house or in a tree, the opening to the north-east. This protects against driving wind and hot sun during the breeding season. Take care that the box does not move about in strong winds. If the nest box is attached to a living tree, use metal strapping around the tree rather than thin wire. Birds, especially parrots, like to clamber all over their nesting sites and could catch their feet between the wire and the box or tree. Do not use nails in living trees, use non-rust screws. Reattach the box every couple of years to help prevent injury to the tree.

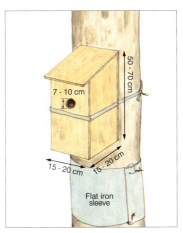

Nest box suitable for rosellas and lorikeets

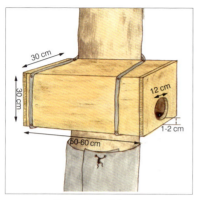

Nest box for kookaburras

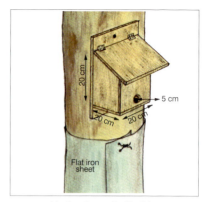

Nest box for smaller kingfishers

Nest box for barn owls

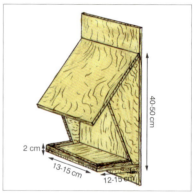

Nest box for swallows

Nest box for tree-nesting ducks

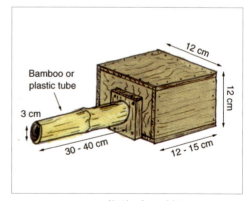

Nest box for pardalotes

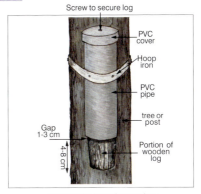

Nest box for brush-tail possums

Nest box for insectivorous bats

Bush rocks and rockeries

Rocks should not be removed from their natural resting places in the bush. Those covered in **lichens** or **moss** are beautiful natural objects and look superb in the right setting. Very often though, plants growing on rocks require quite precise conditions for growth and survival, and slowly die when put into garden situations. Many animals (such as skinks and other lizards, snakes, frogs, small marsupials and native rodents) need rocks for shelter, for breeding sites or to sun-bask. Numerous native invertebrates (such as snails, slugs, millipedes, centipedes, scorpions, spiders, beetles and ants) need the rocks as living places and for food collection, and are part of the food web that includes many frog, reptile, bird and mammal species. Precious soil is in danger of erosion when rocks are disturbed. By buying from commercial outlets for bush rocks we only encourage their removal from the wild, even if the rocks come from private property. Only when taken from places destined for road works, housing development or other drastic alteration should bush rocks be removed from the wild.

Rockeries have to be designed carefully to appear natural. There are few garden designs more hideous than rockeries where rocks stand up like jagged teeth, or headstones in a graveyard. Rocks should appear as if they now rest where they fell, or where they eroded out of the surrounding rocks and soil. Sedimentary rocks, such as sandstone, should lie so that the strata are more or less parallel, undulating or inclined. Similarly with the 'bedding' of metamorphic rocks such as slate, phyllite and schist. It is unwise to mix together rocks of different origin. Rock boulders, such as granitic tors, should lie not stand; and spalds should look as though they have flaked off in situ. River rocks look best when they appear as they would in the pebble bar of a stream. Rocks really look much better when partially covered with appropriate plants. See pages 206 to 212 for a list of native rockery plants.

Planting to attract butterflies

Butterflies are a delightful component of nature. In our subtropical part of the world butterflies can be seen at any time of the year, most of them flying during the warm seasons. Butterflies (and moths) have two stages that require food - the larval stage (caterpillar) and the adult. The larvae usually eat leaves, and adults feed on nectar, pollen, fruit juice and plant exudate ('sap'). To encourage butterflies into our gardens we can provide for the caterpillars and the adults by planting appropriate species. Most butterflies also drink water and will visit ponds and bog areas to drink from floating leaves and wet sand.

Butterflies are attracted to flowers by colour and scent. Most plants in flower, whether native or introduced, will attract butterflies to our gardens. Even if we have not one plant, butterflies will fly past in search of food and mates, or during migration flights, but they will not be enticed to stay. Not as many plants will attract female butterflies in search of plants on which to lay their eggs, and males in search of these females. Here is where native plants are important, although there are many introduced plants that provide food for the caterpillars of some of our native butterflies. Introduced citrus species are good examples of this, and so is the camphor laurel tree, though we should not be tempted to plant or retain camphor laurels - beautiful trees but terribly invasive weeds.

| Blue tiger | Tailed emperor | Big greasy | Common crow |

Some common butterflies of Pine Rivers

Another introduced plant that attracts female butterflies to it is the introduced Dutchman's pipe (*Aristolochia elegans*). The female of the large and beautiful Richmond birdwing lays her eggs on this vine and the caterpillars die when they eat the leaves. We should all ensure that we do not have this plant in the garden and instead, we should plant the native species *Aristolochia praevenosa*, the Richmond birdwing vine.

Richmond birdwing vine

Male Richmond birdwing butterfly

Another group of plants that attracts many beautiful butterflies is the **mistletoes** - parasites of trees and shrubs. All the local mistletoes are native species and are well adapted. Well adapted parasites do not usually kill their hosts. A tree can be host to quite a few mistletoes and not be severely affected. Thus we should not cut mistletoes from our garden plants - they do practically no harm yet provide food for a great many nectar-feeding birds, fruit-eating birds (such as the delightful songster, the mistletoe bird), insectivorous birds and butterflies.

Mistletoe - plant parasite but a useful plant in the garden

Mistletoebird - spreads its food supply

Common jezabel

Northern jezabel

Mistletoes attract native fauna

Often mistaken for a butterfly is Australia's most colourful **moth**, the Joseph's coat moth (*Agarista agricola*) that flies during the day. Its spectacular caterpillars have bands of white, orange and black and feed on the leaves of native grape vines (*Cayratia spp* and *Cissus spp*)

Larva of the Joseph's coat moth on slender grape (Cayratia clematidea)

Joseph's coat moth (Agarista agricola)

CHAPTER **7**

Nature Strips and Footpaths

Areas in front of house blocks offer us opportunities to create habitat and corridors along streets and roads. We have to take some precautions when planting in this area. Factors to consider include the width of the street-side strip and the presence or absence and location of power lines, communication cables, sewerage pipes, water mains and footpaths.

Some desired characteristics of plants for street planting are:

- having non-invasive roots.

- being of small to medium height. Height is important to consider when there are overhead lines.

- being tolerant of heavy pruning. Some trees that grow to considerable height in the wild, or when left to grow unchecked, can, with pruning, be kept to the required proportions.

- being hardy and long lived. Some shorter-lived plants can be planted among others that form a permanent foundation.

- having a non-suckering habit. Species that produce growth (suckers) from surface roots can be a nuisance on nature strips.

- being local native plants or non-invasive native plants from elsewhere in Australia.

- not having harmful spines, irritant sap, poisonous fruit, etc.

Backhousia citriodora as a street tree   Pittosporum rhombifolium   Buckinghamia celcissima

Some hints on planting in the nature strip

- Draw a plan showing the location of underground and overhead service structures, high pressure water outlets, footpaths, etc.

- Consult the local council to see if permission is required and to find out where to plant. Generally, if there are overhead cables, planting between and in line with supporting poles will avoid putting plants where future footpaths or bikeways may be located.

- Select local native species that have the above desired characteristics (see species list Appendix 4, pages 224 to 226).

- Plant a variety of species to increase the benefits to local wildlife. A monoculture (one species only) does not supply the range of foods for wildlife, in a variety of seasons, that several species do.

- Remember that this area is public property and objects and structures that may obstruct public access, such as rocks, fences and gardens, should not be put here.

- Consult with neighbours to extend plantings to in front of their houses. If plants have been grown from seed and there are some spare, offer these for free.

- Use tree guards or tall stakes if there is pedestrian traffic. Short stakes may not be seen by pedestrians.

- Cater for special wildlife species by selecting plants that provide food and other requirements for these. For example, if there is room, plant koala food trees (see page 89) if koala habitat with koalas occurs nearby.

Environment-friendly layout designs for housing developments

Education of developers and landscape designers in the value and care of bushland, and the landscaping potential of many local native plants, could result in housing developments that are more ecologically sound. It would greatly help the general public if there were more examples to follow of **better species selection** and **environment-friendly landscape design**. It is possible to design housing development layouts to provide **very wide nature strips** along all streets, with smaller areas for house blocks. This would enable developers to retain or re-establish natural bush on both sides of streets to provide wildlife habitat and corridors, and yet not decrease the overall numbers of house blocks. In developments where block sizes are planned to be large this could be an easy and ideal way of retaining bushland. The species to be planted on these wide nature strips, being situated on public land, could be controlled by local laws. More house holders would then be encouraged to become involved in caring for and learning about bushland, especially if given helpful information.

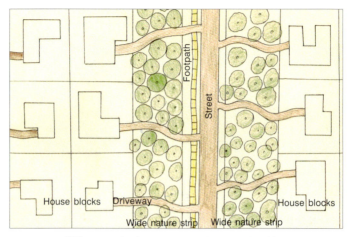

Wide nature strips along streets to provide bushland corridors

An alternative or addition to the above could be the requirement that **houses be set a long way back from the street**. On larger blocks especially, this would give greater scope for people to retain more native plants, particularly larger trees.

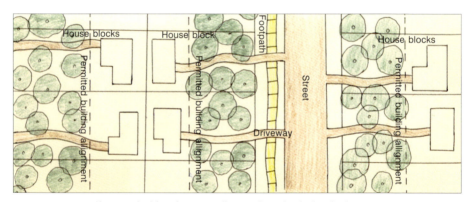

Houses set back from the street to allow retention and replanting of native trees

Another option would be to leave strips of natural or re-established bushland behind house blocks to form corridors midway between streets (and thus between house blocks). This would be particularly appropriate for establishing **corridors along gullies and larger streams**.

A list of local native plants and native species from elsewhere, suitable for planting along nature strips, is provided on pages 224 to 226.

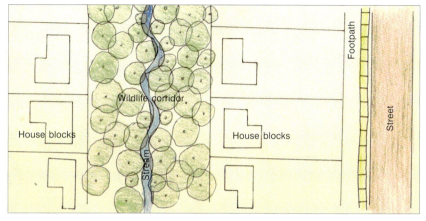

Corridors of bushland between streets and houses

Protecting and enhancing nature strip vegetation and wildlife corridors

Sensitive environmental planning and better practice in development of housing projects results in residents having natural habitat with trees, shrubs, vines, and understorey plants on their land, or in nearby nature strips and wildlife corridors. These precious remnants of our local Australian bushland need to be protected so that the native animals dependent upon them will be here in the future. By applying the following suggestions we can help to ensure the health of these environments:

- plant **local native species** only, or non-invasive native plants from elsewhere (see plant lists in appendices).

- gradually cull **introduced plants** and invasive plants from elsewhere in Australia (see pages 237 to 247) and replace these with local native plants.

- do not use fertilisers; or use them sparingly and only organic ones and those low in phosphorous.

- keep **mowed areas** to a minimum to encourage the survival of native grasses and low-growing native plant gems.

- do not pile **grass clippings**, other organic mulch or soil around the bases of trees and shrubs. This encourages fatal collar-rot fungal diseases.

- do not use **chemicals** of any kind. It is normal for plants and parts of plants to be eaten by animals such as insects, or to die. It is also normal for spiders and other predatory native animals to live in and maintain a natural balance in gardens and bushland.

- if you feel the need to establish gardens with **exotic flowers and shrubs**, keep these near the house and not in natural areas. Do not use any plants that are known to invade bushland (see pages 237 to 242).

CHAPTER

8

Special Animals of the Pine Rivers Shire

All native animals are special, even those that at times may cause economic damage (dingos, king parrots and wallabies), annoy us by disturbing our sleep or peace of mind (koels, possums, frogs and cicadas) or ruin the paint work of our vehicles from above (lorikeets and fruit bats). Sadly, unless we are more careful, some of them (hopefully not too many) in the future will have gone; and we will miss them. Who would not love to see Tasmanian tigers and paradise parrots still living in the wild? There is a chance that dingos, glossy black cockatoos and some others could go the same way, just as tiger quolls have done.

Koala *Phascolarctos cinereus*

The Pine Rivers Shire is one of the few places in Australia where koalas can still be seen regularly in fair numbers in semi-rural and residential areas close to a large metropolitan area. We should be very conscious of this and realise just how lucky we are. Unless we change the way we are destroying, little by little, their remaining habitats and severing their dispersal corridors, the sad time of no more koalas will be upon us. This will be a great pity because, even with our continuing urban growth, we can still make room for koalas by growing their food trees in our gardens, along our streets, in parks and on farms. It will be necessary though for us to control their enemies, domestic dogs, and slow down as we drive along streets and roads when they are on the move.

The koala is a **high profile animal** - they are cute and all the world loves them. There are many other animals that need help to survive - much more so than the koala. However, by protecting the needs of koalas we also provide for other species. The koala therefore **brings attention to the environment** and our duty to conserve it.

Koalas eat the leaves of only a limited number of species of trees. The most important ones in the local area are included in the following list.

Heed these signs in our Shire - look out especially for the koalas

CHAPTER 8

Koala Food Species of the Pine Rivers Shire

Scientific Name	Common Name	Comments
Eucalyptus biturbinata (E. punctata)	Grey Gum	Large tree
Eucalyptus crebra	Narrow-leaf Ironbark	Medium to large tree
Eucalyptus grandis	Rose Gum	Very large tree
Eucalyptus (C.) intermedia	Pink Bloodwood	Medium tree
Eucalyptus (C.) maculata	Spotted Gum	Tall slender tree
Eucalyptus microcorys	Tallowwood	Large tree
Eucalyptus molluccana	Gum-topped Box	Large tree
Eucalyptus pilularis	Blackbutt	Large tree
Eucalyptus propinqua	Narrow-fruited Grey Gum	Large tree
Eucalyptus resinifer	Red Mahogany	Large tree
Eucalyptus robusta	Swamp Mahogany	Medium tree
Eucalyptus saligna	Sydney Blue Gum	Very large tree
Eucalyptus seeana	Narrow-leaf Red Gum	Small and medium forms
Eucalyptus siderophloia	Grey Ironbark	Large tree
Eucalyptus tereticornis	Qld Blue Gum species	Large tree; a favourite
Lophostemon confertus	Brush Box	Large tree

Trees marked (C.) are now regarded as Corymbia, not Eucalyptus

How to help koalas survive:

- Do not let your dog roam, especially at night.

- If there is a koala in your house yard, restrain your dog and leave the koala alone.

- Retain koala food trees whenever possible and/or plant more food trees.

- When building fences, make these koala friendly to allow koalas to travel from tree to tree, to mate, or to disperse after the breeding season. Timber fences allow koalas to climb. If a fence is not easy to pass, lean logs up on either side, and plant trees close together on either side. Neighbourly cooperation may be needed. Remember, other kinds of wildlife, including ones that cannot climb, may need to pass through fences as well.

- Take special care while driving at night in koala country, particularly in the breeding and dispersal periods - between early spring and late summer.

- If you find an injured or sick koala, leave it alone (they scratch and bite) and contact the Department of Environment (3202 0200).

Platypus *Ornithorhynchus anatinus*

Though not often seen, the platypus is still quite common in streams of the Pine Rivers catchment. They prefer fresh water but also live in brackish water. Platypuses are active at dawn and dusk but may also be observed in the daytime, especially on cloudy days. They lie low on the water surface and glide smoothly along before submerging with a typically mammalian up-and-down diving roll.

The platypus is one of the only two kinds of monotremes - **egg-laying mammals**. The eggs (usually two) are laid in a burrow in the bank of the stream. The mother incubates the eggs and, after hatching, the young are fed on **milk** until they leave the nest at about four months. Platypuses feed on invertebrates sifted from the bottom mud and water by use of the **duck-like bill**. The male has two poisonous spurs on his back legs and so platypuses are therefore best left alone.

Degradation of stream banks and **pollution** of water by insecticides and other chemicals (from gardens, farms and factories) are the main threats to the continued survival of these **wonders of the world**. Needing to breathe at the surface, platypuses die quickly when caught in fish traps and nets.

Platypus

Powerful Owl *Ninox strenua*

The powerful owl is Australia's largest owl. During the day it shelters in tall forest trees and in dense vegetation along timbered creeks. It is shy and rarely seen. At night it hunts for roosting birds, gliders, possums and fruit bats. It often roosts while holding the headless remains of one of its victims under one foot.

For a long time this owl was credited with making a terrifying screech, but this is more likely a call occasionally uttered by the much smaller barking owl. The powerful owl's call is a loud 'woo-who'. Powerful owls nest in hollows in trees, usually high above the ground. The female does all of the incubation of the two eggs, that hatch after 38 days.

Though powerful owls are fairly rare birds, they seem to be holding their own. To enable them to survive, we need to ensure that enough habitat remains for their prey animals to be numerous - powerful owl pairs require large territories. Being at the top of food chains, they are in danger of poisoning by chemicals magnified at each link in the chain.

CHAPTER

Problem Animals

From time to time, people perceive some native animal species to be nuisances. Many of the problems we have with animals, we have brought upon ourselves. Sometimes the problem is all in our heads. Usually the animal is simply acting by instinct, often in a changed environment. In other instances the animal acts in a manner that we have trained it. Some of us become so infuriated with a problem animal that we call for the eradication of the species. It is very sad to think that people can be so intolerant, inflexible and self-centred. They assume that every other creature in the environment should act only to please us; and that animals doing things we do not like should not exist. We have encroached upon the animals' environment - they, as well as we, must live with the environment. It may be a case of 'live and let live', or even, 'get a life'.

Introduced animals that compete with, prey upon, or spread diseases and parasites to our native animals are problem animals, even though many of us are unaware of their existence. Though many of them are beautiful and beautifully adapted, they have to be controlled for the sake of our natural environment.

A List of Problem Animals

Animals	Problems	Solutions
Ants	Come into house	Leave no food particles; wipe metho across trails
Cicadas	Males' loud calls	Don't listen; listen to music on head phones.
Flies	Walk on food; crawl upon us	Install fly screens. Outdoors - apply lavender oil
Lawn Grubs	Kill patches in lawn	Ignore - hatchet wasps will parasitise grubs, birds will eat them; put wet bag or towel on lawn overnight & lift in morning to kill grubs.
Hatchet Wasps	Fly over lawn	Ignore and enjoy. These beautiful wasps do not sting unless held, but they control lawn grubs.
Mosquitoes	Female bites; spreads disease	Install fly screens. Outdoors - apply lavender oil; put blue-eyes (fish) in ponds; remove old tyres, & containers holding water and larvae. Do not use plants that retain water (eg some bromeliaeds)

Animals	Problems	Solutions
Mud-dabber Wasps	Carry mud into house	Install fly screens. Outdoors - leave mud nests until after hatching. Wasps control spiders and moths, and pollinate plants.
Paper Wasps	Sting when we go too near nest	Burn (carefully) nests of only those down low, leave others. Wasps control pests and pollinate plants.
Spiders (in/on house)	Come into house; build webs under eaves & verandahs	Install fly screens; catch huntsman in plastic jar & release; catch house spiders on feather duster; spiders eat flies, mosquitoes & roaches. Outdoors - leave webs or use broom - chemicals kill wagtails, skinks, geckos & bats - these eat insects & spiders.
Spiders (in garden) Orb-weavers	Build webs across paths	Leave if not in way; these only bite if harassed - not dangerous; orb-weavers eat insects.
Funnel Webs & Trapdoors	Active at night; bite if annoyed	Leave alone unless in areas used at night.
Garden Snails (Helix) & Slugs	Eat garden plants	Do not use snail bait - harms pets & blue-tongued skinks that eat snails & slugs. Use saucers of stale beer to kill. Do not kill flat-coiled snails - these are carnivorous & eat pest snails & slugs.
Striped Marsh Frogs	"Tock, Tock, Tock, ..."	Don't listen, or listen & enjoy; listen to music on headphones; build frog ponds away from bedroom windows. All frogs eat insects.
Green Treefrogs	Croak; sit on windows at night	Totally harmless. No frogs (or toads) cause warts. Frogs eat insects. Enjoy calls - herald rain.
Cane Toads	Cause fear(?); harm animals; eat pets' food	Catch & freeze; get over fear; give pets just enough food or remove excess. Remove eggs (long ribbons of slime with black dots) from water. Remove tadpoles (small, black & in groups in shallows) from water.
Snakes in garden	Cause fear	Leave alone - snakes eat mice & rats; most are harmless; or call Dept of Environment 3202 0200. All snakes are protected by law.
Pythons in ceiling	Cause fear	Leave alone - pythons eat rats & mice; all are non-poisonous but will bite if annoyed; or call Dept. of Environment 3202 0200.
Lizards in garden	Cause fear	Leave alone - all are harmless; get over fear. Lizards eat insect pests. Blue-tongues eat snails.
Brush-tail Possums	Live in ceiling - noise Run on roof	Close hole(s) to ceiling after dusk; put nest boxes in garden; have professional trap & relocate.

Animals	Problems	Solutions
Birds	Peck at windows	Put paper or cardboard along window to stop reflection; or cut-out of big-eyed owl; or plastic snake.
Birds	Fly into glass doors & large windows	Put transfers of leaves/stems/flowers/pattern on glass to break flight-path scene.
Birds	Call at night or early	Don't listen or listen and enjoy; play soft music or use headphones.
Feral Pigeons	Nest on ledges; spread lice	Catch & kill humanely - introduced vermin.
Scrub Turkeys	Rake up garden plants etc	Wait until late summer to plant; put a pile of leaves or compost heap where you can tolerate a mound; use tree guards or rock piles around plants. Scrub turkeys are wonders of the bird world.
Butcherbirds	Chase small birds; annoy & kill caged birds	Do not feed butcherbirds; plant low & medium shrubs, some spiny, for small birds. Encourage neighbours to do likewise.
Noisy Miners	Chase & harass small birds	See butcherbirds. Leave no food scraps about.
Crows	Call at dawn; call at any time; harass small birds	Don't listen; get out of bed & enjoy the morning; play soft music; listen to music on headphones; plant under-storey & spiny plants for small birds; clean up scraps. Crows control insects, rats, mice & toads, and clear away scraps & carrion.
Currawongs	As for crows	See crows.
Magpies	Chase and peck people	Do not annoy, chase or throw things at magpies; hold twigs above your head; put large eyes on back of your hat or cap. Useful birds.
Spur-winged Plovers	Chase people	Keep away from nest & young. Useful birds.
White Ibis	Nuisance on sports fields; take food at public & private out-door eating areas; sometimes aggressive	Clean away all scraps; do not feed; give dog just enough food or remove excess.
Hares	Chew newly planted shrubs, trees and crops	Use tree guards and plastic sleeves around small plants. Have professionals trap and destroy. Introduced vermin.
Foxes	Destroy native animals	Do not leave uneaten dog food outside at night. Fox-proof the fowl house. Pen lambs and kids at night & during daytime when first born. Have professionals trap and destroy.
Dingos	Kill small livestock	Pen small livestock at night. Dingos control foxes, feral cats, hares, rats & mice, & maintain balance in natural environments.

Tourism - The Woolshed, Ferny Hills (PRSC)

CHAPTER **10**

Acreage Blocks

The zoning of larger blocks of land as **rural residential**, **park residential** or the new zoning category, **forest residential**, allow those of us who choose to live in pleasant natural surroundings to do so. Much of the wildlife habitat of the Shire is on private property and so we have a great opportunity and responsibility to help preserve our precious bushland and the wildlife dependent upon it.

Many acreage blocks are not connected to a sewerage system. **Effluent** is disposed of by way of various types of **septic systems** or more modern on-site treatment plants. It is essential that each system has sufficient inbuilt capacity to treat the likely output of the household. Guidelines for home owners are available from Council. Regular **maintenance** of these systems is essential to make sure that they do not allow contaminated water to flow out into gullies and streams. Grease traps and septic trenches need **regular inspections**. It is important to study carefully the maintenance manual for a particular system and to carry out all instructions fully. Down-stream water quality is at stake.

Hints for protecting and enhancing the natural environment on large and acreage blocks:

- Select a house site on the block so as to cause the least impact on the natural environment.

- Preserve natural bush as much as possible, and with a variety of habitats consisting of trees, shrubs and ground covers.

- Replant with local native plants. Also, if habitats are suitable, grow some rare and endangered native species of south-eastern Queensland.

- If a traditional garden is desired, confine it to the area around the house. See pages 232 to 235 for information on colourful natives to use instead of the usual exotics.

- Select non-invasive garden plants.

- Make the area of lawn as small as possible and design it to aid in fire protection.

- Retain areas of natural grasses and small native plants. Do not mow these areas as they contain some delightful plants and are important habitat for native animals.

- Retain habitat trees - the ones with hollows that provide shelter and nesting sites for many native animals.

- If you own a dog, fence off a yard around the house, or put the dog on a wire run. Keep it on a leash at all times that it is outside the yard. This will protect wildlife species on most of the property. See pages 107 and 108.

- If you own a cat, keep it inside at night and in a large out-door cage during the day unless it is under your direct control. See pages 106 and 107.

- If you keep grazing animals, fence off natural areas and stream corridors, and use tree guards.

Fenced-off natural area protected from stock

Tree guards are needed in pasture areas

- Do not build fences across wildlife corridors. Make fences koala friendly. See page 89.

- Use artificial nest boxes to make up for the shortage of tree-hollow nesting sites in the wild, but do not use this as an excuse to remove old and hollow trees. See pages 79 to 81.

- Take steps to protect your house in the event of a bush fire. See pages 128 to 131.

CHAPTER 11

Residential Development & Building with the Environment

Though many **developers** claim to be 'environmentally aware' and 'green developers', this is rarely the case. The actual devastation wrought upon the environment when developments are under way, and when completed, demonstrates, time and time again, the truth of this. We cannot blame developers alone. As they often point out, "We only provide what the public wants". The problem is that many people, who would love to have a little piece of natural bushland, are denied the opportunity. Others only have ideas as to what they want, in a garden or streetscape, from what they have seen in developers' adds on television (showing some bushland in the far distance) and in periodicals that rarely feature native bush gardens. Education of both the public and developers is therefore essential. If we are to save many of our native wildlife species during urban development, we must address the needless transformation of bushland and rural areas into sterile and artificial replicas of illustrations from American or European home-garden magazines.

Landscape architects and engineers, with some exceptions, must also shoulder much of the blame for the sad lack of developments that illustrate environmental best practice. They could and should lead the way. People simply need more good examples to emulate. Better planning and design and more appropriate procedures in construction are required at almost every stage of development. Sensitivity is usually lacking in the selective clearing of land, the retention of native plant species and the protection of wildlife corridors, stream bank vegetation and natural habitats. Rather, a blitzkrieg, scorched-earth policy, involving the eradication of all plants and the total modification of the natural topography, is too often used.

'Selective' clearing

Housing development where the environment
is highly modified.

CHAPTER **11**

Environmental concern is rarely evident in the selection of species for street planting, and in the landscaping around sales offices and of display villages. Even the naming of developments, and of the streets and parks within, sometimes shows poor imagination and no feel for local history and the regional environment.

Not good environmental landscaping

Choice of trees, shrubs, ground-covers and vines, for planting in **public parks and gardens** and along **streets and roads**, is too often a case of 'what we have', rather than what is most appropriate. **Main roads** especially, too often have verges and centre-spaces planted with species that detract from or are incongruous with the natural landscape. Construction of highways, roads and streets destroys so much bushland that, for the sake of our natural environment and landscape, we should have a policy of replanting local native species where ever possible.

Poor selection of street plants

Jacarandas, poincianas, leopard trees, Norfolk Island pines, poinsettias, oleanders, and exotic bauhinias and pines, are not natives. They alter the appearance of the countryside and provide little for native animals; and some are invasive. All can be replaced with excellent local native trees and shrubs, such as silky oak, flame tree, wheel-of-fire, hoop pine, lilly-pillies, eucalypts, brush box, other grevilleas, bottlebrushes, melaleucas, banksias and a great number of lesser-known locals. Lomandras, crinums, dianellas, hibbertias and myoporums are much more appropriate than Japanese honeysuckle, dietes, exotic lilies and other introduced plants. Native vines, such as bower-of-beauty, wonga vine, scrambling lily and wombat berry, used instead of exotics, are ideal for planting along sound-barrier fences.

The reason given for choosing oleanders and other exotics ahead of natives, for planting between highway lanes, is that birds might be attracted to native plants and killed by traffic. Honey-eaters and small insectivorous birds are rarely killed on highways. Birds that are killed are those that fly low with direct flight, such as kingfishers, and those, such as butcher birds, that are attracted by insects and other animals struck by cars.

Recently in the Pine Rivers Shire, developers, landscape architects and engineers worked together with Council officers to plan and produce developments friendly to the environment. These won State and National awards for good environmental practice. Features of these developments include retained, enhanced and re-established wildlife corridors; retention of treed skylines; natural measures for stream-water quality control; natural area parkland; and cabinet timber plantations of local indigenous trees. These best-practice developments set good examples for other projects in this and other local government

Award winning environmental development in Pine Rivers Shire

areas. All we need to do when we buy these blocks is to think about how, in our building, landscaping and living styles, we can help to continue the protection, already begun, of our beautiful and unique natural environment.

Builders too could take more care and use measures to decrease the amount of damage their activities inflict upon the environment. Studies show that one storm can wash as much as four truckloads of soil from a normal-sized house block if the developer or builder has not taken appropriate measures to control erosion and sedimentation. Sediments and pollutants washed down from building sites adversely affect wetlands, waterways and coastal habitats. Cement, paint, thinners, detergents, plaster and termite-treatment chemicals washed into aquatic habitats may kill wildlife. Deposition, of soil, mud and sand, decreases the effectiveness of storm water channels and pipes, and causes silting of streams and beaches. Repairs are costly.

Bare soil needs protection

People constructing new homes can assist in protecting the environment by insisting that contractors or architects supervise the practices of their workers, subcontractors and suppliers to ensure environmental best-practice. Regular inspections of the building site also help.

Surveys of residents by the Pine Rivers Shire Council continue to indicate that the rural nature and natural landscape values of the Shire are important criteria for people in their decisions to settle and remain here. It would be a tragedy for us if, during development, we destroy the very thing that makes this shire an attractive and pleasant place to live.

Practices of subdivision planners and developers who work with the environment:

- Consult with Council Environmental Services Section first.

- Obtain and make use of information about local plants, local plant communities and the native animals dependent upon these.

- Whenever possible, ensure the preservation and restoration of wildlife corridors, streams and natural habitats.

- Where possible, begin the selective clearing only after the layout of blocks has been determined. This allows the retention of trees, shrubs and ground cover plants in areas where they are more likely to be retained by the new owners. Vegetation can be left on nature strips, but house pad sites may be cleared. Natural rock outcrops and habitat trees then also will have some hope of being saved.

- Retain the natural contours of the land as much as possible to keep earthworks to a minimum.

- Stage developmental phases to keep soil exposure to a minimum and reduce erosion during construction.

- Retain natural stream characteristics and riparian vegetation.

- If flow paths need modification use structures such as boulders, riffles and meanders to cause ripples and rapids for oxygenation of the water, and to create pools and point-bars to provide habitats and refuges for aquatic wildlife.

- Retain, as far as possible, the natural patterns of storm water flow.

- Go around rather than through or into nearby natural areas, such as wetlands, heath and woodlands during construction phases.

- Use degraded areas for access pathways rather than sensitive high-value areas.

- Place stockpiles on cleared and degraded areas, not areas of good habitat.

- Use flagged stakes, and picket and wire fences to outline and confine work sites.

- Locate sports fields, if they are to be sited in natural areas, on the edge rather than towards the centre.

- Route pathways, bike tracks and roads, when passing through natural areas, near the margins not through the centre. If possible, skirt sensitive habitats. Similarly, paths should not go close to habitat trees. This is to ensure that these old and hollow trees do not have to be lopped or cut down for safety reasons.

- Revegetate natural areas with local plant species.

- Landscape roads, streets, sales offices, display areas and homes by using appropriate local native plants and non-invasive native plants from elsewhere, preferably those from South-east Queensland.

- Plant a quick-growing temporary crop, such as rye, on slopes formed in thick soil and poorly compacted sediments during cut-and-fill operations and road and street construction. Alternatively, cover slopes with sheets of pegged hessian or rip-rap (made of organic material) and plant with local native, slope-binding plants (See pages 228 to 230 for list). Encourage and enhance natural regeneration on rocky, secure slopes created during development.

Natural regeneration on a rocky cutting

Hydro-mulch and cover-crop on slope

- Use sediment barriers around areas of exposed soil, sediments and rock, to trap soil, silt and sand, and to prevent deposition into streams, storm-water channels and onto public roads and streets.

Sediment barriers should be used and maintained

Benefits if subdivision planners and developers work with and for the natural environment include:

- the continuation into the future of the preferred natural Australian landscape values of the Pine Rivers Shire.

- the survival of our unique and precious wildlife.

- lower development costs.

- increased aesthetic appeal and recreational potential of natural areas and waterways of the Shire and Moreton Bay.

- a more marketable product.

- provision of good examples of responsible environmental practice and management for other developers and the public to admire and emulate.

- attraction of public and government commendation with the associated benefits of awards, industry leadership, influence on the practices of industry peers, and future contracts and sales.

- protection of our waterways and coastal ecosystems from degradation and pollution.

- the long-term health of our seafood industries and amateur fishing.

- reduction of the need of costly downstream dredging and clean-up of waterways, stormwater drains and pipes.

Destructive road construction practices

Practices of builders who work with the environment:

- Minimise disturbance of the site when excavation is required. This retains vegetation that decreases erosion and filters sediments from run-off. It also preserves plants, some rare and many desirable, and enhances the appearance of the site.

- Flag or fence off the limits of the work site so that as little as possible of the property is degraded by machinery, stock piles and building waste.

- Use sediment barriers (such as geotextile fabric and straw bales) above and below the building site. Barriers above direct water flow around the site and those below prevent wash of soil, silt and sand onto streets and into stormwater channels.

- Plant cut-and-fill slopes, if made up of loose soil and sediment, with a quick, annual cover-crop, such as rye, to help prevent erosion.

- Locate stockpiles of soil, sand and gravel entirely on the site, preferably in a degraded spot, and erect a sediment barrier on the down side.

- If possible, restrict access and exit of vehicles to only one point, the future location of the driveway. Here, put down gravel to form an all-weather surface and to help prevent soil being carried onto the street.

- Connect the storm-water downpipes temporarily before putting on the roof. When a downpipe is removed for wall building, in case of rain, place a sheet of iron on the ground below to take the force of the falling water and to carry water onto grass.

- Store building waste in already degraded areas, preferably in mini-skips for regular removal.

- Clean up concrete and mortar waste on degraded grassed areas, well away from the street, to prevent cement entering gutters and stormwater pipes.

- Wipe wet paint brushes onto newspaper and dispose of the paper and paint properly. Wash water-based paint on degraded grassed areas. Wash oil-based paint in turps, and dispose of this properly.

Benefits to builders of building with the environment include:

- a safer, more inviting, attractive and pleasant work site.

- favourable public comment, satisfied customers and possibly, new clients.

- less loss of stockpiled soil, sand and gravel.

- less mud to clean up in wet weather and less dust in the dry.

- less erosion of the site and therefore less filling of gullies and cleaning up of deposited sediment.

- no scattered piles of building-waste that need machinery to clean up.

- less pollution of waterways and natural habitats.

- retention of native plants and habitats for native animals.

South Pine River - Highvale (PRSC)

CHAPTER

12

Pets

Studies show that the keeping of pets has considerable benefit to the health of their carers. Humans have kept animals as pets for many thousands of years - it is part of our nature and culture to do so. Association with other animals as pets brings us many advantages, such as companionship and protection. For the pets themselves, this pet-owner relationship is an on-off alliance - the pet doing its own natural thing in the surrounding environment for a lot of the time. Even our most domesticated breeds still retain many instincts that enabled their survival in the wild, without the aid of humans.

Keeping a pet or pets involves **responsibilities** that unfortunately some pet owners do not take seriously enough. There are responsibilities to the animal, to neighbours, to the other people our pets come in contact with and to the environment. We should provide a good home, adequate and suitable food and water, care and exercise for our pets. We should also ensure that other people do not suffer inconvenience and annoyance caused by noise, smell, deposits of droppings, or other activities of our pets, especially in their own or in public places. We need also to prevent our pets from killing or maiming native animals.

Cats

Cats are hunting animals whose behaviour in play involves the honing of skills for catching prey such as mice, rats, marsupials, birds, reptiles, frogs and insects. **Domestic** cats hunt no matter how well fed, in spite of what many devoted owners claim. **Feral** cats now live in almost all terrestrial habitats in Australia, the majority living entirely on what they can catch in natural ecosystems. Other ferals live in and around rural and urban human habitation and live partly on scraps and pet food put out for their domestic cousins and pet dogs. As well, there are cats that are at times domestic pets and at other times feral. Feral and semi-feral cats spread many serious diseases to other cats, especially ones that are not de-sexed. There is absolutely no doubt that domestic and feral cats do enormous damage to populations of Australia's native animals.

Suggestions that have been proposed to protect native fauna from predation by cats include:

- de-sexing all cats except those in registered catteries.

- requiring that all cats be belled. Even with a bell, cats still learn to hunt successfully. Two bells may be necessary.

- limiting the number of cats to 1 or 2 per household.

- restricting all cats to their owner's property.

- restricting all cats to within their owner's house and large outdoor cages.

- banning all cats (and all other pets) from some developments in or near sensitive natural areas.

Dogs

Dogs have natural hunting instincts. No matter how well fed, they will play with, chase, torment, attack, maim and kill many kinds of native animals - such as frogs, lizards, snakes, birds, marsupials and other mammals. They wander about their territories and, when these are abnormally small as in most domestic situations, explore surrounding areas. This is particularly so in dogs that are not de-sexed. Dogs instinctively want to protect their territories and defend their owners. Different breeds of dogs react differently and dogs receive different training. They are therefore unpredictable and many people are afraid (and with good reason) of those that wander the streets and other public places, especially in packs. Dogs attack domestic and farm animals such as sheep, goats, cattle and horses, often at night and far from their home yards. In natural areas, dogs contaminate the environment with droppings, scare wildlife (if only by their scent), become lost and annoy other visitors.

Suggestions that have been proposed to protect native fauna from predation by dogs include:

- de-sexing all dogs except those kept as stud animals in registered kennels.

- limiting the number of dogs to 1 or 2 per household.

- restricting all dogs to their owner's property except when on a leash.

- banning all dogs (and all other pets) from some developments in or near sensitive natural areas.

- banning all dogs from natural areas.

To help ensure our dogs are environmentally friendly we should:

- surround the property with a dog-proof fence.

- keep the dog in a restricted yard or on a wire 'run' if the property is large or has wildlife such as bearded dragons, stone curlews, quail, wallabies and koalas.

- teach the dog not to bark except as required. This may mean taking the dog to obedience training.

- train the dog (from puppy-hood) not to chase wildlife of any kind, but do not trust it out of your sight.

- keep the dog on a leash whenever it leaves its own yard.

- take plastic bags or special 'poopa-scoopas' to pick up droppings when taking the dog for walks; and dispose of these properly in a bin.

- leave the dog at home when visiting natural areas.

Grazing animals when kept as pets, especially on small properties, usually need some supplementary feeding, at least during the late winter and spring dry seasons, and in times of drought. This means that extra nutrient is being added to the environment. **Droppings** that become concentrated in sheds and pens can be collected and, after rotting or composting, used in the growing of plants such as vegetables, fruit trees and rainforest species. This can decrease the amount of **nutrient** being carried into streams during rain.

It is important to **fence off streams** so that grazing animals do not eat, trample and destroy riparian vegetation. During floods, plants in this zone protect the banks from erosion. **Drinking water** should be available for stock, away from streams. Stock are healthier for drinking clean water. When stock drink at streams their tracks become the foci of gully erosion. They also bring weeds - in their droppings and on their fur. For the sake of the environment, we should fence off portions of our properties to preserve and/or restore natural areas, otherwise the activities of our domestic animals will destroy much of the value of the area to which they have access. We should not fence across streams nor across natural corridors; and we should allow access, if possible, of native animals to our fenced natural areas. See page 97.

All grazing animals, unless protected by suitable fencing may be attacked by roaming domestic **dogs**. **Dingos** also can cause problems in areas linked by corridors to large natural areas. Foxes will take the unprotected offspring of small grazing animals.

Sheep, goats, cows, horses and donkeys are the most kept grazing animals, but more recently people keep such creatures as emus, ostriches, deer, alpacas and camels.

Sheep and goats

These animals, as pets, should only be kept on properties that are suitably fenced **to keep them in**, and to **keep out dogs**. Dogs, particularly at night, no matter how well behaved at home, by instinct will chase, play with and eventually injure or kill sheep and goats.

Goats, notwithstanding popular belief, will not eat everything. Similarly, sheep have their likes and dislikes in plant food. The plants that they do like are targeted and those not to their liking are less frequently eaten, or are ignored. The end result is that blue billy-goat weed, flannel weed, lantana and other unpalatable and undesirable weeds become the dominant plants in paddocks and yards. We then need to control the weeds. Sheep and goats, unless in large enclosures destroy most small native plants. What they do not eat they rub, push and chew until the plant is ringbarked. The only ways to retain patches of native bush and to protect saplings and newly planted shrubs and trees are by **fencing** and by the use of **tree guards**. See page 97.

Horses, donkeys and cattle

These larger pet animals also need to be kept in **adequately fenced** properties. When **straying** onto roads and streets they pose a real danger to themselves and to motorists. Dogs will also harrass even these big animals, and cause them injury.

Horses, donkeys and cattle also graze selectively, eating out native grasses and most small herbaceous native plants while leaving undesirable plants to proliferate. They do considerable damage to shrubs and trees. Horses, when hungry will dig up grass roots with their hooves. Horse, goat and donkey manures are particularly friable, and readily wash into watercourses. None of these animals can be regarded as friends of the Australian environment. All lean on, rub against and damage trunks of trees and shrubs, removing lower branches and bark. It is therefore necessary to **fence** them out of the natural areas we wish to protect and to use substantial **tree guards**.

Poultry

Fowls and ducks need to be properly penned to protect them from roaming dogs. Foxes are prevalent in even closely settled areas. Though mostly nocturnal, foxes will take chickens and ducks even during the day, particularly from late winter to late spring - before and during the foxes' breeding season. Cats, carpet snakes and hawks, such as goshawks, will eat chicks. Adequately fenced coops are needed to house chicks while they are small. In forested areas we may be lucky enough to have to protect chicks and even adult fowls from the rare but very interesting brush-tailed phascogale; although this loss would be a worthwhile sacrifice.

It is important that food stores be kept in vermin-proof containers and that **rats and mice** do not have easy access to food put out for poultry. Similarly, table scraps given to but not eaten by them should be raked up before dark and composted. Sparrows, feral pigeons and spotted turtle doves are also pest species attracted to chook food.

Poultry **manure** when rotted or composted is ideal to use as fertiliser for vegetable gardens, orchards and rainforest plots. Care should be taken not to let it contaminate ponds, dams and waterways. It is rich in phosphorus and can promote the growth of blue-green algae. Do not use any fertilisers containing phosphates on plants of the proteaceae family, such as banksias, grevilleas and hakeas. Free ranging poultry feed on pests and their scratching helps aerate the soil.

CHAPTER **13**

Farming with the Environment

European settlement in Australia introduced a degree of land degradation never before seen here. Agricultural and pastoral practices have culminated in a situation where 'more than half the country now requires soil conservation treatment' and 'land degradation is costing the nation at least $600 million a year in lost production and restorative action. Other estimates put the figure at two or three times that amount' (R. Clark, 1992, p. 6).

In the past we have sought to correct soil conservation problems through engineering solutions rather than to change the practices that caused the problems. Today and into the future we should seek ways of rural production that are in harmony with conservation principles. If we do not, farming cannot be **sustainable** in the long term and, as time goes on, rural land will either become less and less productive or the environment more and more polluted. A worse but likely scenario is that, unless we change harmful farming practices, the land will lose its productive ability and, as well, the environment will become massively polluted.

Good farming practices should be attuned to the characteristics of **each farm** as a whole, to the **surrounding farms** and to the entire **catchment** in which they occur. Farms cannot be run on sound ecological principles in isolation. Management practices on nearby farms may be causing problems for farmers elsewhere in the catchment. Similarly, no farm should be operated without consideration of downstream or upwind effects on water and air quality, natural ecosystems and human populations. Problems such as loss of native species and genetic diversity, pests, weeds, salinity, acidity, toxic algae and water pollution are concerns of the whole community and should be tackled as such. **Landcare** and **Greening Australia** groups were set up to implement and coordinate restoration programs with the involvement of farming communities. Similarly, **integrated catchment management groups** were established to enable a unified approach to catchment problems.

To ensure that agricultural and pastoral systems are sustainable and will not decrease the ability of future generations to produce adequate food, we need to use management techniques that minimise damage to the environment.

Some general management techniques for rural properties (to make agricultural and pastoral industries sustainable, stable and ecologically sound) include:

-   retention and restoration of natural vegetation along streams (including small gullies) and on hillsides as wildlife habitat and to control erosion. Planting of rainforest species in belts approximately 30 metres wide along major streams will use some of the best cultivation and grazing areas but will provide major protection for the water quality.

- retention of old hollow trees which provide shelter, breeding sites and refuge for birds, insectivorous bats, marsupials, reptiles and treefrogs.

- leaving fallen logs and branches and rocks in paddocks as habitat for echidnas and other ground-frequenting animals. In non-agricultural land, fallen logs strewn along the contours catch litter, slow erosion, aid deposition of soil, facilitate water infiltration and increase wildlife habitat.

- planting of shelter belts and wind breaks of local tree and shrub species and suitable non-invasive native species from elsewhere in Australia. These should be strategically located to provide wildlife corridors and habitat, and to minimise the drying and chilling effects of winds.

- control or eradication of invasive plant species and feral animals that threaten the survival of native species.

- control of farm dogs and cats, especially at night, to prevent attacks on wildlife species.

- establishment of farm dams and flow channels along contours from one dam to the next in accordance with 'keyline farming' principles to retain as much fresh water as possible and to help prevent soil erosion.

- constructing fences that allow wildlife to move between habitats and along corridors.

- fencing off of saline areas and planting salt tolerant vegetation above the salt line to lower the watertable.

- rehabilitation of saline areas by planting with a succession of salt marsh and, later, salt tolerant shrub and tree species.

- burning off only between May and mid-August and in the late afternoon on evenings when dew is expected. Fires will then be self-extinguishing. Many such fires will establish a patchwork, in irregular shapes, of burnt and unburnt areas. Permission from the local rural fire warden will need to be obtained to do this.

Management techniques that make agriculture more friendly to the environment include:

- retention of crop stubble to make use of organic content and to protect soil.

- cultivating less often, to decrease exposure of soil to rain, run-off and wind.

- direct seeding methods of planting crops and pastures.

- contour ploughing to decrease gully erosion on slopes.

- crop rotation to include legume crops, grazing and fallowing.

- testing soil moisture so that irrigation is only done when necessary and to the degree required by the crop.

- drip irrigation rather than wasteful sprinkling and flooding methods.

- organic farming where pesticides and inorganic fertilisers are not used.

- use of organic fertilisers, such as those generated on the farm (or other farms), and treated sewage. These materials are already in existence and it is better to use them for production rather than to release them directly or indirectly into streams or the sea.

- use of no more than optimum amounts of fertilisers for crops, to reduce pollution of ground water and streams.

- use of biological controls instead of chemicals to counter pest species.

- encouraging natural predators of pests by establishing natural habitats close to fields. Nest boxes for owls and insectivorous bats can help. See pages 79 to 81.

- use of pest-resistant crop varieties.

If it is felt that pesticides cannot be eliminated from use then:

- use the most environmentally-friendly pesticides such as those that are bio-degradable, short-lived and target-specific.

- use pesticides most effectively by applying when target species are most vulnerable and by using optimum concentrations, amounts and frequencies.

- follow carefully the instructions for safe use and disposal of containers and unused remnants.

Management techniques that make pastoral industries more friendly to the environment include:

- control of stocking rates to within carrying capacity determined by poorer seasons.

- de-stocking in times of drought so that land is not grazed bare.

- rotation of pastures to spell paddocks for regrowth and regeneration, to help the control of parasites, such as ticks and parasitic worms, and to allow understorey plants to provide habitat for native animals. This necessitates the fencing of pastures into paddocks.

- fencing off along streams to prevent grazing of in-stream and stream-side vegetation to decrease erosion and to protect water quality.

- fencing of laneways for stock movement so that traffic occurs where there is least chance of damage and erosion.

- choosing tick-resistant breeds to make it unnecessary to use chemicals for cattle tick control.

- farming native animals such as emus and kangaroos. These animals have much less impact upon the environment than do cattle and sheep. Emu farms are already producing, and kangaroos and wallabies are culled and processed for human consumption.

Advantages gained by establishing natural vegetation along streams, in windbreak plots and for shelter belts:

- Stock have shade in hot weather and protection from cold winds.

- Soil and crops are protected from the drying effects of wind.

- Erosion is decreased.

- Leaves and fallen litter absorb and retain rain water. Thus there is less run-off and so less flooding. Streams are more permanent.

- Farm dams lose less water by evaporation.

- Trees are not isolated, so animal droppings are not concentrated under the few trees that provide shade for stock.

- More habitat means that there are more native animals. Many of these control insects, such as beetles, stick insects, caterpillars and grasshoppers, that defoliate trees.

- Old dying trees have replacements coming along.

- Property values increase along with the beauty of the landscape and higher numbers of wildlife.

- Opportunities for diversification are greatly increased.

Some income generating products and enterprises for diversification include:

- timber produced by selective thinning and harvesting of commercial species. (See list of species suited to local conditions on pages 195 to 204 and 216 to 218).
- mulch
- honey
- bush tucker
- essential oils
- wildflowers
- seeds, seedlings and potted plants
- eco-tourism

Day visits with interpretation, to rainforest and other habitats, night spot-lighting, and longer stays on farms, camping or in cabins are some possibilities. Natural areas in national parks and state forests are becoming loved to death and crowded out as Australia's tourist industry grows. There is increasing interest in our natural areas both from overseas visitors and Australians. It is possible to establish substantial habitats of rainforest, open-forest and other local plant communities in less than ten years, starting from bare ground.

Forest (centre, left) established on bare, degraded land in less than 15 years.

Native animals and pest species as food

The acceptance of many more **native animals** as sources of excellent low-fat and low-cholesterol food is only a matter of time. In the future we may farm many species. Some of these animals at the moment are considered **pests**, and some are **wastefully destroyed**. Others are rare and becoming more so. Farming them may be the best (or only) way to ensure their survival. Many **pest species** are at present killed in large numbers and wasted as a source of food. Because of our upbringing we may at present have qualms about eating some species, but Aborigines regard many as delicacies. Other cultures also have a high regard, as food, for some animals in Australia. Some possibilities include: worms, grasshoppers (locusts), cicadas, crickets, moths, 'witchetty' grubs, yabbies, cockles, mussels, snails, whelks, eels, frogs, snakes, goannas, skinks, tortoises, galahs, cockatoos, feral pigeons, turtle doves, possums, wallabies, kangaroos, donkeys, fruit bats, rats and mice. Had enough? Remember, many of us until fairly recently would never have contemplated eating octopus or snails, or frog legs.

Cycling (PRSC)

CHAPTER **14**

Weeds

Weeds are plants growing in places where they are not wanted. Some are native plants but by far the greatest number are those from other countries. They usually succeed better in Australia than in their places of origin because here they do not have the natural controls of their homelands - the diseases, parasites and predators. The number of species of weeds that are found in our precious bushland increases each year. Some plants are introduced by accident when seeds come in with imported goods. Others arrive with people who bring them in deliberately in goods they do not declare. A great number, sadly, are garden plants gone wild. Some are dumped in bushland. The seeds of others are carried by the wind, or parts wash away during rain. The seeds are spread far and wide by birds and flying foxes. It is time that we placed curbs on the importation of new species of garden and pasture plants until research has been done to determine their potential as weeds. Today's favourite garden plant is likely to become tomorrow's invasive weed.

Unfortunately, many of the plants long known to be environmental weeds, such as camphor laurel, African tulip, ochna, broad-leafed pepper and umbrella tree, are still freely available from many nurseries, even those run by government agencies. One very well known talkback radio garden expert recently proclaimed that mock orange (*Murraya paniculata*) was the plant that he most recommended for garden use. It is fast becoming a major problem in local bushland, especially rainforest. Look at the plants chosen to landscape many government buildings and the beds between road lanes of highways. Here we notice such weeds as honeysuckle vine, creeping lantana and Singapore daisy.

A weed control program for natural bushland and gardens

Many people make the decision to clean up their weeds, and then attack the problem with much enthusiasm. They try to do it all at once and concentrate on the areas of greatest infestation. If they finish the job they are exhausted, or worse, in no time at all, there is massive regrowth of the same or different species. This scheme may be all right for small areas and where there are few weeds, but for bigger areas and where there are lots of weeds there is an easier and more effective method.

To control weeds in bushland more effectively:

- Begin in the areas of healthiest bush where there are fewer weeds, and work towards the more infested areas. This way, we are helped by the bush itself.

- Use the most appropriate methods of control for the particular weeds (see pages 237 to 242.)

- Cause as little disturbance as possible to the habitat.

- Replant with local native plants and/or allow natural regeneration.

- Continue follow up work if necessary - and it usually is.

- Do not use machinery for weed control. This causes too much habitat disturbance and promotes growth of weeds at the expense of native plants.

In a regional sense, the best way to suppress weeds is by means of **biological control**. We use the organisms that normally control them to do just that. Introducing organsims from other countries to control weeds or animal pests is fraught with danger to the environment. Much research is necessary to determine whether or not the organism we hope to introduce will itself become a problem. The introduction of the cane toad to control cane beetles is a notable example of not doing enough research. An outstandingly successful introduction for biological control is that of the cactoblastis moth, which very quickly controlled prickly pear.

Chemicals are often used in weed suppression. This should be the last resort rather than the first, and done with the greatest of care. The 'best' chemicals (weedicides/herbicides) to choose are those that are least toxic to animals and break down quickly to harmless products. Glyphosate is a good example of this but even here care must be taken. If a desired plant is **accidentally sprayed** with a herbicide containing glyphosate, wash it as soon as possible with dirty water.

Using chemicals for weed control:

- Read the instructions carefully and follow them exactly. This includes directions for use, personal safety and storage.

- The most effective times for treating weeds are when they are growing vigorously.

- Spraying with non-selective chemicals (such as glyphosate) can produce areas of bare soil. This can result in new crops of weeds. Cutting off of annual weeds before they set seed is a better option.

- Spray foliage only when there is little or no wind, where there is much weed cover and no (or few) desired plants. It is often best to cut off some species, wait for vigorous new growth and then spray. This is then done when the plants are low to the ground and there is less chance of drift affecting other plants. Use other methods of control for weeds that are not susceptible to the 'safer' chemicals.

- Cut stems and paint with herbicide when a tree or shrub is to be cut down. It is also useful for vines that have climbed over other plants. *Immediately* after the plant is cut or sawn through, the top of the stump is painted with the chemical.

- Chipping and dabbing with herbicide is used if a shrub or tree is to be left standing to die. Use an axe or tomahawk to cut downwards through the bark to the inner live tissue, all around the stem. Dab *immediately* with the chemical. Allow a minute or so and then apply some more herbicide into the cuts.

- Stem scraping and painting is used for vines with aerial tubers, many of which would drop if the plant was disturbed. *Immediately* after the bark of the stem is scraped off all around, to reveal the underlying tissues for about 10 centimetres, it is painted with the herbicide. Leave it to die without disturbance.

Using mechanical methods to remove weeds:

- Hand pulling is used on small young woody plants, such as seedlings of trees and shrubs, and some grasses and herbaceous weeds that have shallow root systems. In wet weather, older and larger ones may become easier to pull. Hand tools, shovels and picks can be used to assist in removal. Practically all very young weeds can be pulled out, but take care not to leave behind corms, bulbs or tubers if they have already formed.

- Digging is used to remove the tubers, bulbs, corms and lignotubers. Plants can regenerate from these underground structures left behind if the plants are pulled. Take care to remove all parts.

- Lifting and cutting is used for plants that scramble along the ground, roots forming where stems touch the ground. Stems are raised, the roots cut and the whole plant removed. Many of these plants break easily into parts, any of which may start a new colony.

Protecting our environment by quarantine

Because the Australian continent was for so long separate, Australian natural communities evolved in isolation from those of the rest of the world. There are a great number of animal and plant diseases and pests that we do not have in Australia but which are major problems overseas. Today's rapid and frequent movement of people and goods to and from most parts of the world greatly increases the chances of undesirable organisms entering Australia. Not having had any previous contact with these, many populations of plants and animals in Australia would be devastated if these organisms gained entry. This is why we have **quarantine regulations** - to protect our native species, our crops, our farm animals and our pets. We also need this protection from exotic diseases, pests and parasites.

Some **diseases** that could decimate our native and domestic animals, if ever they reach Australia, include Newcastle disease, foot-and-mouth disease and rabies. Controlling these would be made even more difficult by the presence of feral animals.

We have recently seen, with the spread of papaya fruit fly, how the introduction of an unwanted insect can have drastic economic effects on our country. Even within Australia there are species, both native and exotic, that are present in one region but which we do not want to spread elsewhere. Cattle ticks are an example. At this very moment, a native insect from north Queensland is attacking and killing pandanus palms in south-east Queensland. It is thought to have been brought south in potted pandanus palms. A native wasp is now being introduced from north Queensland in an attempt to biologically control the problem.

When entering Australia we need to ensure that we comply with all requirements of the quarantine regulations. This is equally true **when travelling within Australia** from one region to another. Remember, plants and animals, soil and rock can contain eggs and spores and microscopic organisms. Take special care for the sake of our environment.

CHAPTER **15**

Recreation and the Environment

We need places to relax, to expend excess energy, to keep fit and to take our minds off other matters of life. Recreation is part of healthy living, and special areas are set aside and facilities provided for these sports and pastimes. Natural areas are increasingly being recognised as locations for passive recreation, such as bird watching, plant studies, eco-tourism, interpretation and education. The different recreational activities vary in their impacts on the environment but some have quite severe effects.

Sports fields

Almost invariably, sports fields consist mostly of areas of lawn. These lawns are mowed often - some very often. Following the American example, many sporting fields are cultured and clipped to resemble picture postcard scenes of artificial green, particularly golf courses, bowling greens and some sports ovals. It would make very interesting but disturbing reading to see the annual total amounts of fertilisers, herbicides, fungicides and insecticides applied to maintain these 'beautiful' facilities. Imagine the effects of these chemicals, most of which end up in ground water, waterways and ultimately, aquatic life-forms. And think about the quantities of water and mower fuel consumed.

Sports fields do not all have to be the environmental disasters that many are. Let us look at how we can make them more compatible with the environment.

Golf Courses

The first golf courses in Scotland were rough and ready places, little altered from natural fields. Today we have highly modified courses, some of them nothing like the original bush habitats that they replaced. The 'better' golf courses consist of vast fairways, mowed, rolled and manicured. Greens are as smooth as billiard tables and bunkers are of clean, white or yellow sand. Water traps are ponds, pools, lakes and streams - crystal-clear and sky-blue - tributes to the chemicals that maintain them. No insect, worm, or leaf of any but the desired grass in the appointed place dare show itself. The roughs are hardly rough and new shrubs and trees are not usually those of value as wildlife habitat.

Golf courses do not usually favour a wide variety of species.

Would it make a great deal of difference to the course as a place to play the game or as an attractive landscape if the grassed areas were not emerald green the whole year? Would it really matter if there was the occasional dead patch with dollar spot, or if hatchet wasps flew about in search of lawn grubs? The green keeper would be sacked, the members and associates devastated and overseas visitors aghast! Or would they?

Golf courses as wildlife refuges and corridors

Occupying such large areas and often located within urban areas, golf courses have much potential as important wildlife habitats and corridors. In fact, with retained or re-established natural bushland, many golf courses could become showpieces of environmental management and focal points of eco-tourism for local and overseas visitors. Trained staff could take interpretive tours through habitats such as rainforest, open forest, heath-land and wetland ecosystems. Topics of educational value could include, birds, plants, bush tucker, ecology, Aboriginal and pioneer culture and, at night, spotlighting of frogs, birds and mammals.

To make golf courses more friendly to the environment:

- mow fairways less often.

- in the roughs remove all imported grasses and other weeds. Mulch and plant with local native grasses, ground covers, shrubs, trees and climbers.

- water less often and more effectively, preferably at night with recycled water from lakes, ponds and dams within the course or from tertiary water-treatment facilities.

- retain mature and old trees in all but places where falling branches could endanger people. Trim dangerous branches rather than destroy the whole tree. Put in place nesting boxes designed for a variety of animals. See pages 78 to 81.

- use no inorganic fertilisers and a minimum of organic ones.

- remove weeds manually, not chemically, in areas of lawn and in bunkers. Recent tests have shown that flame weeders, that use heat to sear and kill weeds, are only one percent less effective than chemicals at killing weeds.

- use no insecticides or fungicides at all. Natural predators will gradually return to control pests.

- do not provide motorised buggies to players except those who are physically handicapped. After all, golf is supposed to be played for exercise.

- plant rainforest, using local species and non-invasive native species from elsewhere (see pages 181 to 204), along streams and lower boundaries of the course. Rainforest plants will thrive on and use nutrients that otherwise will flow away, on the surface or via ground water, to pollute aquatic ecosystems. These rainforests in time will provide an important resource for the club.

Bowling greens, ovals and sporting fields

These facilities can also be made less damaging to the environment by applying the relevant suggestions from the list above regarding golf courses.

Power boats and jet skis

There are places suitable for activities that make use of these machines, but often their use damages the environment and decreases the amenity of the surroundings for others. Some users of power boats and jet skis are not aware of this. Some simply do not care.

Power boats and jet skis produce considerable **wash** when they travel at high speeds. This causes severe **erosion** problems to stream banks and shoreline vegetation. Even a 'tinnie' with an outboard motor can have a considerable impact. Jet skis do not function at low speeds and so should not be used in creeks and rivers. Boating people who care always observe **speed limits**. There are heavy fines for those who ignore them. People fishing from river and creek banks do not appreciate the disturbance caused to their tackle. Another problem, for people living or relaxing near where these water craft are used, is the **noise**. Grease, **oil** and fuel spills are other concerns.

Fishing

Fishing has always been a pleasant pastime. No fish ever taste as good as the ones we catch ourselves. Everyone who loves fishing will be only too pleased to do all they can to protect the environment. Protecting the environment helps ensure that we will still have plenty of fish well into the future.

With the advent of **nylon fishing line**, discarded and lost line became a real and serious threat for wildlife. Previous to this, natural fibres used in fishing lines rotted away quickly. Nylon, out of sunlight, lasts for centuries. Nylon line can entangle, choke and starve fish, crabs, birds and mammals.

Boating people who care always observe speed limits

It is pleasant to take a snack to eat while we fish; and so easy to throw away the **rubbish**, including plastic bags. These readily blow away and are hard to retrieve from the water. Rings of metal and plastic from drink cans and packing often trap wild animals. Plastic rings should be cut and disposed of properly.

To protect the environment while fishing:

-   take all rubbish home for correct disposal. Take some of other people's rubbish as well.

- take care not to let plastic bags blow into the water - animals such as turtles eat these and die.

- feed unused bait to the fish but take it out of the container first. Take the container home for correct disposal.

- do not feed bait, fish or fish gut to birds such as cormorants, pelicans, gulls and herons. They become nuisances and it disrupts their ecology.

- do not leave any fish hooks or lines.

- when travelling in creeks and rivers observe speed limits (less than 6 knots) so wash does not damage banks.

- observe size and number limits for fish and crustaceans. We want to go fishing and take a successful catch in the future as well.

Four-wheel-drive vehicles and trail bikes

Tracks and trails made by vehicles travelling through the bush can very soon become paths along which **gully erosion** occurs. When these tracks become very rough or impassable, alternative tracks are used, and the same processes are repeated. In a relatively short time there is major damage done to the environment - **soil** is washed away, small plants are destroyed, large ones are undercut and toppled, invasive **weeds** are introduced and silting of streams occurs downstream. Users of four-wheel drives and trail bikes are very often responsible for this kind of damage. In places where these vehicles are allowed, sensible and careful drivers take care that their activities do not impact too much on the environment.

Four - wheel drive damage

To use trail bikes and four-wheel-drive vehicles responsibly:

- keep to designated areas where trail bikes and four-wheel-drive vehicles are allowed.

- keep to designated tracks and trails and do not start new tracks. Inform authorities or land owners if fallen trees or rocks block paths.

- take rubbish home for correct disposal and take some of other people's as well.

- do not injure or remove any plants or animals.

- make sure no oil, grease or fuel is spilt or discarded in the bush. Damaged tyres should be taken home.

- leave gates as they were - open if already open; closed if found closed.

Camping

Camping, whether on private property, on forestry land, crown land or in national parks involves responsibilities. We should no sooner want to spoil a lovely environment for other people than we would want others to do so for us.

Ways of camping with minimum impact on the environment include:

- taking all rubbish home for correct disposal.

- placing the fire in a cleared area if campfires are permitted and there are no provided fire pits.

- extinguishing fires before leaving. Use of portable spirit stoves for cooking is preferable to burning wood from the bush.

- taking care not to injure or remove any plants or animals.

- leaving pets at home. These frighten wildlife, annoy other visitors and may become lost.

- keeping to walking tracks (if provided).

- not using soaps, shampoos or detergents in or near streams.

- not feeding wild animals. This can make them sick, dependent or aggressive.

- where there are no facilities, disposing of human waste by first digging a hole with a shovel and then burial. This should not be closer than fifty metres from any stream.

- taking care not to introduce weed seeds on clothes, footwear or tyres.

- not using generators or engine-driven compressors if in hearing range of other visitors.

- filling and covering all traces, holes and ruts, made during the visit, before leaving.

North Pine River - Lees Crossing (PRSC)

CHAPTER

16

Fire

Because of the nature of most bushland ecosystems in Australia, anyone living in or near natural areas of forest, woodland or grassland should be aware of the dangers when **bushfires** burn at the wrong time of year. We should be prepared, especially in seasons when the risks of bushfire are greatest.

In residential suburbs far from natural areas, the risk from bushfires is minimal because of the close proximity of streets and roads that act as fire breaks. However, even when we live at considerable distances from bushland, we need to take many of the same precautions as people whose houses are adjacent to fire-prone areas.

Without fire in bushland, fuel loads of combustible materials (grass, leaves, twigs, bark, logs and branches) accumulate. After a spell of dry weather and when strong winds are blowing from the fire towards houses, burning fragments carry for hundreds of metres. Embers can set alight leaves and twigs in roof guttering, even kilometres away. Fires from embers may also start in garden mulch, wood piles and rubbish in backyards.

Destructive fires can result when we burn off during unsafe burning times

We need to be aware that authorities must carry out **burn-off operations**. Fires lit at appropriate times reduce fuel loads and decrease the risk of wildfires during later danger periods. The smoke of bushfires is an inconvenience to many people, especially those with respiratory problems, and fire officers take every means to inform residents of impending burning operations. It is much better to face the troubles resulting from smoke of controlled fires than to have to tolerate the same annoyance together with the terrifying danger of wildfires lit by vandals. Wildfires are not only potentially devastating to human life and property but they generally occur when native animals have eggs or young.

In this region, the safest and the most environmentally sound time to burn is generally between mid-autumn and late-winter. During this period ground temperatures are lower, leaf and grass litter still contain moisture, ground vegetation is still partially green and there is less strong wind. Also at this time, when the dew-point is high, fires lit in the afternoon are cool, and usually die out later in the evening when the air temperature falls and dew forms. Many such fuel-reduction fires, lit periodically throughout these months, can establish an irregular mosaic of burnt and unburnt patches. Animals that live on or near the ground thus always have places to shelter, and there are patches of green regrowth - food that stimulates them for the coming breeding season.

The desired cool fire pattern of burnt and unburnt areas of habitat

At the end of winter and in spring, westerly winds dry out the mature grass and litter. This is normally the driest part of our year and, until summer thunderstorms bring rain, the fuel load in unburnt areas is tinder dry. This is also the time that accidental fires, and those lit by vandals, are most likely to occur. With a mosaic of burned areas already established these unplanned high-temperature fires burn only in the patches where there has not been a fire for a considerable time - where there is ample dry fuel. The regions burned by these hot fires now become part of the mosaic. Some plant species need hot fires and, without them, eventually die out, as do some animal species dependent upon them. This is how we can use to advantage the actions of vandals and careless people - actions, it seems, we will never be able to control.

It seems ridiculous that every three to eight years, especially in parts of New South Wales and Victoria, tragic losses of life and property occur when extremely hot fires burn out thousands of hectares. Well before conditions become critical over vast areas, appropriate and adequate use should be made of fire, during safe burning times each year, as a matter of routine. This would protect people and their property, and benefit natural communities. We have a lot to learn from past Aboriginal use of fire. Here in South-east Queensland, humid weather and thunder storms give us some protection, but in drought conditions we also can face extreme fire danger. Fuel-reduction burning must be carried out at correct times well before this situation is upon us.

To make your home safer in the event of a bushfire:

Before the bushfire season (before mid-August):

- clear the roof-gutters of leaves and twigs, and then do it regularly.

- fit external metal flyscreens to windows, door-openings and vents in eaves and roof. (Fibre-glass mesh melts readily)

- enclose the under-house area and cover vents with metal flyscreen.

- remove combustible materials (eg firewood and timber) from near the house, or store in an enclosed space.

- store highly inflammable materials (eg petrol, oil and paint) in an enclosed space well away from likely fire sources.

- face safety valves of LP gas cylinders away from the house.

- have ladders, suitable to reach the roof (inside and outside), ready for use in times of fire danger.

- install and maintain garden hoses long enough to reach all parts of the house and nearby garden areas.

- if town water is not connected, keep an adequate reserve of water (10,000 + litres) for fire emergency and install and maintain a pressure pump (petrol or diesel). Water from swimming pools, dams and creeks is suitable. Contact the local fire brigade for compatible fitting sizes.

- establish lawns, driveways or paved areas as firebreaks around the house perimeter, especially between the house and the source of possible fires.

- plants next to the house should be no higher than the guttering and should be of species least likely to burn. (See list of fire retardant plants, pages 252 to 270)

- organic mulches should not be used near the house. They should be kept moist, if possible, when there is evidence of approaching bushfires.

- inorganic mulch, such as pebbles and river rocks, can be used near the house and other buildings.

- if you live adjacent to bushland, do not prevent access along Council firebreaks. Contact the Council if access is hindered (eg by fallen timber).

- have an appropriate, well-maintained, fire extinguisher in an easily accessible place.

- keep the batteries for the radio, mobile phone and torches charged.

- maintain adequate bushfire insurance.

- decide well before a bushfire arrives whether to leave early or to stay in the house.

During the bushfire:

- do not panic.

- phone the local fire brigade as soon as possible to make sure they know of the fire.

- fill baths, laundry tubs, sinks, buckets and other containers with water.

- turn off power and gas.

- close all external doors and windows and seal gaps with wet towels and cloth.

- dress in long woollen or heavy cotton clothing, a balaclava or hat, gloves and heavy boots.

- plug the downpipe holes in roof-gutters with tennis balls (or drink cans) wrapped in cloth and fill the gutters with water.

- hose the walls and the garden on the side of the house facing the approaching fire, then take the hoses inside.

- move the curtains and furniture away from the windows.

- move verandah furniture, bedding, blinds, etc inside the house.

- stay inside away from the windows when the fire-front arrives.

- put a ladder to the manhole and buckets of water in the ceiling.

- soak blankets, towels and bags to beat out fires.

- soak handkerchiefs and tea towels to use as smoke masks.

- after the passing of the fire-front, hose out any fires around the house including inside the roof. Keep checking inside the ceiling well after the fire has passed.

- if the house is burning and the fire cannot be put out, wait as long as possible and then leave. Go towards where the fire has been and wait there.

What to do when trapped in a bushfire while driving:

- do not panic.

- pull off the road where there is a clearing or less vegetation.

- stay in the car.

- switch off the ignition; switch on the hazard lights and headlights.

- close vents, windows and doors, but leave doors unlocked.

- keep down below the window level, preferably under a woollen blanket.

- after the passing of the fire-front, if there is too much heat or fumes in the car, get out and go towards where the fire has been and wait there.

What to do when trapped in a bushfire while walking:

- do not panic.

- cover the entire body surface, if possible with woollen or cotton cloth.

- move across the slope away from the fire front, and then downhill to where the fire has passed.

If the fire-front cannot be avoided:

- look for a hollow in the ground, a gully, dam or creek and lie face down behind a bank, rock or large solid log, especially where there is less fuel (grass, twigs, branches). If there is loose sand, gravel or rocks, use these as cover. Stay there until the fire has passed.

- do not shelter in a water tank, the water may boil.

What to do when family members or friends are in a bushfire area:

- do not panic.

- do not drive (or go by other means) to where they are.

- phone the local fire brigade to find out details and to give the name(s) of the person(s) and your name and phone number.

- stay by the phone and a radio and wait for news.

Planting For Fire Protection

Different plants vary in their **flammability**. Some burn fiercely, while others ('fire-retardant' species) will only burn after pre-heating and drying. No plant is fireproof and all will burn in severe conditions. Some exotic plants and some native plants contain resins and volatile oils and, when they catch alight during hot fires, can increase fire intensity.

The most common cause of buildings catching alight during fire is **embers and sparks** blown ahead of the fire-front by wind. Fire-retardant plants in groups, rows and wind breaks around buildings can help in protecting property during fire, but must be used in conjunction with other fire protection measures to be fully effective. Properly used, they can decrease wind speed and turbulence, catch sparks and embers, decrease fire intensity and absorb radiant heat energy that can cause other plants and structures to burn.

Fire-retardant plants do not ignite as readily as most others. Some have a **high water content** in their leaves and, especially if they are watered well when bush fires are likely, can reduce the intensity of a fire. Many rainforest plants, fruit trees, fruit shrubs, fruit vines, vegetables, **fleshy-leafed** plants and salt-marsh plants are examples. Some plants, such as salt-marsh plants, mangroves and some casuarinas have a **high salt content** that makes them fire-retardant, but some will burn fiercely in very hot fires. Unfortunately, many fire-retardant species are not fire-resistant and are severely set back or die after fire exposure.

Plants that ignite easily during fire include those with **stringy and papery barks** and those that seasonally cast their **barks in strips and sheets**. Many gum trees, stringy-barks and paperbarks are like this. Trees and shrubs, such as melaleucas and leptospermums, that produce **many twigs and dead branches**, can increase fire intensity when they ignite, and should not be planted too near buildings. Similarly, conifers, eucalypts, melaleucas and leptospermums, that contain high levels of **resins and volatile oils**, should not be planted on slopes down from and near buildings in fire prone areas.

Fire barriers of fire-retardant plants should be planted so that they cross the likely paths of possible fires. They are particularly important on downhill slopes from buildings. They can be separated from other rows of retardant species or other plants by cleared areas such as lawns, paved areas, vegetable patches, orchards, driveways, swimming pools, tennis courts and so on. Similarly, in larger blocks and in rural areas, closely cropped pasture strips, cultivation and green crops can provide these fire-break areas. Fire can travel quickly across dry lawns, stubble and low pastures during a fire, so systematic watering of these areas is a useful strategy during fire seasons.

CHAPTER **17**

Water Use

The water cycle

The sequence of processes whereby water particles continually circulate through the hydrosphere (the water in the oceans, seas, lakes, streams, soil and rocks), the atmosphere and living things (the biosphere) is known as the water cycle. Nearly all the energy that drives this cycle comes ultimately from the sun. The following diagram shows simply how the water cycle works.

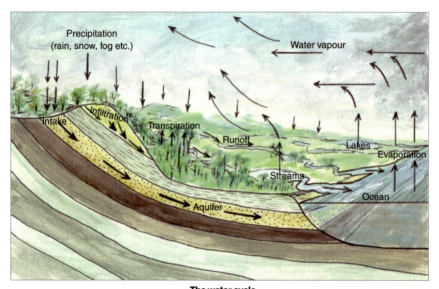

The water cycle

'Town' water

Water used for homes and industry costs money. It is us, the rate and tax payers, who must pay. If we have rainwater tanks or if we use bore water, we pay for the necessary equipment, such as tanks, pipes and pumps, as well as upkeep; but this is entirely at our own cost and then the water is free. For those on 'town' water, everyone using it shares in the total cost of the water used.

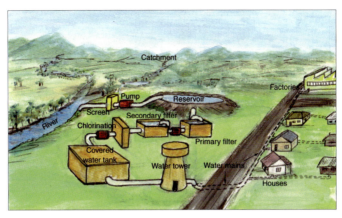

Supplying our water

It pays us all to conserve our water. With our present and predicted rates of population growth, unless we come to terms with our overuse and waste of water, we will need to build more water-storage dams, filter stations, reservoirs and pipelines. These are costly - economically, environmentally and socially. The earth's average rainfall is 660mm per year; Australia's is 430mm, yet we use more water per head of population than almost anyone else on earth. See 'Australia the driest continent', pages 166 & 167.

Things we can do to conserve water

In public places:

- turn off taps and drink-fountains that are left running.

- report leaks, dripping taps and running toilets to the Council as soon as possible.

In the bathroom:

- convert to a dual-flush toilet cistern.

- check that the toilet is not continuing to flow. Do this by putting food-colouring in the cistern. If the toilet is not flushed and the colouring enters the bowl, there is a leak to be fixed as soon as possible.

- do not use the toilet to flush away tissues, wrapping paper, cigarette butts and the like.

- turn off the tap while brushing your teeth.

- during and after shaving, rinse the razor in some water in the basin, not under a running tap.

- take a bath instead of a shower; or shower no longer than 4 minutes. Bathtubs are being made smaller to save water. By washing hair in the basin, rather than under the shower, we can save much water.

- fit a water-saving rose in the shower recess.

- insulate hot-water pipes so less water is used while we wait for the hot water.

In the laundry:

- arrange to wash clothes in the washing machine only when there is a full load.

- front-loading washing machines use less water than top-loading ones. Next time, select a front-loading machine.

- if it is always moist around the washing machine there may be a leak.

In the kitchen:

- if the sink has two compartments, use water in one for rinsing instead of rinsing dishes under a running tap.

- if using a dishwasher, wait until there is a full load before doing the dishes, otherwise wash small amounts by hand.

- use a bowl or saucepan of water when peeling and cleaning vegetables instead of doing this in the sink under running water.

- garbage disposal units waste large amounts of water and put extra strain on the sewerage system. It is best not to use them. Use a compost bin instead.

- aerators on taps decrease flow and save water.

- when having a drink of water, rather than running water at the sink until the water is cool, keep some water in the refrigerator for drinking.

In the garden:

- allow the lawn to reflect the weather by letting it turn brown in dry times. It will not die but will green up again when it rains. By watering less we make the lawn more able to tolerate dry times.

- if we feel we must water lawns, gardens and shrubberies, water at night when there is less loss by evaporation. One occasional good soaking is much more beneficial than many brief sprinklings. This encourages plants to form deep root systems, making them less dependent on artificial watering.

- decrease the area under lawn and replace with natural areas of native grasses, low shrubs (heathland), shrubs, forest trees (using plants suited to the garden dimensions), rockeries, and paved areas.

- do not water during and after good soaking rain.

- watering by spraying the leaves is not beneficial to plants. It is the roots that need water. Micro-sprays and drip-water systems use much less water, and allow it to soak in without wasteful run-off.

- group plants according to their water requirements. Plants that do not need watering are then not watered unnecessarily.

- choose from the list of many suitable local native plants - they tend not to need artificial watering once established.

- use mulches to retain soil moisture and to deter weeds. Do not use mulches of wood, bark or leaves near house walls; use pebbles or gravel instead. Wood with moisture, in contact with the ground, encourages subterranean termites, the termites that attack wood of houses.

- weeds compete with other plants for soil moisture. Pull them out.

- watering of garden paths, driveways, footpaths and roadways is absolute waste of water.

- use a broom rather than the hose to clean or sweep paved areas, pathways, driveways, footpaths and street channelling.

- a trigger control on the hose spray will cause less waste of water. After use, switch off the water at the tap in case the hose leaks or fittings come loose.

- there is no need to fertilise a lawn; and therefore no need to 'water it in'. Most of the fertiliser ends up elsewhere (carried away in solution as we water); and anyway, it's only a temporary fix.

- wash the car on the lawn by using water from a bucket; and then use the hose only to rinse-off.

- a cover over a swimming pool will decrease loss of water by evaporation and keep the water warmer. It will stop leaves from blowing in and be safer for young children.

In general:

- leaking pipes and dripping taps cause the loss of much water. Even a slow dripping tap can waste 20,000 litres in a year. A water meter provides an easy way of determining if we have leaking pipes. Turn off all taps and read the water meter. After about three hours, read the metre again. If no water has been used the reading should be the same. If not, then we have to find the leak and fix it.

- changing the washers usually fixes dripping taps. If this does not solve the problem, contact a plumber.

CHAPTER **18**

Water Use, Abuse and Pollution

Water that goes down the sink or is flushed away in the toilet is still part of our environment. It either becomes part of sewage destined for a treatment plant or it goes into a septic system. From there it re-enters the water-cycle.

Sewage consists mostly of water - 20 litres of raw sewage contains less than a table spoon of dirt. The pollutants in it include organic matter, nutrients and pathogens (J. Simpson, 1996, p. 10). In sewage there are many micro-organisms or 'germs', most of them harmless and needed in the processes that break down sewage in treatment plants and septic tanks. Some kinds of micro-organisms though, are **pathogens** - they can cause disease in plants and animals, including humans. Pathogens in sewage are of four kinds - bacteria, viruses, protozoans and helminths. Authorities take special care to ensure that these organisms do not find their way from sewage into drinking water or to places such as streams and beaches where people swim.

Bacteria

Bacteria and fungi are the decomposers in all ecosystems. They are absolutely necessary for life to function. They break down the remains of dead organisms and return nutrients back to the environment, to be used again by other organisms. Bacteria assist some plants to convert atmospheric nitrogen into nitrogen compounds needed by other organisms. Some cause the fermentation process. Some bacteria live where there is oxygen (aerobic bacteria) and others where there is none (anaerobic bacteria). They occur in our bodies and enable us to digest our food; and make some vitamins for us. A few though, cause disease. Two well known pathogenic ones, associated with polluted water, are those that cause typhoid *(Salmonella typhi)* and cholera *(Vibrio choleri)*.

Viruses

Viruses are much smaller and simpler than bacteria. They cannot reproduce unless they are inside particular cells of specific host organisms. Outside of its host, a virus resembles an inorganic substance. Only a few virus particles are enough to cause an infection, unlike bacterial pathogens that need more than a million. Swimming in or ingesting water contaminated with sewage can result in a twenty-four hour gastric complaint caused by a virus.

Protozoans

Protozoans are single-celled animals. Most are free-living organism of aquatic habitats such as in ponds, pools and soil. Some occur in other organisms as harmless symbionts but a few are pathogens. Two protozoan pathogens are giardia and cryptosporidium. These cause symptoms of vomiting and diarrhoea that, in individuals of low resistance, may be severe. Protozoans form resistant phases (called cysts) in the presence of chemicals and other harsh environmental conditions. Cysts have to be filtered out during the treatment of drinking water.

Helminths

Helminths are roundworms and flatworms, not all microscopic, some of which are parasites. Tapeworms and parasitic nematodes (roundworms) live in the digestive systems, blood vessels, lymph glands or other tissues of infected animals, the eggs passing out in the faeces or from open sores of the host. Untreated sewage may contain eggs of these parasites and be the source of human infection in polluted areas.

Blue-green bacteria (algae)

Blue-green algae (which are more correctly called blue-green bacteria) are single-celled organisms which, in fresh water containing high levels of nutrients, may increase rapidly ('bloom') and produce toxins harmful to humans. It has been shown that detergents and human waste are the major contributors to a phosphorus build-up in waste water, and that blue-green algae depended entirely on the release of phosphorus into standing water bodies, and sunlight (P. Jones, Faculty of Environmental Science, Griffith University, 1993). The need to limit development in catchments in close proximity to water-storage dams is highlighted by these findings, especially if septic systems are used for waste processing. Blue-green algae in streams and dams become a problem mostly in summer during drought periods. Good rainfall and water movement help to destroy infestations.

Treatment of water containing blue-green algae is expensive and involves removing the cells by microfiltration, adsorption of toxins using activated carbon, and breakdown of toxins using chlorine dioxide and ozone.

In the Pine Rivers Shire, sports fields at Brendale are watered at night with water from treated sewage. In this way the phosphate in the water can be used as fertilizer, and that not used by plants combines with the soil. Phosphorus removal from sewage is possible but expensive.

Towns such as Moore, Linville, Toogoolawah, Kilcoy, Esk, Lowood, Laidley and Gatton are above the Mt Crosby Weir from which at least some of the water for residents of Brisbane and the Pine Rivers originates. Lake Kurwongbah and the North Pine Dam are other sources of water for the Pine Rivers Shire and there are many residents in these catchments who have septic systems. Good treatment and testing procedures of water are therefore necessary to ensure the quality and safety of water supplies.

Sewage Treatment

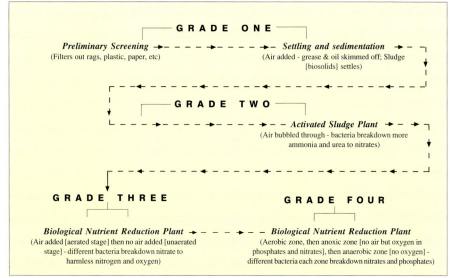

Steps in the treatment of sewage

Treatment of sewage to produce high quality water

The smallest particles can be removed from effluent water by passing it through smaller and smaller porous fibres. Even sodium and chlorine ions (as in salt water) can be removed. These processes together with other necessary treatments can produce high quality water from sewage. Such production of high grade water is very expensive but necessary when towns upstream discharge their wastes into rivers.

Disposal of other waste into toilets

We should not put objects such as rags, nappies, condoms, tampons and sanitary pads, newspaper, etc, down the toilet. These cause problems because they do not biodegrade readily and can block pipes and filters, adding to the expense of maintenance and repair. There is no real need for us to use patterned, coloured or bleached (pure white) toilet paper. Uncoloured, unbleached paper does the job just as well, yet does not involve manufacturing processes and chemicals that can harm the environment. Similarly, chemicals such as solvents, oils and fats, detergents, antiseptics and pesticides, poured down the sink or toilet, upset the biological processes that break down wastes in sewage treatment plants and home septic systems. Cleansing agents, deodorants and other chemicals used for toilet bowls that are connected to septic systems should be those designed for septic systems. The septic tank contains bacteria that break down human waste and toilet paper. Chemicals can kill these bacteria and cause failure of the system.

Grey water

Grey water (that which comes from the bathroom and laundry) contains substances such as dirt and grease as well as detergents, soaps and water softeners. This water is suitable for watering lawns, gardens and shrubberies but goes into the sewerage system in sewered areas. Fats and oils in grey water passing through sewage treatment works are costly to remove. Air bubbled through the sewage, and chemical additives, cause fats and oils to float so that they can be skimmed off. In unsewered areas, grey water passes through a grease trap. This should be cleaned out regularly to keep it working efficiently.

Storm water

Water from the roofs of houses and other buildings flows into stormwater drains that also take run-off from roads and streets. This water then flows into streams. Some people (illegally) connect their storm water to the sewerage system. This can cause sewerage pipes to overflow or burst during times of high rainfall and discharge **raw sewage** into streams and even onto streets.

Never pour substances such as garden and household chemicals, oil, solvents and paint down stormwater drains. These poisons flow to streams and then coastal waters and kill or taint commercial and amateur fishery stocks, such as fish, crabs, prawns and oysters. This is one reason why it is better to wash the car on the lawn rather than on the street.

Curbing and channelling along streets and roads is designed to take rainwater to stormwater drains, hence to streams and then to the ocean. Oils, fuels and fuel additives (such as lead) and soot from vehicles, together with rubber particles from tyre wear, are washed to aquatic ecosystems with stormwater run-off. The more vehicles that use our ever-increasing areas of roads and streets, the greater the amounts of these pollutants. What is the capacity of our natural environment to tolerate these changed conditions? And what values do we place on the natural communities that are affected?

Waste from industry

Primary, secondary and tertiary industries produce wastes that can pollute our environment. Waste substances from industry must be disposed of properly if we are to protect aquatic habitats.

Manufacturing industries that use metals and their compounds produce mostly inorganic wastes. For example battery factories produce wastes that may contain lead, zinc or nickel; electroplating industries may generate metal wastes containing chromium. Inorganic wastes from other industries include compounds of arsenic, cadmium, silver, copper and mercury.

There are laws that require industries producing wastes to dispose of them in appropriate ways or to pre-treat them before adding them to the sewerage system. Illegal dumping can also result in industrial wastes entering sewerage systems. However, much of the heavy metal waste that becomes part of sewage is derived from domestic sources. Inorganic compounds in sewage end up as part of the solid waste (sludge) of sewage treatment. In too high concentrations, metal waste in sewage can kill the bacteria needed for the breakdown processes in sewage treatment, and can decrease the options of sludge disposal, which otherwise, after preparation, can be used as fertiliser.

In the past, for example in Japan, people have died from eating seafood contaminated with heavy metals, particularly mercury. Biological magnification occurs as poisonous metals are passed through food chains so that the largest fish contain concentrations in their flesh that are very high. In the human body many metal poisons are accumulative and continued eating of contaminated food leads eventually to poisoning. Tests on fresh fish samples from markets in New South Wales and Victoria, showed that some large fish contained mercury levels two to three times that considered safe for consumption. No mercury was found in samples taken in Queensland (A Current Affair, Channel 9, 01.12. 97). We must not be complacent and hope that it 'can't happen here'.

Primary industries and some manufacturing industries produce **organic wastes.** Dairy farmers, pig farmers and horse trainers wash out cow bails, sties and stables respectively. Cattle feedlots also produce much manure and urine. Many primary producers use farm manure as fertiliser or for production of methane for energy, however much animal waste still finds its way into streams. Sugar refineries, butter factories, tanneries, paper mills and sawmills are just a few factories that generate organic wastes; and some produce inorganic ones as well. Some of these treat their waste and recycle the water. Food outlets also create organic waste that has to be disposed of. The waste of fish and chip shops particularly is not suitable for treatment in sewage plants and is taken to special landfill sites.

Osprey House Environmental Centre - Dohles Rocks (PRSC)

CHAPTER **19**

Other Forms of Pollution

We have discussed water pollution in the previous chapter. All forms of pollution are interconnected, just as are all ecosystems of the earth. Rain washes pollutants from the atmosphere and from the land into streams. Some polluted water soaks into the ground and ultimately reaches the sea. Polluted water kills aquatic life; and these dead organisms rot, producing gases that pollute the atmosphere. Pollution, apart from making our environment less attractive and less pleasant to live in, affects the survival chances of other organisms and, ultimately ourselves.

There are some phenomena that we may describe as '**natural pollution**'. Smoke from bushfires, dust from wind erosion, ash and gases from volcanic eruptions, methane from swamps and odours from rotting dead organisms are examples of pollutants that were here well before us. In the past, natural processes rectified the effects of these natural occurrences. Human-induced pollution though is becoming so great that we can no longer rely on nature to heal itself. Affluent societies, such as ours, use more and more resources and produce ever-increasing amounts of waste; and human populations are increasing.

'Natural pollution'

Air Pollution

Pollutants added to the air include those resulting from manufacturing industries, electricity production, road, rail and air transport, burning of bushland, spraying of pests, and many others. Some effects of air pollution are quite obvious - smoke and smog haze, unpleasant odours, respiratory problems for susceptible people, and defoliation of plants. Other effects go unnoticed by the majority of people - damage to the ozone layer, long-term health problems (such as cancers), increased greenhouse effects, and loss of species.

Smoke haze

Industrial air pollution

Burning of fossil fuels

The amounts of coal (carbon), gas and petroleum products (hydrocarbons) that are burnt continues to increase each year as south-east Queensland becomes more populous and manufacturing industries grow. When pure and burnt completely, these substances produce carbon dioxide and water; as we do when we respire. However, because of incomplete burning, impurities in fuels and the presence of gases other than oxygen in the air, poisonous substances result.

Carbon dioxide is non-poisonous but is one of the major greenhouse gases, causing the earth to retain more of the sun's heat. Thus the temperature of the earth rises slowly with time. **Carbon monoxide** is produced when fuels burn in oxygen-deficient air. This is a deadly gas, preventing our red blood cells from taking oxygen to our tissues.

Engine exhausts also release **hydrocarbons** when fuels do not burn completely. Keeping engines well maintained ensures that they operate at maximum efficiency, waste less energy and produce less pollutants. Emission-control modifications to engines (such as catalytic converters) help to remove substances other than carbon dioxide and water.

Because vehicle engines burn fuels at high temperatures, nitrogen and oxygen taken into combustion chambers combine to form **nitric oxide.** In the atmosphere nitric oxide reacts with ozone to form **nitrogen dioxide** which, in sunlight, produces more nitric oxide and ozone. **Ozone**, even in low concentrations, is very poisonous, irritating the eyes, throat, nasal sinuses and lung tissues. It can aggravate bronchial diseases and asthma, affecting young children and old people especially. Ozone also reacts with hydrocarbons and nitrogen compounds in polluted air to form another harmful and distasteful substance, **peroxylacyl nitrate**.

Normally, warm air rises and takes atmospheric pollutants away from where they can harm us here close to ground level. Sometimes though, a layer of cold air can form near the surface, trapping polluted warmer air below it. This is known as a **temperature inversion**. The mixture of pollutants resulting from the action of sunlight, atmospheric pollutants and fog is called **photochemical smog.** Regions with frequent warm, sunny days are most susceptible. In some cities of the world people wear gas masks in times of heavy smog pollution. We usually associate severe problems of this kind with cities such as Los Angeles and Tokyo, but in South-east Queensland we have topographical structures (coastal lowlands backed by nearby mountain ranges) similar to these places. We do not (yet) have the high population, high level of vehicle use and intensive industry, but we already experience a degree of this type of pollution.

Photochemical smog is a health hazard - it can happen here

Temperature Inversion

Sulfur in fuels, when burned for example in furnaces, produces **sulfur dioxide**, a poisonous gas with a pungent odour. Sulfur dioxide reacts with atmospheric oxygen and water to produce sulfuric acid; and acid rain. It can cause paintwork to bleach, crack and peel, and stonework to become stained and eroded. It also reacts with the moisture in our eyes, nasal sinuses and respiratory tracts, causing pain, inflammation and disease. Plants are affected by sulfur dioxide and even small amounts can cause leaf diseases and defoliation.

Lead, as tetraethyl lead, is still added to some petrol to enhance the performance of engines of older vehicles. Use of leaded petrol adds to the amount of lead in air, particularly near busy streets and highways. Lead is a cumulative poison, each dose adding to that already in the body and, especially in young children, can affect intellectual development.

Less use of cars decreases the need to build enormous networks of roads and freeways. The infrastructure needed for cars and the associated traffic make urban living less pleasant as well as destroying great areas of natural bushland and cutting wildlife corridors.

To decrease the amount of pollution caused by private vehicles:

-   take public transport, instead of using a private vehicle, whenever possible. Public transport generates much less pollution per person carried. As more people use public transport it becomes cheaper and services are extended.

- join a car pool. Car pooling decreases the number of one-occupant vehicles on the road, saves money and cuts output of pollutants.

- use steady driving techniques, as opposed to aggressive, rapid acceleration and deceleration. These not only help save on petrol and vehicle maintenance but create much less pollution.

- use unleaded petrol in all vehicles suited to its use and, if feasible, convert engines to use unleaded petrol.

- keep the correct air pressure in tyres. This will save petrol and decrease tyre wear.

- service vehicles regularly to ensure that emission of pollutants is kept to a minimum.

- use a bicycle instead of a car for travel to work, to shops, to natural areas, or to visit friends. Bicycles cause minimal pollution. As well, cycling is healthy exercise. A healthy walk is also an alternative to a short trip in the car.

Cars, motor bikes and trucks are not of course the only burners of fossil fuels that produce pollution. Trains, buses, tractors, boats, ships, planes, factories and power stations also add their wastes to the atmosphere, soil and water. Our modern way of life demands the production of energy by using fossil fuel, but if we all do a small part in decreasing wasteful energy consumption, the overall change will be enormous and make a real difference to the environment.

The greenhouse effect

Our atmosphere regulates the entry and exit of radiation from the earth. It acts like a greenhouse. If it were not for the atmosphere, temperatures on the surface of the earth would vary each day from freezing to extremely hot. Life as we know it could not exist. Throughout the history of the earth, since life first became possible, average temperatures have varied but not greatly - only a few degrees Celsius. This is enough though, when world temperatures are higher, to melt polar ice and cause expansion of the water of oceans. As well, during cooler times, the polar icecaps grow and ocean waters contract. Since the beginning of the industrial revolution (approximately 150 years ago), we have continued to burn more and more fossil fuel, increasing the content of carbon dioxide in the atmosphere by about 30 percent. We have also destroyed vast areas of forest, much of the wood being converted to carbon dioxide by burning. Carbon dioxide is a 'greenhouse gas' - it acts like the glass on a greenhouse, or like a blanket, decreasing the escape of heat by radiation. Other greenhouse gases, produced by industry and vehicles, include methane, nitrous oxide and ozone, a form of oxygen.

For the last two million years or so the earth has been experiencing glaciation. Ice ages have alternated with interglacial periods. We are now in the midst of one of these inter-glacial times, world temperatures are higher and the sea level is well above average geological levels. Sea level is still rising but we do not know if this is because of increased amounts of greenhouse gases in the atmosphere or whether this would have occurred anyway. Maybe our production of these gases forestalled the onset of the next ice age. Most scientists, however, tend to agree that we will see a rise of sea level of between 50 centimetres and 1.5 metres in the next thirty years, unless we can decrease our output of greenhouse gases. A sea level rise of this magnitude would devastate highly populated low-lying regions of the world. Island nations, such as those in the Pacific, could be flooded out. Australia burns coal to generate most of our electricity and this adds greenhouse gases to the atmosphere.

The ozone layer

High in the atmosphere, between 20 and 40 thousand metres above the earth, is a layer of ozone, a gas made up of molecules consisting of three atoms of oxygen. This layer filters out much of the sun's dangerous ultra-violet rays and without it we would suffer much more sunburn and skin cancers. Above Antarctica, in the last few decades, the ozone layer has become thin, and the area of thinning is increasing in size. A group of chemicals called chlorofluorocarbons (CFCs), released into the atmosphere, destroys ozone molecules. CFCs were commonly used in air conditioners, refrigerators, some aerosol spray containers, in cleansing agents and in foam plastics. New technology for these products is replacing CFCs.

Dust is another component of atmospheric pollution. It is produced by traffic on unsealed roads and by machinery during construction projects, such as the building of roads and dams. Here, in dry weather, watering is usually used as a means of alleviating the production of dust. Cultivation on farms also results in dust in the atmosphere, particularly during dry and windy conditions. Occasionally we have severe dust haze when winds bring dust from arid inland areas. Although dust storms have always existed, much of the dust that blows from inland areas is the legacy of inappropriate farming methods. These include clearing of vegetation, over-stocking, burning-off at wrong times and denudation of land by introduced feral pests, such as rabbits and goats.

Smoke has been a typical part of our landscape since Aborigines first used fire as a means of ecological modification. Most of Australia's terrestrial ecosystems depend for their health and diversity on fires of various intensities and frequencies. We must therefore learn to live with fire as part of our environment. A policy of fire suppression is not the answer, whether in urban or rural areas. It is instead a recipe for disaster. With no fire there is a build-up of fuel (logs, bark, twigs, leaves and undergrowth).This ensures that the fire that does occur, and occur it will, will be very hot and potentially dangerous, especially if it occurs during hot, dry and windy conditions. It is during these conditions that bush fires are most likely to start, if left to chance, accident or vandalism. We see and hear with sad regularity the news of death and destruction wrought by wildfires in Australia (See Fire, chapter 16, pages 126 to 131). If it was possible to prevent bushfires, our natural communities would gradually change and many species, plants and animals, would be replaced.

The burning of rubbish in domestic **incinerators** is no longer allowed. This caused much smoke in the suburbs. It was also the source of many neighbourhood disagreements. Burnable rubbish may be disposed of via the wheelie bin or by transporting it to the local tip, but suitable organic matter, such as leaves and grass clippings, is better put in the compost heap. Compost can be used instead of fertiliser. This is more environmentally friendly, as well as making economic good-sense. (See Composting, pages 158 and 159.)

Domestic stoves that use wood as fuel are no longer often used for cooking, though many people still use wood as fuel for **barbeques**. **Wood-burning fire places** provide warmth on cold winter nights. These wood-burning appliances can be a source of smoke pollution.

Inefficient fires and poor quality fuel produce much smoke

To decrease smoke production when using wood as fuel:

-    make sure the stove or fireplace is properly installed and well-maintained.

-    do not use green or moist wood.

-    wood of some tree species produces much smoke. Test unknown wood types for smoke production by burning dry, small amounts. Do not use those that prove to be smoky. These usually do not produce good heat anyway.

-    when lighting the fire, use crumpled newspaper or fire-starters beneath plenty of dry small twigs, woodchips or pine cones. When the fire is burning well, stack on larger pieces of wood (but not too large too soon) and leave plenty of space for air circulation.

-    do not burn chemically-treated wood. This can release very toxic materials into the atmosphere, or our homes or food.

Land development is another source of smoke. When land is being cleared for rural development, it is the usual policy to stack and burn the remains of felled trees and shrubs. Regardless of the method of doing this, it generates much smoke. On land other than rural land, any burning of cleared vegetation is required to be pit-burnt. Plant remains are burned in a large pit into which air is forced from a large steel pipe. Because of the high temperatures generated, smoke is virtually eliminated.

However, burning all forest material is wasteful. Useful materials that are burned include hollows that can be used in gardens for wildlife, firewood, wood suitable for carving, and logs and root stocks useful as landscape features. The leaves, twigs and smaller branches are also valuable for mulch. Developers could win friends and possibly encourage sales by making these materials available (on site, or from a local council centre) to buyers of allotments in the development, or to other local residents.

Pit-burning - to eliminate smoke

Land Pollution

It is very pleasant to live in natural surroundings, but much of what we do changes our surroundings, not always for the betterment of ourselves nor other species. Some of these changes are unseen but others are visual.

Visual pollution

Most of us would agree that pieces of wrapping paper, empty cartons, bottles and cans, food scraps and cigarette butts left lying in parks, streets and along footpaths are not pleasing to the eye.

Smoke from land-clearing does not only occur in Indonesia

Garbage, thrown into bushland, strewn along country roads and washed up by the tides, is not what the vast majority of people prefer. Yet, to accumulate the vast amounts of litter that we can see almost any day of the week, there must be many careless people amongst us who think nothing of throwing rubbish away just anywhere.

Wrappings, cartons and cans, left after that picnic or snack by the river, in the park or near the beach, do not simply disintegrate or disappear. Some may be carried short distances by animals such as dogs, rats or crows, but unless picked up by someone, rubbish usually blows or washes eventually into streams. Take a short walk past a mangrove area to see just what great amounts and variety of rubbish end up in the sea. Even as far back as 1970, Thor Heyerdahl recorded bottles, plastic containers, cans and oil slicks on 43 of the 57 days he spent sailing across the Atlantic Ocean on a papyrus raft. It is unlikely that things have improved since then.

Because much of the litter and rubbish that is dumped along roads and streets washes into gullies and down stormwater drains, measures to intercept it are put in place along streams. Gross pollutant traps and trash racks collect larger materials, especially in times of increased flow.

Accumulated rubbish is periodically removed and disposed of properly. Detention basins and artificial wetlands are designed to prevent the downstream flow of finer sediments, and to allow aquatic plants to take up nutrients.

Pollutant traps and detention basins protect downstream environments.

It is not just the aesthetic component of visual pollution with which we should be concerned. Plastic bags and six-pack holders, fishing lines, aluminium cans and ring pulls do not decompose readily. Some will take hundreds of years to decay and many are lethal to animals that become entangled in or eat them. For example some of our rare sea turtles eat jellyfish and mistake plastic bags for food.

Rubbish dumped on the beach

Rubbish dumped in the bush

Do we really love our country?

To decrease litter pollution:

- we should always put rubbish into bins provided. If there are special recyling bins, put rubbish into the appropriate ones. See recyling pages 157 and 158.

- where there are no bins provided, or if the bins are full, we should take our rubbish with us. In many natural areas, authorities provide no bins at all because, with the provision of bins, many people bring rubbish here for deposition, or they keep putting rubbish into already full and overflowing bins.

- do not take a dog into natural areas. When walking a dog along the footpath or in a park (on the leash of course) pick up all droppings.

- take vehicle registration numbers of people seen dumping rubbish. Dob in a dumper.

- do not use unnecessary or excess wrapping and packaging of food for picnics, lunches or snacks. Reusable containers are better.

- when shopping, choose products that do not have unnecessary, excessive or misleading wrapping or packaging.

- write letters of complaint to companies who use unnecessary, excessive or misleading wrapping or packaging.

- buy food that is packed in recyclable containers (See recycling, pages 157 to 158), or ask for it to be wrapped in grease-proof paper only.

- join in the local Clean-up-Australia Day program.

- quit smoking. Cigarette butts are very common litter.

Graffiti is another form of visual pollution. Some individuals may consider that 'tags', initials and attempts at artistic expression are somehow clever when painted, carved or scratched onto prominent surfaces. However, most people regard graffiti as vandalism, pathetic and immature. Graffiti on walls and fences, paths and signs defaces private and public property. On trees, rocks and cliff faces it degrades things of natural beauty and makes our world a sadder and uglier place. Names scratched into the bark of trees can be a source of fungal and viral infections that can eventually kill the trees. A great deal of rate-payers' money is used in cleaning up the mess that these defacers of the environment create.

Advertisements nailed to trees, and bill boards on frames in roadside paddocks of outer suburbs and in country areas also detract from the beauty of the surroundings. Have we allowed ourselves to become conditioned to the presence of these objects; and should we?

Is this art or vandalism?

A selfish act can kill a tree

Landscapes can be degraded by various other forms of visual pollution. Some people with vested interests may not agree, but the vast majority of people would regard a prominent quarry scar on the side of a hill as a blemish on natural scenery. On the other hand, most would agree that we need rock materials derived by quarrying. Similarly, extractive industries, that carve up river banks and flats and destroy stream-side vegetation, supply us with sand and gravel. Are we willing to pay more for these essential building materials if we have these industries moved to other locations? And what of the people who will then be affected, and the decline of their visual amenity? Most people can appreciate the need for some landscape degradation if we see the commencement of suitable rehabilitation programs early in the life of the operation.

Gravel extraction

Quarry

Necessary evils in the short term but rehabilitation should begin early

Should we allow **housing developments**, or indeed the occasional house, to be built on the tops and slopes of our most outstanding forest-clad hills and mountains? These buildings intrude into the natural scenery of our skylines and horizons. If we do allow them, should we require that they be landscaped and suitably painted so as to lessen the visual impact?

Townscapes can be visually polluted by garish and ugly **advertising** signs. As we drive along roads through inner and outer suburbs, do we take notice of the profusion of signs and advertisements above, in front of and on either side of each and every shop, car yard and service station? We do not; and so most are entirely unnecessary. They serve only to promote the disfigurement of our urban scenery. Does it serve any purpose to have strings of bunting flying over real estate shops and car yards? Is it necessary or effective to have boards of the day's specials strewn along the roadside for fifty metres each side of fruit and vegetable outlets? Could it not be better to have a limit of two signs on the outside of any one establishment? We would then be much more likely to see and focus upon the intended messages. It is very unlikely that any town with this overkill of signage could win a tidy towns competition.

Many new suburbs have their phone, electricity and TV cables underground. In older suburbs (and some new ones as well) these are above the streets on poles. High voltage electricity transmission lines and their pylons are a part of every developed country's infrastructure. Do they add to the visual pollution of our towns, cities and rural areas or do they add a certain charm to the landscape? Have these unnatural parts of our environment been with us so long that we no longer see them as intrusive; and should we? Of course there are also the added factors of radiation pollution associated with magnetic fields induced by alternating currents; and microwaves.

Is this advertising overkill?

CHAPTER **19**

Will we become used to all this? Have we already?

Sound (noise) pollution

When does sound become a form of atmospheric pollution? Can some natural sounds, sounds that have always been with us, be considered pollution? Is it not strange how selective we can become about what we tolerate in the way of noise? There are some sad people who allow natural sounds to irritate them. One small striped marsh frog's intermittent 'tock, tock, ...', is enough to keep some people awake. Others find this sound relaxing. Crows, cawing at daybreak, annoy and keep some of us from sleep. There are some people who become so irritated as to call for the eradication of crows. How sad? On the other hand, many people thank the birds for preventing them from sleeping their lives away and for giving them the opportunity of enjoying the best part of the day. Some people curse willy-wagtails and koels that call at night. These same birds sooth others of us back to sleep as we listen, feeling thankful that we could be so fortunate as to have such lovely creatures with us in our world.

Calls of native birds such as lorikeets, spangled drongos, noisy miners and magpies pester and even frighten a few persons. Cicadas, crickets and grasshoppers drive some of the populace to distraction. So do we call these sounds pollutants?

Many of us can still remember the times when nearly every family had a dozen or so chooks in the backyard and, at least one rooster. No one seemed to notice then that the roosters all around the neighbourhood began to crow well before dawn. Poultry around (and in) households has been part of human existence for thousands of years. A few decades ago, once the frequency of roosters in the suburbs began to fall, the number of people who were familiar with the early calls of chook-yard cocks decreased. It was then that complaints about the crowing of the neighbours' roosters began to rise, leading to the almost universal ban on the keeping of all but a few hens - without a rooster. Could it be that people's intolerance of their neighbours and of each others' differences were the real reasons for the suburban rooster getting the chop, and for a crowing cock in town to be considered sound pollution?

Many people are willing to put up with all manner of artificial sounds. Noisy vehicles, loud television sets and stereo systems, and booming fireworks from the local sports fields are some of the noises we accept, albeit reluctantly. Most of us do not complain about the occasional loud late party near our homes, but are not so forgiving when these events happen often.

In relation to the amount of sound pollution we have to tolerate in our environment, some of us are more fortunate than others. If a sound is fairly constant we become habituated to it; that is, we learn not to react to it, and only if it stops do we notice. Those of us who live near a major highway, train-line or under the flight path of an airport, become, after a time,

Plantings help to improve the 'look' of sound barriers

habituated to the polluting sounds. Sound barrier walls, built along highways, help alleviate the problem of excess noise. Rows of trees and shrubs between highways and houses help through some sound absorption and by hiding the source of the sound.

To decrease the amount of noise pollution:

- keep mufflers and manifolds on vehicles and mowers in good condition.

- do not accelerate so as to cause car tyres to screech. This not only shortens the life of tyres, wastes petrol, pollutes the atmosphere with toxins and noise, but indicates a lack of intelligence.

- do not blow the car horn as a parting gesture when leaving a residence, especially at night.

- decrease the amount of lawn so that less time is needed to mow it, or perhaps a manual push mower is all you need.

- do not buy nor use noisy unnecessary machines such as petrol driven edger-cutters and leaf sweepers.

- keep stereos, radios and television volumes down so that they do not annoy neighbours. Close windows next to nearby neighbours. If only one person is listening, headphones could be used.

- practise the drums, saxophone, opera singing or electric guitar with the windows closed and use a fan to keep cool.

- do not take radios or ghetto-blasters to natural areas - other people go there to appreciate the sounds of the natural environment. We can too. If we simply cannot do without the music, sports report or talkback show, we should use headphones.

- fit a super car stereo system, play it at mega-decibels and deafen yourself and your passengers but keep the windows wound up fully.

Light Pollution

The duration of natural daylight varies through the year - longer night-time in the winter and longer daylight hours in the summer. Plants and animals respond in various ways to the relative lengths of daylight or darkness. Flowering and growth of plants, and breeding and migration of animals are affected by the stimuli of changing periods of light and darkness.

Insects such as moths and beetles, attracted to artificial light sources, in turn attract bats, nocturnal birds, frogs and toads. Where there are street lights, some of these animals become road kills and are fed on by other animals, many of which are also killed by vehicles.

In modern towns and cities artificial light affects natural environments and has an influence upon our lives. Is it necessary to have as much light from street lights? Do we need to light as many rooms in office buildings twenty-four hours a day? The generation of electricity for these lights consumes fuels and produces pollutant wastes. The glow from cities and towns at night decreases the visibility and beauty of the stars and moon in the night sky, and it is not until we go out into the country that we appreciate what we in town have lost.

There are many ways in which artificial light intrudes upon our lifestyles. A bright exterior light at night may be very annoying to neighbours. Car lights may shine intermittently through our windows. The floodlights of sports fields and golf practice-ranges extend the period of twilight for many neighbouring houses. Shrubs and trees strategically positioned can be used to screen out intrusive light, but to be effective these may need to be planted in otherwise undersirable sites and have unwanted effects.

A lot of rubbish

Australia, per head of population, produces more rubbish than all but a few other countries of the world. We go to the shop for an article that is wrapped in aluminium foil or plastic, contained in a cardboard box that is also covered by plastic. The person at the checkout then puts it into a plastic bag for us.

More and more of the things we use are of the **disposable** kind - lighters, razors, pens, cameras, nappies and containers. Many other goods, not designed to be disposable, are dumped because it is cheaper to get rid of them rather than repair them. Ours is a throw-away society. Much of what we throw away can be reused, but it is not, and about one quarter of this is packaging, much of it unnecessary. What happens to all this rubbish after the garbage truck comes?

Most rubbish taken **to land-fill sites** is buried. In the compacted anaerobic conditions within dumps decomposition can be very slow. In the USA, rubbish uncovered after 50 years in a dump contained still-recognisable sandwiches with butter and green lettuce. Buried plastics are likely to last for thousands of years. Noxious materials, such as oil, paint, solvent, asbestos and pesticides, are now taken to special facilities where some are treated, some destroyed and others stored. Most of these will need to be stored indefinitely. For very many years these substances were thrown into rubbish tips along with everything else. They are a worry for the future of aquatic environments. There are many other problems associated with this system of waste management.

We are quickly running out of sites suitable for land-fill. These have to be close enough to towns and cities to keep the cost of transport low. In the past, wetlands, mangroves and areas of infertile soil were regarded as worthless and therefore good sites for refuse tips. This often was not the case and time will tell as to what seeps out of these places. The most important requirement of a tip site is that it should be contained within **impervious sediment or rock** so that the surrounding and underlying regions are not contaminated by infiltration from the dump. It is usual to have drains around the perimeters of rubbish dumps so that the materials that leach out can be pumped back. **Leachate** is tested so that seepage of any hazardous substances can be intercepted before damage is done to the adjacent environment.

To decrease long-term pollution problems of tip sites and the need for land-fill space:

- recycle as many things as possible (see Recycling, pages 157 & 158).

- choose goods that are packed in recylable containers.

- compost as many plant and food wastes as possible (see Composting, page 158).

- do not shop for waste - avoid goods with unneccesary packaging.

- before throwing away old or broken appliances, toys, books, records, spectacles, etc, ring charity organisations. Many things can be fixed and used again.

- choose paper goods made from recycled paper - writing paper, envelopes, toilet paper, greeting cards, etc.

- reuse envelopes, and staple together paper, printed on one side, as note and scribble paper.

- when shopping, take your own shopping bag or basket and refuse plastic bags.

- toxic materials (pesticides, sump oil, solvents, etc) should be disposed of properly. In the Pine Rivers Shire phone 3205 0776 for information about disposal of these substances.

Capped tip sites

When a tip site is full, the top and sides are capped with clay so that rainwater cannot percolate down into the underlying waste. If this happens seepage from the tip will increase and contamination may spread. Old tip sites are often used as **sports fields** but increasingly they are being landscaped with selected natural vegetation, to become picnic grounds and environmental areas - and being high, the views are excellent. We are restricted in what can be grown on old dump sites because trees with deep roots can break through the capping layer and allow surface water to penetrate. There are suitable native plants that we can use - ones that have no tap roots and those with spreading fibrous roots.

Not all 'rubbish' is rubbish

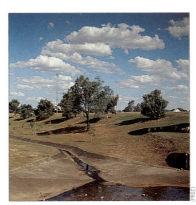

What lurks below; and is it escaping?

The breakdown of organic matter in rubbish dumps produces gaseous material, some useful, especially **methane**. Left to seep into the atmosphere, methane can damage the protective ozone layer in the upper atmosphere. However, it is an excellent fuel and some closed dumps are being tapped and the methane added to domestic gas mains for energy production.

Recycling

Much of what we threw away in the past was not useless. Numerous old dumps now contain a lot of buried valuable materials. The manufacture of many goods uses non-renewable resources and consumes energy, so, by recycling, we **decrease pollution** and **save resources and energy**. The Pine Rivers Shire Council is a leader in recycling, being one of the first local governments to introduce the two-wheelie-bin collection system for sorting recyclable articles from other rubbish. The list of articles and substances collected for recycling in the yellow-topped recycling bin includes **glass bottles and jars** (with lids removed)**, certain plastics such as drink and ice-cream containers, aluminium and steel cans, cardboard and paper**. Articles that are not recyclable and that should not be put into the recycling bin include crockery, plastic bags and disposable nappies. These items should be put into the rubbish bin.

Recycling bin - pioneered by Pine Rivers
Shire Council

Articles suitable for recycling

Tip site recycling

At council tips, materials such as sound timber, metals and articles such as bicycles, tricycles, prams, toys, etc are removed. Prunings and vegetable matter are shredded and made into mulch and compost. This can be made available to members of the public.

Recycling industries

There are other used-materials that are **recycled by various private firms**. Waste engine **oil** is treated and made ready for reuse. Used **tyres**, if they are in sound condition, are retreaded. If not they can be made into a range of products such as door mats, flooring and footwear.

The **waste from grease traps** of food processing plants, restaurants and other food outlets is converted into organic fertiliser and protein stock-food. Some organic waste is composted and turned into potting mix.

Methods are being pioneered and tested for processing materials in landfill sites by using them as **furnace fuels** and then using the ash remains to make **building blocks**.

Composting

A lot of **recycling can be done at home**. Valuable products that can be composted should not be put into the rubbish bin to be taken away and buried. This uses scarce land-fill space unnecessarily. Garden prunings, lawn clippings, weeds, leaves, peelings of fruit and vegetables, tea leaves, tea bags, coffee grounds and egg shells are all suitable for composting. The occasional watering and addition of soil helps the process. It only takes about six to eight weeks for garden and kitchen wastes to be converted to rich, odourless compost for pot plants, the garden or shrubbery. With two compost bins, the compost from one can be in use while the other is busy composting. Compost bins can be bought cheaply from the Council (phone 3205 0776) or they can be constructed easily using timber or old pallets.

Earthworm farm kits

Earthworm farm kits, made from recycled plastic, can be bought cheaply from the Council (phone 3205 0776). These can use almost all vegetable wastes from the kitchen. There are no associated bad odours. The worm castings are perfect as an additive to potting mixes and mulches. The liquid produced is excellent for watering plants in pots and the garden. Instructions for use come with the kits, but there is minimal effort required. The worms, that do all the work, breed profusely. Excess ones can be added to the garden, used as fishing bait or sold for profit.

Compost bin made from recycled plastic

Earthworms - sign of a healthy garden

Worm farm - converts kitchen waste into valuable additives for the garden

CHAPTER **20**

Saving Energy and Resources

Nearly all energy available to living things in the natural environment comes initially from the sun. This passes through an energy cycle beginning with green plants using sunlight. First-order consumers (herbivores) gain their energy by eating plants. Energy then passes to higher consumers when they eat other animals or other animals and plants. Humans are, of course, part of this cycle, but we also make use of other forms of energy. We do this to produce light and heat, provide transport, cook food, manufacture goods, enhance communications and so on. Some of this energy comes from hydro-electric generators, some from nuclear power, some from the sun, some from the burning of wood, but most comes from the burning of '**fossil fuels**' - coal, oil and gas.

There are two **problems** related to the burning of fossil fuels. Firstly, it takes millions of years for fossil fuels to form. They are finite resources, so eventually they will become more and more scarce and increasingly costly to obtain. Secondly, the burning of fossil fuels produces wastes such as water, carbon dioxide, carbon monoxide, nitrogen dioxide, nitric oxide and ozone (see pages 143 to 145). Most of these products are harmful to the environment, either because they are greenhouse gases (see pages 145 & 146), they destroy the ozone layer (see page 146) or they are toxic.

There are some very important reasons why we should **conserve energy**. By doing so we can **decrease pollution** of the environment, and we can help to **make our fuel reserves last longer**. Another factor to consider is that, by conserving energy, we **save money**.

Designing and building energy-efficient homes

Houses can be designed and built to save energy. This will pay dividends because, for the entire life of the house, the owners will be more comfortable and save much expense in cooling, heating and lighting.

Some factors to consider when building energy-efficient homes:

- The shape and size of a house affects its energy needs. Square, small, compact houses are more energy-efficient than large, long, irregular-shaped ones. Many of our houses are unnecessarily large.

- Correct orientation of a house with respect to movement of the sun can conserve energy. See pages 60 to 62. Windows and skylights facing north to north-east allow in heat and light during winter. Overhanging roofs can shade these from the heat of summer. Elongate houses are best aligned east west.

- Orientation of windows with respect to prevailing breezes allows through-circulation and helps to cool the house in summer.

- Verandahs can shade and protect the house walls and provide cool living spaces in the summer.

- Insulation in the walls and ceilings of homes can greatly decrease heat-gain in summer and heat-loss in winter. A 75 mm thick layer of good insulation material in the ceiling of a home can decrease the cost of cooling in summer and heating in winter by as much as thirty percent.

- Insulate the hot water tank and pipes and place the tank as close as possible to the kitchen sink, or next best, the laundry.

Ways of saving energy in the home:

- Insulate the house by use of insulation in the walls and in the ceiling.

- Stop air leaks at all windows and doors to maintain heat in winter.

- Turn off lights that are not in use.

- Use fluorescent bulbs instead of the older light bulbs, especially where light is needed for long periods. Though these cost more they last ten times longer and use thirty percent less energy.

- Use low wattage bulbs in areas where bright light is not needed.

- Use natural light from skylights, open the shutters and blinds and draw the curtains instead of using artificial light.

- Turn off television sets and computers when not in use.

- Use ceiling fans and mobile fans instead of air-conditioning units. Fans use a lot less energy. Moving air makes a person feel several degrees cooler.

- In the house in cold weather, wear warm clothes or put extra blankets on the bed. Electric blankets and electric heaters use a lot of energy. It takes three times the amount of fuel to generate electricity to produce the same amount of heat as from fuel burned in the home.

- Cook with gas rather than electricity. It is cheaper and produces less pollutants.

- Install a solar hot water system. Solar panels should face north at an angle of 33 degrees in the Pine Rivers Shire.

- Insulate the hot water tank and pipes and place the tank as close as possible to the kitchen sink.

- Use off-peak electricity for the hot water system.

- Turn the temperature control on the hot water system down in summer and up in winter.

- Heat only as much water as needed for tea or coffee, and cook food with as little water as possible.

- Boil different vegetables at once, separated in the one pot. Use a lid. Pots should have thick, wide bottoms. Pressure cookers are very efficient.

- Decide what you want before opening the fridge and do not open the oven during cooking.

- Use the cold water or warm water cycle when using the washing machine.

- Use a clothes line instead of a clothes drier.

- Plant or retain trees in positions to shade the house in summer, to allow the sun to shine in during winter and to protect the house from cold or hot winds.

Remember:
- *Every energy-using appliance has an energy-saving position on the controls. It is called OFF.*

Alternative sources of electrical energy production

Most of Australia's electrical needs are produced by the burning of coal. This produces toxic materials and greenhouse gases (see pages 145 & 146). There are alternative ways of generating electricity that are less harmful to the environment. As fossil fuels become more expensive to use some of these methods of electricity production will become more viable economically.

A small amount of electricity is produced in Queensland by **hydro-electric** stations, but our scope for more is small because we have so few high waterfalls with sufficient year-round water flow. As well, damming of rivers destroys large areas of natural habitat above the dam, and alters aquatic habitats below.

Wind mills have been used in Australia since the early pioneering days for pumping water. There is potential in the future to make much greater use of this non-polluting method of utilising the energy of winds to generate electricity.

Solar energy is being used more and more and eventually will become one of our major sources of electrical energy. We have many sunny days during the year so we are well placed to be at the forefront of pioneering this free and non-polluting resource.

Australia has a large proportion of the world's uranium, used in some other countries to produce most of the electricity they consume. We could easily make use of this resource to generate most or all of our electrical power requirements, but there are some important considerations to be taken into account. Though **nuclear power plants** do not produce any toxins or greenhouse gases they have to be run extremely carefully to ensure no leaks of radiation that could severely damage the environment. As well, the waste products of nuclear fuel are extremely dangerous and at present we have no safe way of disposing of them. They have to be stored and prevented from contaminating the environment, virtually forever.

Tree Planting (PRSC)

ANOTHER TRAY OF   NURSERY
QUALITY PLANTS
FROM A MEMBER OF

PART THREE

UNTIL

Now

CHAPTER **21**

A Land of Extremes

Australia - the oldest continent

Australia is the oldest continent on Earth. Our most ancient rocks outcrop in Western Australia. They were formed more than 4 thousand million years ago and are the core of the continent. Since then, every few hundred million years, the Australian continental landmass has grown eastwards. This process involved deposition of sediments on the ocean floor, uplift of those sediments to form enormous fold-mountains, weathering and erosion of the uplifted rocks, and re-deposition to begin the cycle again. The last phase of accretion, about 250 million years ago, added the Great Dividing Range and present coastal plain to the older continent.

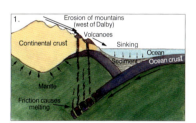
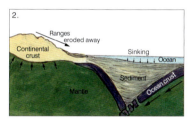

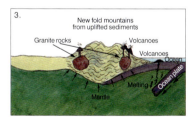

Geological development of South-east Queensland

Australia - the most infertile continent

For hundreds of millions of years this rock-recycling process continued, leaching and washing soluble minerals to the sea and making Australia's soils some of the most infertile on Earth. They are typically deficient in nitrogen, potassium, phosphorus, and sometimes trace elements. The occasional addition of rocks of more basic composition, such as basalt, andesite, serpentinite and gabbro, during periods of vulcanism and igneous intrusion, provided parent rock that could give rise to very fertile soils.

Australia - the most geologically stable continent

Australia is moving northwards at about 8 centimetres a year - about half as fast as our hair grows. However, earthquakes and volcanic eruptions are rare. This is because Australia is within its tectonic plate and away from its plate boundaries. Other continents have plate margins along their coastlines or within their land masses, and it is along plate margins that earthquakes and volcanoes mostly occur. The earthquakes that do occur in Australia are usually along old fault lines. They are due to minor isostatic adjustments of the crust, the result of imbalances created after long periods of erosion and deposition. Australian mountains were once the magnificent heights of the much-younger Andes, Rockies and Alps, but because of their age are now mere hills, eroded almost flat. The last major volcanic eruptions to affect South-east Queensland occurred during the Tertiary Period - about 25 million years ago. These eruptions occurred in the vacinities of Mt Warning, the Darling Downs, Mt Glorious and the Glasshouses. Soils resulting from these lavas are some of our most fertile.

Source of South-east Queensland's richest soils

Australia - the driest inhabited continent

Australia's mountain ranges are too low to force clouds to heights great enough to shed all of their water as rain. The Great Dividing Range, which includes our tallest mountains, crosses the path of the prevailing south-east trade winds. Though laden with moisture after blowing across the Pacific Ocean, they yield only some of their potential as rain, and mostly on the eastern coast. The lack of higher inland ranges means that the interior tends to become drier as we go west. The other high rainfall areas in Australia where seasonal winds bring moisture from the ocean are the south-west corner of Western Australia and the west coast of Tasmania. These are under the winter influence of the roaring forties. Tropical monsoons bring summer and autumn rain to the northern areas of Cape York Peninsula and Northern Territory. In summer and autumn, irregular and unreliable cyclonic influences can result in high rainfall, especially in the north and east of Australia.

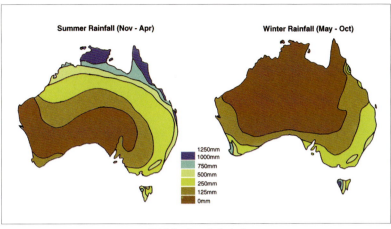

Rainfall patterns in Australia

One of the most important factors influencing the climate and long-term weather patterns of Australia is the phenomenon known as the El Nino Southern Oscillation (ENSO) - the **El Nino Effect**. Temperature patterns of oceanic water and air in the Southern Hemisphere periodically reverse. This induces conditions over the southern continents that result in periods of drought, sometimes lasting for years, or seasons of numerous and often severe cyclones and flooding rains. Australian plants and animals evolved with these environmental conditions, adapting to increase their chances of survival. We too now live with this environment.

A land 'of drought and flooding rains' - South Pine River

Australia - the long-isolated, island continent

All of the continents of the earth, in the distant past, formed one super-continent - **Pangaea**. It was possible then for many groups of terrestrial plants and animals to spread to most parts of this huge land mass. About 200 million years ago Pangaea began to separate into two - the great southern continent (Gondwanaland or Gondwana) and the great northern continent (Laurasia). Many land organisms now became restricted to one or other of the massive continents on which they lived.

Break-up of Pangaea

Gondwana, consisting of Africa, Madagascar, India, South America, Antarctica and Australia, began to break up about 120 million years ago. Australia was the last continent to separate from Antarctica - some 45 million years ago. It then drifted north on its crustal plate in total isolation until 15 million years ago when it began its collision with south-east Asia. Even so, the land on the Australian plate is still separated from that of the Asian plate by narrow straits of very deep water.

Australia's unique flora and fauna

During Australia's long period of isolation, many of our plants and animals evolved separately from those of the rest of the world. The marsupials, monitor lizards, and honeyeaters reached their pinnacle of genetic diversity here. The monotremes occur nowhere else (except in New Guinea, which is connected to Australia during times of lowered sea level). The remarkable mound-building birds are almost entirely restricted to our continent. Many plant genera such as the acacias (wattles), eucalypts and casuarinas, now typical of our landscapes, proliferated. Some groups of fauna and flora which may have been present before the break-up of Gondwanaland continued to survive here - the emu and cassowary, the cycads. Many flourished and are now some of our most representative groups - the Proteaceae family (banksias, geebungs and grevilleas), the parrots (lorikeets, rosellas, grass parrots and cockatoos).

Australia - a special place

We indeed have a special country here, in many ways the envy of the rest of the world; but how much do we know about it? How much do we appreciate it? And how can each one of us help to preserve it for future generations? Do we want our beautiful and unique landscapes to continue to be degraded, altered and replaced? Is our own different and distinctive flora to be crowded out by overseas species - ones we plant deliberately or that become feral? Will our unique animals, which survived and adapted during tens of millions of years of isolation on that long journey northwards, resist the onslaught of invading exotic species?

CHAPTER
22
South-east Queensland

A region of rich diversity

This area is biologically one of the richest in Australia. From the coast to the mountains in the hinterlands we pass through a range of habitats - beaches, mangroves, tidal creeks and rivers, marshlands, brackish and freshwater swamps and lagoons, grasslands, woodlands and forests. The numerous parent rock-types and topography ensure a wide variety of soils - some poorly drained, some porous, some infertile and others rich, some shallow and some deep. This area is included in what has been called the Macleay-Macpherson Overlap, where the Torresian and Bassian biological distributions come together. Plants and animals from sub-tropical areas occur here together with those of the temperate south.

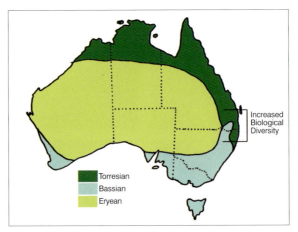

North meets south

The role of geology in diversity

The natural community of plants and animals that live at a particular place is determined ultimately by the geology - past and present. This includes the earth movements, volcanic activity and sedimentation. The resulting parent rocks influence the soils formed from them. So does the climate; and climate is largely dependent upon location on the continent. The former positions of continents and parts of continents, on the Earth's surface, determined previous climates. The resulting plant communities sustain particular animal communities. Land forms and topography also play important roles in the distribution of living things: so does the presence of other organisms and those that have lived before. All of these factors influence the activities and population of humans. In turn, we impact, as we have in the past, upon the success or otherwise of particular species of plants and animals.

Geological History of South-east Queensland

Before 370 million years ago - ocean deposition:

In this region, before 370 million years ago, the Pacific coast of Gondwana (still part of Pangaea) was farther west - somewhere near where Dalby is today. West of this were high fold mountain ranges with streams flowing eastward across coastal plains and depositing sediments onto a continental shelf and into a deep, sinking trench farther east. This trench, the Tasman Geosyncline, was the subduction belt where the Pacific plate slid down under the Australian plate. All of what is now the Great Dividing Range, the coastal plain, the islands off the coast and the continental shelf did not exist. This was all deep ocean.

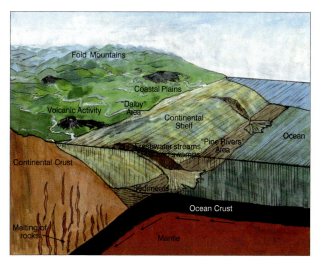

South-east Queensland, before the birth of eastern Australia

From 290 to 240 million years ago - uplift of fold mountains:

For tens of millions of years the mountain ranges west of about Dalby eroded away and the deep trough filled with sediments. These came mostly from the eroding continent but others were scraped off the ocean floor. There was also some addition from volcanic activity. The whole subduction process was becoming clogged. Between 290 to 240 million years ago the sediments of the trough were pushed up and compressed, forming new mountain ranges attached to the older continent. The variously altered rocks, compacted and heated during uplift, now form the basement on which all other rocks in this region have accumulated. See diagrams, pages 165.

From 240 to 220 million years ago - faulting, vulcanism and intrusion:

After the clogging of the subduction belt and uplift of the trough sediments, the geosyncline possibly moved farther to the east in the Pacific Ocean. This caused instability within the crust in the south-east Queensland region, resulting in earth movements that gave rise to volcanic eruptions and intrusion of granitic magma. About this time, in the early Triassic, part of the mountain belt gradually subsided forming the Esk Rift. This collapsed valley separates the Main Range (or Yarraman Block) in the west from the D'Aguilar Block to the east. Later subsidence resulted in a corridor between the D'Aguilar Block and the Beenleigh Block to the south. This may have allowed a river, the fore-runner of the Brisbane, to flow through to the coast. One short episode of violent eruptions in or near the Brisbane area produced hot frothy lava that flowed down some valleys to form deposits of welded tuff. The emplacement of granitic rocks helped to stabilise the old geosynclinal belt, welding it to the older continent.

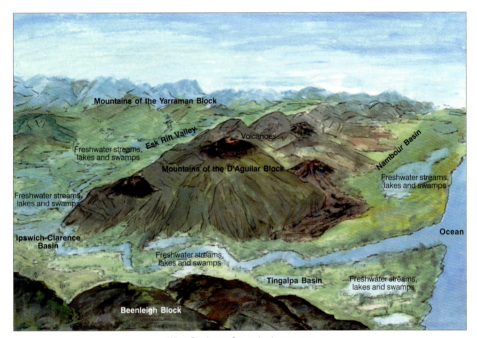

When South-east Queensland was young

In the Pine Rivers area we see magnificent views to or from the D'Aguilar Range, the remnants of the ancient, towering mountain ranges. The flaky and foliated rocks, often with beds and veins of quartzite, that outcrop in many parts of the shire are phyllite. The clayey 'dirty 'sandstone containing small rock fragments is greywacke. These rocks, derived from the sediments of the old ocean trough, produce infertile soils. North-west of Petrie the darker more basic flaky rock is greenstone, altered from volcanic material. It weathers to form fertile chocolate soils. Greenstone is quarried at Petrie and Narangba. It is crushed and used for rock aggregate and to construct retaining walls.

There is evidence of volcanic eruption about 220 million years ago at Jollys Lookout, where boulders of andesite outcrop.

At Samford, Mt Samson and Dayboro granitic rocks occur. These igneous intrusions (plutons) cooled slowly kilometers under the surface, forming course-grained rocks. This attests to the initial height of the old land surface and the amount of erosion since 240 million years ago. The plutons have weathered and eroded so that we now have granitic amphitheatres - almost circular or oval patterns of hills surrounding these wide valleys.

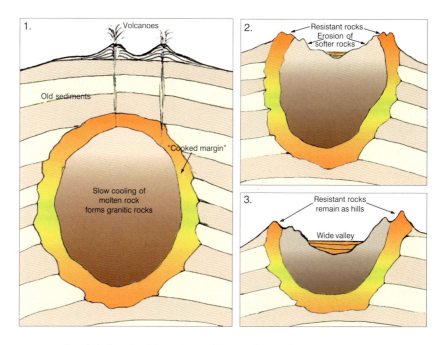

Steps in the formation of the granite amphitheatres of Samford, Samsonvale and Dayboro

The resulting sandy soils of the valleys are well drained and relatively fertile. Ground water is plentiful and sweet. Quarries in these areas supply decomposed granite, and boulders (tors) for rock walls and landscaping.

From 220 to 180 million years ago - freshwater deposition; streams, lakes and swamps:
On the new terrestrial land-surface, streams, at first short and fast-flowing, carried large fragments. With prolonged erosion, the land surface gradually matured and streams flowed greater distances over flat, broadening valleys. Immature sediments which gave rise to conglomerates and coarse sandstones were followed by those forming finer sandstones, siltstones, shales and coal. Intermittent uplift in mountain areas rejuvenated streams and caused repetition of these sedimentary sequences. Slow sinking of the basin itself (the Moreton Basin) resulted in great thicknesses of sediments.

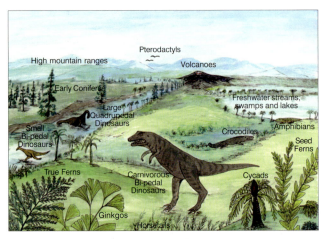

Triassic-Jurassic Park

By the Jurassic Period (200 million years ago) the Moreton Basin was more or less continuous with the Nambour Basin to the north-east. Fossil remains show that highly evolved and diverse plant life lived in these two basins, including groups such as the true ferns, the 'seed ferns' (now all extinct), cycads, ginkgos and horsetails. The earliest species of Araurcaria, ancestors of the Hoop Pine, appeared at this time. Animal life included large amphibians and dinosaurs - plant eaters and carnivores (A. Simpson in W. Willmott and N. Stevens, 1992, p. 21).

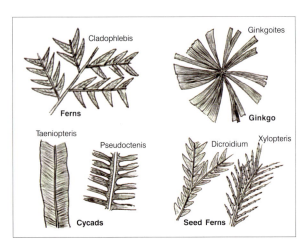

Triassic-Jurassic plants

In the Pine Rivers area north from Dohles Rocks and Petrie, sedimentary rocks (mostly sandstones and some conglomerates) were deposited in the Nambour Basin. These have been eroded to low country and weathered to give, in some places, laterite soil with red iron-rich pebbles. At Narangba low-plasticity, light-firing clays are quarried for brick making. Pebbly laterite and conglomerate have provided material suitable for gravel roads.

65 to 45 million years ago - new basins form:

After a long period of erosion, new freshwater sedimentary basins formed in several places in South-east Queensland. This may have been due to instability in the crust caused by tension in the ocean plate east of Australia. The sediments, deposited into shallow swamps and lakes, are now sandstone, siltstone, shale, limestone and oil-shale. These are sometimes inter-bedded with basalt flows, reflecting the instability at the time.

The dominant vegetation was now the angiosperms (flowering plants), and the mammals had replaced the dinosaurs. Fossils are uncommon but include remains of freshwater species of lungfish, modern bony fish, a turtle, ostracods, bivalved molluscs and crustaceans. Plant remains include some species similar to today's banksias and eucalypts. It is thought that the climate was warm and moist and rainforests extensive.

In the Petrie and Strathpine areas the fine, soft, mostly unconsolidated sediments have eroded to form slightly undulating plains. Deposits at Strathpine supply dark-firing, plastic clays for brick making.

28 - 20 million years ago - volcanic eruptions:

Further tension in the crust east of Australia may have caused local instability that led to numerous volcanic plugs and basalt flows in South-east Queensland. The volcanic plugs, such as the Glasshouses, consist of rhyolite and trachyte and are more resistant to weathering than their surroundings. Much of the basalt lava flows and underlying older sediments have been weathered to produce laterite soil profiles. This suggests a very seasonal rainfall pattern that caused a rising and falling of the watertable. Overall, the climate seems to have become drier as Australia continued to drift northwards. Open forests and dry vine scrubs replaced, in many areas, the more luxuriant rainforests of the past. The marsupials were an abundant and diverse group.

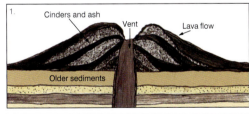

1. Cinders and ash
Vent
Lava flow
Older sediments

Volcanic eruptions occurred at Mt Glorious and Mt Mee. The resulting red soils are very fertile, and rainforests have probably clothed these areas since soon after the flow of lava. Some quarries at Mt Mee have supplied basalt for road metal.

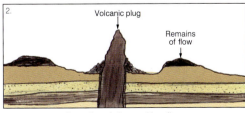

2. Volcanic plug
Remains of flow

Formation of plugs and lava flows

Erosion has been the dominant geological process in South-east Queensland since the cessation of volcanic activity around 20 million years ago. The present landscapes reflect the varying resistance to weathering and erosion of surface rocks, as well as the location and orientation of zones of weakness within them.

2 million years ago to the present - a time of sea level change:

The last 2 million years have been a time of glaciation. Ice ages have alternated with times of higher temperatures. During ice ages, sea level falls and shore lines move seawards as ice accumulates at the poles and ice sheets cover land in polar and near-polar regions. During interglacial periods, polar ice melts and sea level rises covering low coastal land.

In the last 200 thousand years Moreton Bay, which at its deepest is only 40 metres, has emptied at least five times. When the last ice age was at its peak, between 19 and 13 thousand years ago, Moreton Bay was a coastal plain through which the Brisbane River flowed, joined by its tributaries, the Pine and Caboolture Rivers, before entering the sea about 25 kilometres east of Cape Moreton (Willmot & N. Stevens, 1997, p27).

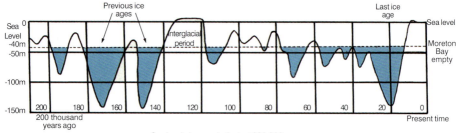

Sea level changes in the last 200,000 years
(After M. Jones, in W. Willmott and Stevens, 1997, p. 27)

Recession of the shoreline exposed the off-shore sand that is normally moved northwards by longshore currents. Exposed sand now dried out and was transported by winds to form large sand hills, initially where obstacles such as rhyolite hills occurred. Stradbroke and Moreton Islands were created in this way.

Because of the lowered base level of erosion, streams could now cut down into their beds and carry larger gravel fragments seawards. As the world began to warm up and the sea level to rise again, the coastline moved inland once more. Streams now deposited sediments of large fragments farther upstream, and on top of these, sand, silt and mud, refilling the deepened riverbeds.

Dredging of the North and South Pine River beds and nearby flats supplies enormous amounts of the sand and gravel needed for concrete manufacture for construction purposes in the Brisbane area.

After the last ice age the sea level continued to rise until the thermal maximum about 6000 year ago. Sea level was then about a metre higher than it is today and the sea inundated low-lying areas along today's coastline. Sluggish streams brought fine sediments such as clay, silt and fine sands to the sea. Tidal action transported and then deposited these sediments, building the almost flat, low-lying wetland areas that we see today along parts of the coast. Sulfide deposits in old mangrove soils can cause pollution problems when these coastal areas are disturbed.

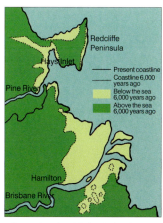

Lowered sea level during the last ice age

The sea level began to fall after 6000 years ago and continued to do so for several thousand years. It is now rising again, and in the last 80 years has risen about one millimetre each year. Predictions are that the sea will continue to rise, possibly at an increasing rate. This increased rate is thought to be caused by the addition to the atmosphere of gases, such as carbon dioxide, adding to the greenhouse effect. The burning of fossil fuels, such as coal, natural gas and petroleum, is responsible for the greatest addition. The clearing of the Earth's forests, which help convert carbon dioxide to oxygen, is also thought to be responsible for an apparent increasing greenhouse effect.

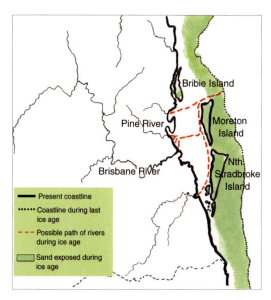

Coastal land covered by the sea 6000 years ago

Geological time scale and events in the Pine Rivers area

Era	Period	Years 10^6 mya	Local Geological History	Local Sites of Outcrops
Cainozoic	Quaternary	2	Ice ages - sea level changes; coastal deposition and erosion - acid sulfate	Pine R. Lowlands
	Tertiary		Seasonal rain - laterisation - red yellow & white soil profiles	Mt Mee, Kallangur, Narangba
			Volcanoes - plugs and lava flows	Mt Glorious, Mt Mee
		65	Sand, silt, clay, oil-shale & lime-stone; interbedded basaltic lavas	Strathpine
	Cretaceous	144	Erosion of surface rocks Mild folding of sedimentary layers	
Mesozoic	Jurassic	213	Large active streams - gravels, sands and some silts Freshwater lakes, swamps, streams - gravels, sands, silts, clays and plant debris	Dohles Rocks
	Triassic	248	Violent eruptions and granitic intrusions before stabilisation of the crust	Jollys Lookout, Samford, Dayboro & Samsonvale
	Permian	286	Material in trough compressed, uplifted, hardened and folded	Kurwongbah, D'Aguilar Range
Palaeozoic			Subduction belt clogged by sediment & material scraped from the sea floor	
	Carboniferous	360	Deposition continues in ocean trough - mud, clay, sand, silt, silica, basaltic tuffs and lavas	North of Petrie
	Devonian		Whole area under ocean - deposition of sediments and volcanic material in deep ocean trench. Coastline near Dalby	

Appendices

North Pine Country Markets - Petrie (PRSC)

Planting List for Rainforest Gardens

Form: S = Shrub; T = Tree; P = Palm; V = Vine; G = Grass; Se = Sedge; H = Herb; eH = epiphytic Herb; aH = aquatic Herb; eO = epiphytic Orchid; tO = terrestrial Orchid; eF = epiphytic Fern; tF = terrestrial Fern; Gc = Ground cover

Comments: L = colourful new leaves; Fl = Flowers; Fr = 'Fruit'; Sc = scented flowers; Sp = spiny; Bi = Birds attracted; Bf = Butterfly larvae food; Pi = Pioneer species or can be used as such.

(-) = may not occur naturally in Pine Rivers Valley but has not proved invasive.

Rainforest Plants for Small Gardens

Scientific Name	Common Name	Form	Comments
GYMNOSPERMS			
Zamaceae			
Lepidozamia peroffskyana	Shining Burrawang	S	Orange seeds
Macrozamia lucida	Pineapple Zamia	S	Orange seeds Bf
MONOCOTYLEDONS			
Agavaceae			
Cordyline petiolaris	Broad-leaf Palm Lily	S	Fl - white Fr - red
Cordyline rubra	Red-fruit Palm Lily	S	Fl - mauve Fr - red
Cordyline stricta	Slender Palm Lily	S	Fl - mauve Fr - black
Amaryllidaceae			
Crinum pedunculatum	River Lily	H	Pi Fl - white Fr - green
Doryanthes palmeri (-)	Spear Lily	H	Fl - red
Proiphys cunninghamii	Brisbane Lily	H	Fl - white Fr - green
Araceae			
Alocasia brisbanensis	Cunjevoi	H	Sc Fl - cream Fr - red
Gymnostachys anceps	Settlers Flax	H	Fl - purple Fr - red
Pothos longipes	Pothos	V	Fl - cream Fr - red Bi
Typhonium brownii	Stinking Lily	H	Sc - unpleasant Fl - white Fr - green
Arecaceae			
Archontophoenix cunninghamii	Picabeen Palm	P	Fl - purple Fr -red Bi Bf V. Tall
Linospadix monostachya	Walking Stick Palm	P	Fl - cream Fr - red Bi Bf
Commelinaceae			
Aneilema acuminatum	Aneilema	H	Gc Fl - white/mauve
Aneilema biflorum	Aneilema	H	Gc Fl - white

Scientific Name	Common Name	Form	Comments
Commelina cyanea	Scurvy Plant	H	Gc Fl - blue
Pollia crispata	Snake Weed	H	Gc Fl - white/blue
Pollia macrophylla	Large Snake Weed	H	Gc Fl - white/blue
Cyperaceae			
Cyperus tetraphyllus	A Sedge	Se	
Gahnia aspera	Saw Sedge	Se	Fr - red Bf
Dioscoraceae			
Dioscorea transversa	Native Yam	V	Sc Fl - green Fr - brown
Lillaceae			
Dianella caerulea	Blue Flax Lily	H	Pi Fl - blue Fr - blue
Dianella revoluta	Flax Lily	H	Pi Fr - blue Fr - blue
Drymophila moorei (-)	Orange Berry	H	Fl - white Fr - yellow
Tripladenia cunninghamii	Bush Lily	H	Fl - pink
Orchidaceae			
Dendrobium gracilicaule	Spotted Orchid	eO	Fl - yellow & brown
Dendrobium X gracillimum	Natural Hybrid	eO	Fl - cream/yellow
Dendrobium monophyllum	Lily-of-the-valley Orchid	eO	Fl - yellow
Dendrobium schoeninim			
(D. beckleri)	Pencil Orchid	eO	Fl - white
Dendrobium speciosum	King Orchid	eO	Sc Fl - cream/yellow
Dendrobium teretifolium	Bridal Veil Orchid	eO	Fl - white
Dendrobium tetragonum	Spider Orchid	eO	Fl - cream
Philesiaceae			
Eustrephus latifolius	Wombat Berry	V	Pi Fl - pink Fr - yellow Bi
Geitonoplesium cymosum	Scrambling Lily	V	Pi Fl - green & white Fr - black Bi
Philydraceae			
Orthothylax glaberrima (-)	Flax Lily	H	Sc Fl - cream/brown Fr - white
Philydrum lanuginosum	Frogsmouth	aH	Fl - yellow
Poaceae			
Oplismenus aemulus	Creeping Beard Grass	G	Gc
Oplismenus imbecillus	Pademelon Grass	G	Gc
Ottochloa gracillima	Ottochloa	G	Gc
Smilacaceae			
Smilax australis	Barbwire Vine	V	Pi Sp Fl - cream Fr - black Bi Bf
Smilax glycophylla	Sweet Sarsparilla	V	Fr - black Bi
Xanthorrhoeaceae			
Lomandra hystrix	Creek Mat Rush	H	Pi Sc Fl - cream Fr - brown Bf
Lomandra longifolia	Long-leaf Mat Rush	H	Pi Sc Fl - cream Fr - brown Bf

Scientific Name	Common Name	Form	Comments
Lomandra spicata	Mountain Mat Rush	H	Fl - cream Fr - orange
Zingiberaceae			
Alpinia arundelliana	Wild Ginger	H	Fl - white Fr - blue Bi
Alpinia coerulea	Native Ginger	H	Fl - white Fr - blue Bi
DICOTYLEDONS			
Acanthaceae			
Graptophyllum excelsum (-)	Scarlet Fuchsia	S	Fl - red
Graptophyllum spinigerum	Samford Holly	S	Fl - cream
Harnieria hygrophiloides	Native Justica	S	Fl - white
Pseuderanthemum tenellum	Pseuderanthemum	H	Fl - lilac Bf
Pseuderanthemum variabile	Love Flower	H	Fl - lilac Bf
Agavaceae			
Doryanthes palmeri (-)	Spear Lily	S	Pi Fl - red/pink & white
Apiaceae			
Hydrocotyle pedicellosa	Pennywort	H	Gc Fl - yellow Fr - green
Apocynaceae			
Alyxia ruscifolia	Chain fruit	S	Pi Sp Sc Fl - white Fr - orange
Carissa ovata	Current Bush	S	Pi Sp Fl - white Fr - black
Neiosperma poweri (-)	Milkbush	S	Sc Fl -white Fr - red
Ochrosia moorei (-)	Southern Ochrosia	S	Sc Fl - white Fr - red
Parsonsia lenticellata	Narrow-leaf Silkpod	V	Fl - cream
Parsonsia lilacina	Delicate Silkpod	V	Fl - cream
Parsonsia leichhardtii (-)	A Silkpod	V	Fl - white
Tabernaemontana pandacaqui	Banana Bush	S	Sc Fl - white Fr - yellow
Aristolochiaceae			
Pararistolochia laheyana	Pipe Vine	V	Fl - cream/mauve Bf
Pararistolochia praevenosa	Richmond Birdwing Vine	V	Fl - cream /mauve Bf
Asclepiadaceae			
Hoya australis	Wax Flower	V	Sc Fl - white Bf
Marsdenia longiloba	Slender Milk Vine	V	Fl - white
Secamone elliptica	Corky Milk Vine	V	
Tylophora paniculata	Thin-leaf Tylophora	V	Fl - pink
Bignoniaceae			
Pandorea florabunda	New sp. Pine R.	V	Fl - white
Pandorea jasminoides	Bower of Beauty	V	Fl - white & pink
Campanulaceae			
Lobelia trigonocaulis	Forest Lobelia	H	Gc Fl - blue

Scientific Name	Common Name	Form	Comments
Capparaceae			
Capparus arborea	Native Caper	S/T	Sp Fl - white Fr - green Bf
Capparis sarmentosa	Scrambling Caper	V/S	Bf Fl - white Fr- red Bf
Celastraceae			
Cassine australis	Red Olive Berry	S/T	Pi Fl - cream Fr - red
Denhamia celastroides	Orange Boxwood	S/T	Fl - cream Fr - orange Bi
Denhamia pittosporoides	Orange Boxwood	S/T	Fl - cream Fr - orange
Maytenus bilocularis	Orangebark	S/T	L Fl - yellow Fr - orange Bi
Convolulaceae			
Dichondra repens	Kidney Weed	H	Gc
Cunoniaceae			
Aphanopetalum resinosum	Gum Vine	V	Pi Fl - green
Vesselowskya rubifolia (-)	Southern Marara	S/T	L Fl - white
Davidsoniaceae			
Davidsonia pruriens (-)	Davidson's Plum	T	Pi L Fl - red Fr - purple, jam
Dilleniaceae			
Hibbertia scandens	Twining Guinea Flower	V	Pi Fl - yellow Fr - red
Dioscoriaceae			
Dioscoria transversa	Native Yam	V	Sc Fl - green Fr - brown
Elaeocarpaceae			
Elaeocarpus reticulatus	Blueberry Ash	S/T	Pi Fl - white/pink Fr - blue Bi
Epacridaceae			
Trochocarpa laurina	Tree Heath	S/T	L Fl - pink Fr - black Bi
Escalloniaceae			
Abrophyllum ornans	Native Hydrangea	S	Sc Fl - yellow Fr - purple
Polyosma cunninghamii	Featherwood	S/T	Sc Fl - white Fr - black
Euphorbiaceae			
Acalypha capillipes	Small-leaf Acalypha	S	Fl - red Fr - brown
Acalypha eremorum	Native Acalypha	S	Fl - cream/pink Fr - brown
Acalypha nemorum	Southern Acalypha	S	Fl - cream Fr - brown
Actephila lindleyi	Actephila	S/T	Fl - yellow Fr - brown
Alchornea ilicifolia	Native Holly	S	Pi L Fl - cream Fr - brown
Breynia oblongifolia	Native Coffee Bush	S	Pi Fl -yellow Fr - red Bf
Cleistanthes cunninghamii	Cleistanthes	S/T	Fl - green Fr - orange
Croton phlebaliodes	Narrow-leaf Croton	S	Fl - brown Fr - brown
Croton verreauxii	Native Cascarilla	S/T	L Fl - green Fr - brown

Scientific Name	Common Name	Form	Comments
Macaranga tanarius	Macaranga	S/T	Pi Fl - cream Fr - green Bi
Mallotus claoxyloides	Scrub Odour Bush	S/T	Sc Fl - green Fr - brown
Omalanthus nutans (O. populifolius)	Qld Bleeding Heart	S/T	Pi L Fl - green Fr - blue
Omalanthus stilligiifolius		S	L Bi
Eupomatiaceae			
Eupomatia bennettii	Small Bolwarra	S	Sc Fl - cream Fr - yellow
Eupomatia laurina	Bolwarra	S	Sc Fl - green Fr - green
Escaloneaceae			
Cuttsia viburnea (-)	Native Elderberry	T	Sc Fl - white
Fabaceae			
Abrus precatorius	Crabs Eye Vine	V	Pi L Fl - pink Red & black seeds (poison)
Hovea longipes (-)	Brush Hovea	S	Fl - purple Fr - brown
Sophora fraseri	Scrub Sophora	S	Fl - yellow
Geraniaceae			
Geranium homeanum	Native Geranium	H	Fl - pink
Grossalariaceae			
Argophyllum nullamense (-)	Silver Leaf	S	L Fl - cream
Lamiaceae			
Plectranthus alloplecttus (-)		H	Fl - blue/purple Rare
Plectranthus argentatus (-)	Silver Native Coleus	H	Pi L Fl - blue
Plectranthus graveolens	Native Coleus	H	Pi L - Sc Fl - blue
Plectranthus habrophyllus (-)	Silver Native Coleus	H	Fl - purple Rare
Plectranthus parviflorus	Cockspur Flower	H	Pi L - Sc Fl - blue
Lauraceae			
Cryptocarya laevigata	Glossy Laurel	S/T	Fl - cream Fr - red Bi
Cryptocarya meisneriana	Thick-leaf Laurel	S/T	Fl - white Fr - black Bi
Leeaceae			
Leea indica (-)	Bandicoot Berry	S	L Fl - white Fr - black
Lythraceae			
Lagerstroemia archeriana (-)	Native Crepe Myrtle	S/T	Pi Fl -white/pink/purple
Malvaceae			
Hibiscus heterophyllus	Native Rosella	S/T	Pi Fl - white & pink/ yellow & red
Melastomaceae			
Melastoma affine	Pink Lasiandra	S	Pi Fl - pink
Meliaceae			
Turraea pubescens (brownii)	Native Witch-Hazel	S/T	Sc - Fl - white

Scientific Name	Common Name	Form	Comments
Menispermaceae			
Pleogyne australis	Pleogyne	V	Fr - black/red
Mimosaceae			
Archidendron lovelliae (-)	Baconwood	S/T	Fl - pink Fr - orange Rare
Monimiaceae			
Wilkiea austro-queenslandica (-)	Smooth Wilkiea	S/T	Sc Fl - yellow Fr - black Bf
Wilkiea huegeliana	Tetra Beech	S/T	Sc Fl - yellow Fr - black Bf
Wilkiea macrophylla	Large-leaf Wilkiea	S/T	L Fl - green Fr - black Bf
Myrsinaceae			
Rapanea howittiana	Scrub Muttonwood	S/T	Fl - white Fr - blue
Rapanea subsessilis	Red Muttonwood	S/T	Fr - cream Fr - blue
Myrtaceae			
Archirhodomyrtus beckleri (-)	Rose Myrtle	S	Fl - pink Fr - yellow
Austromyrtus fragrantissima (-)	Sweet Myrtle	T	Sc - Fl - white Fr - red
Austromyrtus hillii	Scaly Myrtle	S/T	L Fl - white Fr - black Bi
Austromyrtus inophloia	Thread-bark Myrtle	S/T	L Fl - white Fr - black Rare
Austromyrtus aff. lasioclada (-)	Velvet Myrtle	TL	Fl - white/pink Fr - black Bi
Austromyrtus metrosideros (-)		S	L Fl - white & pink Fr - black
Backhousia myrtifolia	Carrol	T	Pi P Fl - white Nutmeg scented leaves
Pilidiostigma glabrum (-)	Plum Myrtle	S	Fl - white Fr - black Bi
Pilidiostigma rhytispermum	Small-leaf Plum Myrtle	S	L Fl - white Fr - black Bi
Rhodamnia acuminata (-)	Cooloola Ironwood	S	L Fl - white Fr - black Bi
Rhodamnia dumicola	Rib-fruit Malletwood	S/T	Fl -white Fr - black Bi
Rhodamnia maidenii (-)	Smooth Scrub Turpentine	S	L Fl - pink Fr - black Bi
Rhodomyrtus psidioides	Native Guava	S	Fl - white/pink Fr - yellow Bi
Syzygium wilsoni (-)	Powder-puff Lilly Pilly	S	L Fl - scarlet/pink Fr - white Bi
Nyctaginaceae			
Pisonia aculeata	Native Bougainvillea	V	Fl - cream
Oleaceae			
Jasminum simplicifolium	Slender Jasmine	V	Sc - Fl - white Fr - black
Jasminum suavissimum (-)	Sweet Jasmine	V	Sc Fl - white Fr - black

Scientific Name	Common Name	Form	Comments
Notelaea lloydii	Small-fruit Mock Olive	S	Fl - yellow Fr - black Bi Rare
Passifloraceae			
Passiflora aurantia	Red Passion Flower	V	Fl - cream/red Fr - green Bf
Passiflora herbertiana	Yellow Passion Flower	V	Fl - white/yellow/pink Fr -green Bf
Peperomiaceae			
Peperomia blanda (leptostachya)	Native Peperomia	H	
Peperomia tetraphylla	Native Peperomia	H	
Pittosporaceae			
Bursaria incana	Prickly Pine	S	Sc
Citriobatus linearis	Black-fruit Thornbush	S	Sp Fl - white Fr - orange Bi
Citriobatus paucifloris	Orange Thornbush	S	Pi Sp Fl - white Fr - yellow Bi
Clematis fawcettii (-)	Mountain Clematis	V	Fl - white Rare
Pittosporum oreillyanum (-)	Thorny Pittosporum	S	Fl - white Fr - yellow Bi
Pittosporum revolutum	Brisbane Laurel	S	Pi Fl - yellow Fr - yellow
Rosaceae			
Rubus rosifolius	Native Raspberry	S	Pi Sp Fl - white Fr - red Bi
Rubiaceae			
Canthium coprosmoides	Coast Canthium	S/T	Pi Sc - Fl - white Fr - black
Canthium lamprophyllum	Large-leaf Canthium	S/T	Sc - Fl - white Fr - black
Canthium microphyllum	Small-leaf Canthium	S	Sc - musty Fl - cream Fr - black
Diplospora cameronii (-)	Diplospora	S	Fl - greenish Fr - black Rare
Ixora bleckleri	Brown Coffeewood	S/T	Fl - white Fr - black
Morinda acutifolia	Veiny Morinda	V	Fl - cream
Morinda jasminoides	Sweet Morinda	V	Sc Fl - yellow Fr - red Bf
Pavetta australiensis	Pavetta	S	Fl - white - Bf Fr - black
Psychotria daphnoides	Smooth Psychotria	S	Fl - white Fr - greenish
Psychotria loniceroides	Hairy Psychotria	S	L Fl - cream/white Fr - yellow Bi
Psychotria simmondsiana	Small Psychotria	S	Fl - white Fr - yellow
Randia benthamiana	Native Gardenia	S	Sc Fl - white
Randia chartacea	Narrow-leaf Gardenia	S	Sc Fl - white Fr - orange
Rutaceae			
Clausena brevistyla (-)	Clausena	S	Sc Fl - white
Microcitrus australasica (-)	Finger Lime	S	Sp Fl - white Fr - green Bi Bf
Micromelum minutum (-)	Grey Bollygum	S/T	Sc Fr - orange/red
Murraya ovatifoliolata (-)	Native Murraya	S/T	Sc Fl - white Fr - red

Scientific Name	Common Name	Form	Comments
Sambucaceae			
Sambucus australasica	Yellow Elderberry	S	Fl - white Fr - orange Bi
Sapindaceae			
Alectryon coriaceus (-)	Beach Bird's Eye	S/T	Pi L Fl - cream Fr - red/ black Bi Bf
Arytera microphylla (-)	Dwarf Coogara	S	Fl - green Fr - yellow
Cupaniopsis newmanii (-)	Long-leaf Tuckeroo	T	Pi L Fl - pink Fr - pink & yellow Rare
Cupaniopsis serrata	Rusty Tuckeroo	S/T	L Fl - white Fr - brown
Cupaniopsis wadsworthii (-)	Dwarf Tuckeroo	S	Fl - cream Fr - orange
Harpullia alata (-)	Wing-leaf Tulip	S	Fl - white Fr - yellow
Mischocarpus sundaicus	Red Pear-fruit	T	L Fl - cream Fr - orange/purple
Sapotaceae			
Planchonella myrsinoides	Yellow Plumwood	S/T	Fl - green Fr - black
Solanaceae			
Duboisia myoporoides	Corkwood	S/T	Fl - white Fr - black Sap poison
Solanum aviculare	Kangaroo Apple	S	Pi Fl - mauve Fr - orange
Solanum densevestitum (-)	Furry Nightshade	S	Fl - mauve Fr - red
Solanum stelligerum (-)	Star Nightshade	S	Sp Fl - mauve Fr - red
Sterculiaceae			
Brachychiton bidwillii	Little Kurrajong	S	Pi Fl - red Fr - fawn Bf Rare
Commersonia fraserii	Scrub Kurrajong	S	Pi Fl - white Fr - brown Suckers
Symplocaceae			
Symplocus baeuerlenii (-)	Shrubby Hazelwood	S	Fl - cream Fr - red Rare
Thymeliaceae			
Phaleria clerodendron (-)		S	Sc Fl - white Fr - red Bi Poisonous?
Phaleria chermsideana	Scrub Daphne	S/T	Sc Fl - pink/white Fr - red Bi
Pimelia latifolia (-)	Rice Flower	S	Fl - white Fr - green
Wikstroemia indica	Tie Bush	S	Pi Fl - green Fr - red
Tiliaceae			
Corchorus cunninghamii	Corchorus	S	Fl - yellow Fr - black V. Rare
Grewia latifolia	Dysentary Plant	S	Fr - brown
Ulmaceae			
Trema tomentosa (T. aspera)	Peachleaf	S/T	Pi Fl - green Fr - black Bi Bf

Scientific Name	Common Name	Form	Comments
Urticaceae			
Elatostema reticulatum	Rainforest Spinach	H	Gc Fl - green
Elatostema stipitatum (-)	Small Soft Nettle	H	Gc Fl - green
Pipturus argenteus	Native Mulberry	S/T	Fl - white Fr - white Bf
Verbenaceae			
Callicarpa pedunculata	Velvet-leaf	S	Fl - pink/mauve Fr - purple
Clerodendrum floribundum	Lolly Bush	S/T	Fl - white Fr - black & red
Clerodendrum tomentosum	Hairy Lolly Bush	S/T	Sc Fl - white Fr - black & red
Violaceae			
Viola betonicifolia	Purple Violet	H	Gc Fl - purple & white
Viola hederacea	Native Violet	H	Fl - blue & white
Vitaceae			
Cayratia acris	Hairy Water Vine	V	Fl - green Fr - black
Cayratia clematidea	Slender Grape	V	Pi Fl - white Fr -black
Cissus opaca	Small-leaf Water Vine	V	Pi Fl - green Fr - black
Winteraceae			
Tasmannia insipida	Pepper Bush	S	L Fl - white Fr - purple

PTERIDOPHYTES

Scientific Name	Common Name	Form	Comments
Adiantaceae			
Adiantum aethiopicum	Common Maidenhair	tF	Gc
Adiantum diaphanum	Filmy Maidenhair	tf	Gc
Adiantum formosum	Giant Maidenhair	tF	
Adiantum hispidulum	Rough Maidenhair	tF	Pi Gc
Adiantum silvaticum	Maidenhair	tF	Gc
Aspleniaceae			
Asplenium attenuatum	A Spleenwort	tF	
Asplenium australasicum	Crow's Nest Fern	eF	
Asplenium bulbiferum	Mother Spleenwort	tF	
Asplenium polyodon	Marc's Tail Fern	eF	
Athyriaceae			
Diplazium assimile	Lady Fern	tF	Gc
Blechnaceae			
Blechnum cartilagineum	Gristle Fern	tF	Pi Gc L
Blechnum indicum	Swamp Fern	tF	Pi Gc
Doodia aspera	Prickly Rasp Fern	tF	
Doodia caudata	Small Rasp Fern	tF	
Doodia media	Common Rasp Fern	tF	Gc L
Cyatheaceae			
Cyathea australis	Rough Tree Fern	tF	Eventually tall

Scientific Name	Common Name	Form	Comments
Cyathea cooperi	CommonTree Fern	tF	Eventually tall
Cyathea leichhardtiana	Prickly Tree Fern	tF	Eventually tall
Davalliaceae			
Davallia pyxidata	Hare's Foot Fern	eF	
Dicksoniaceae			
Calochlena dubia			
(Culcita dubia)	False Bracken	tF	Pi Gc
Dicksonia youngiae	Bristly Tree Fern	tF	
Nephrolepidaceae			
Arthropteris tenella	Climbing Shield Fern	tF	
Osmondaceae			
Todea barbara	King Fern	tF	
Polypodiaceae			
Drynaria rigidula	Basket Fern	eF	Pi
Phymatodes scandens	Scented Climbing Fern	tF	
Platycerium bifurcatum	Elkhorn	eF	
Platycerium superbum	Staghorn	eF	
Pyrrosia confluens	Felt Fern	eF	
Pyrrosia rupestris	Rock Felt Fern	eF	
Pteridaceae			
Pteris tremula	Tender Brake	tF	
Pteris umbrosa	Jungle Brake	tF	
Schizaeaceae			
Lygodium microphyllum	Climbing Maidenhair	tF	
Pellaea falcata	Sickle Fern	tF	
Pellaea paradoxa	Diverse Fishbone Fern	tF	
Thelypteridaceae			
Cristella dentata	Binung	tF	

Rainforest Plants for Medium Gardens

The following plants can be used in addition to the list of plants for small gardens.

Scientific Name	Common Name	Form	Comments
GYMNOSPERMS			
Arecaceae			
Calamus muelleri	Lawyer Cane Vine	P	Sp Fr - flesh pink Bf
Livistona australis	Cabbage Palm	P	Pi Sp Fl - cream Fr - black Bf Tall
Cupressaceae			
Callitris baileyi (-)	Bailey's Cypress	T	Pi Cone - brown Rare

Scientific Name	Common Name	Form	Comments
MONOCOTYLEDONS			
Smilacaceae			
Ripogonum fawcettianum	Small Supplejack	V	Sp Fl - green Fr - black
Smilax australis	Barb-wire Vine	V	Pi Sp L Sc Fl - cream Fr - black Bf
DICOTYLENDONS			
Akaniaceae			
Akania lucens	Turnipwood	T	L Sc Fl - pink Fr - red
Alangiaceae			
Alangium villosum polyosmoides	Muskwood	T	Fl - yellow Fr - black
Alangium villosum tomentosum	Muskwood	T	Fl - yellow Fr - black
Annonaceae			
Polyalthia nitidissima	Canary Beech	T	Fl - green Fr - yellow/red Bi Bf
Apocynaceae			
Alstonia constricta	Quinine Tree	T	Fl - white Fr - brown Bi
Melodinus acutiflorus	Merangarra	V	
Melodinus australis	Southern Melodinis	V	Sc Fl - cream Fr - orange
Araliaceae			
Cephalaralia cephalobotrys	Climbing Panax	V	Fl - purple & white Fr - black
Bignoniaceae			
Pandorea pandorana	Wonga Vine	V	Pi Fl - white/pink/yellow/mauve
Caesalpiniaceae			
Barklya syringifolia	Crown of Gold	T	Pi Fl - yellow Slow at first
Cassia tomentella (-)	Velvet Bean	S/T	Pi Fl - yellow Fr - brown Bf Rare
Corynocarpaceae			
Corynocarpus rupestris arborescens	Southern Corynocarpus	S/T	Fl -white Fr - red Rare
Cunoniaceae			
Callicoma serratifolia (-)	White Alder	S/T	Pi L Fl - cream
Dilleniaceae			
Tecomanthe hillii (-)	Fraser Island Climber	V	Fl - pink Uncommon
Ebenaceae			
Diospyros australis	Black Plum	T	Fl - cream Fr - black Bi
Diospyros geminata	Scaly Ebony	T	Fl - cream Fr - orange Bi
Diospyros mabacea (-)	Red-fruited Ebony	T	Fl - greenish Fr - red Very Rare

Scientific Name	Common Name	Form	Comments
Escalloniaceae			
Anopterus macleayanus (-)	Queensland Laurel	T	L Sc Fl - white Fr - brown
Polyosma cunninghamii	Featherwood	T	Sc Fl - white Fr - black
Euphorbiaceae			
Claoxylon australe	Brittlewood	S/T	Fl - cream Fr - yellowish Bi
Cleistanthus cunninghamii	Cleistanthus	S/T	Fl - green Fr - orange/ red
Croton achronychioides	Thick-leaved Croton	S/T	Sc Fl - green Fr - brown
Croton insularis	Queensland Cascarilla	S/T	L Fl - green Fr - silver
Croton stigmatosus	White Croton	T	L Fl - brown Fr - brown
Petalostigma pubescent	Quinine Bush	S/T	Fl - cream Fr - yellow
Flacourtaceae			
Casearia multinervosa	Casearia	L	Fl - white Fr - orange/ yellow
Choricarpia leptopetala	Brown Myrtle	S/T	Sc Fl - cream Fr - brown
Decaspermum humile	Silky Myrtle	S/T L	Sc Fl - white Fr - black
Hernandiaceae			
Hernandia bivalvis	Cudgerie	T	Pi Fl - white Fr - black & orange Rare
Lauraceae			
Cryptocarya bidwilli	Yellow Laurel	T	Fl - green Fr - black Bi
Cryptocarya meisneriana	Thick-leaf Laurel	T	Fl - white Fr - black Bi
Cryptocarya sclerophylla	Boonah Laurel	T	Fl - cream Fr - black Bi
Cryptocarya triplinervis	Brown Laurel	T	Fl - green Fr - black Bi Bf
Cryptocarya triplinervis var. pubens	Hairy Brown Laurel	T	Fl - green Fr - black Bi Bf
Meliaceae			
Owenia venosa	Rose Almond	T	Fl - white Fr - red
Synoum glandulosum	Scentless Rosewood	S/T	Sc Fl - white/pink Fr - red
Turraea pubescens (*T. brownii*)	Native Witch-Hazel	T	Sc Fl - white Fr - brown
Menispermaceae			
Stephania japonica var. discolor	Tape Vine	V	Pi Gc Fl - green Fr - red
Mimosaceae			
Acacia cincinnata	Wattle	S/T	Pi L Fl - yellow Fr - bluegrey Bf
Pararchidendron pruinosum	Snowwood	T	Pi Sc Fl - white/yellow Fr - orange Bf

Scientific Name	Common Name	Form	Comments
Moraceae			
Ficus coronata	Creek Sandpaper Fig	T	Pi Fr - purple Bi Bf
Ficus fraseri	A Sandpaper Fig	T	Pi Fr - orange Bi Bf
Ficus opposita	A Sandpaper Fig	T	Pi Fr - yellow Bi Bf
Streblus brunonianus			
(S. pendulinus)	Whalebone Tree	T	Pi Fr - yellow Bi
Myrsinaceae			
Rapanea variabilis	Muttonwood	T	L Fl - white Fr - mauve Bf
Myrtaceae			
Acmena smithii (Small)	Creek Lilly Pilly	T	Pi Fl - white Fr - pink/ mauve
Austromyrtus acmenioides	Scrub Ironwood	T	Fl - white Fr - black Bi
Backhousia citriodora	Lemon Ironwood	T	Pi Fl - cream Fr - brown
Choricarpia leptopetala	Brown Myrtle	S/T	Sc Fl - cream Fr - brown
Decaspermum humile	Silky Myrtle	S/T	L Sc Fl - white Fr - black Bi
Metrosideros queens-landica (-)	Golden Myrtle	T	L Fl - yellow Bi
Syzygium hodgkinsonia (-)	Smooth-bark Rose Apple	T	Sc Fl - cream Fr - red
Oleaceae			
Jasminum didymum	Coastal Jasmine	V	Sc Fl - white Fr - black
Notelaea johnsonii	Veinless Mock Olive	S/T	Fl - brown Fr - black Bi
Notelaea longifolia	Large Mock Olive	S/T	Pi Fl - yellow Fr - black Bi
Notelaea microcarpa	Velvet Mock Olive	S/T	Fl - cream Fr - black Bi
Notelaea ovata	Netted Mock Olive	S	Fl - cream Fr - black Bi
Notelaea venosa	Veined Mock Olive	S	Fl - green Fr - black Bi
Pittosporaceae			
Hymenosporum flavum	Native Frangipani	T	Pi Sc Fl - yellow Fr - brown
Pittosporum undulatum	Mock Orange	T	Pi Sc Fl - white Fr - orange
Proteaceae			
Buckinghamia celsissima (-)	Ivory Curl Flower	T	Pi Fl - cream
Grevillea helmsiae (-)		T	Pi Sc Fl - cream Fr - brown
Hicksbeachia pinnatifolia (-)	Red Boppel Nut	T	L Fl - brown Fr - red
Lomatia arborescens (-)	Tree Lomatia	S/T	Sc Fl - cream
Triunia youngiana	Spice Bush	T	Sc Fl - pink/cream Fr - red - Poison
Rubiaceae			
Coelospermum paniculatum	Coelospermum	V	Fr - green/black
Hodgkinsonia ovatiflora	Golden Ash	T	Fl - yellow Fr - black Bi
Rununculaceae			
Clematis glycinoides	Headache Vine	V	Fl - white

Scientific Name	Common Name	Form	Comments
Rutaceae			
Acronychia imperforata	Coast Aspen	S/T	Fl - cream Fr - yellow - Jam
Acronychia laevis	Hard Aspen	S/T	Fl - white Fr - purple
Acronychia pauciflora	Soft Acronychia	S/T	Fl - white Fr - red/black
Acronychia pubescens	Hairy Acronychia	S/T	Fl - green Fr - yellow
Acronychia wilcoxiana	Silver Aspen	S/T	Fl - white Fr - white
Bosistoa pentacocca	Native Almond	T	Fl - white Fr - yellow/brown
Medicosma cunninghamii	Pink Heart	S/T	Sc Fl - white Fr - brown Rare
Microcitrus australis	Round Lime	S	Sp Fl - white Fr - green Bf
Microcitrus australasica (-)	Finger Lime	S	Sp Fl - white Fr - yellow/red Bf
Sapindaceae			
Alectryon connatus	Alectryon	T	Pi Fl - yellow Fr - black & red Bi
Alectryon subcinereus	Wild Quince	T	Fl -pink Fr - black & red Bi Bf
Alectryon subdentatus	Holly-leaf Bird's Eye	T	Fl - pink/red Fr - black & red Bi
Alectryon tomentosus	Hairy Bird's Eye	T	Pi L Fl - cream Fr - black & red Bi
Arytera distylis	Twin-leaf Coogera	T	L Fl - cream Fr - orange & black Bi
Arytera divaricata	Rose Tamarind	T	L Fl - cream Fr - orange & red Bi
Arytera foveolata	Pitted Coogera	T	Fl - cream Fr - yellow & red
Cupaniopsis parvifolia	Small-leaf Tuckeroo	T	Pi Fl - cream Fr - orange Bi Bf
Cupaniopsis shirleyana (-)	Wedge-leaf Tuckeroo	T	Fl - cream Fr - orange & brown Rare
Cupaniopsis tomentella (-)	Boonah Tuckeroo	T	Pi L Fl -white Fr - orange & black Rare
Elattostachys nervosa	Beetroot	T	L Fl - yellow/pink Fr - orange Bi
Elattostachys xylocarpa	White Tamarind	T	L Fl - cream/red Fr - yellow & black Bi
Lepiderema pulchella (-)	Fine-leaf Tuckeroo	T	Pi L Fl - orange Fr - brown Uncommon
Mischocarpus australis	Red Pear-fruit	T	Fl - green Fr - red/orange
Toechima tenax	Scrub Teak	T	Pi L Fl - cream Fr - yellow & black
Sapotaceae			
Planchonella (Pouteria) chartacea	Thin-leaf Plum	S/T	Fl - white Fr - black
Planchonella cotinifolia (Pouteria)	Small-leaf Plum	S/T	Fl - yellow Fr - black

Scientific Name	Common Name	Form	Comments
Simaroubaceae			
Guilfoylia monostylis	Native Plum	T	Fl - yellow Fr - black
Symplocaceae			
Symplocus thwaitesii	Buff Hazelwood	S/T	Fl - white Fr - black
PTERIDOPHYTES			
Cyatheaceae			
Cyathea australis	Rough Tree Fern	tF	
Cyathea cooperi	Common Tree Fern	tF	
Cyathea leichhardtiana	Prickly Tree Fern	tF	

Rainforest Plants for Large Gardens, Acreage Blocks, Parks and Farms

The following plants can be used in addition to the lists of plants for small and medium gardens.

Scientific Name	Common Name	Form	Comments
GYMNOSPERMS			
Araucariaceae			
Agathis robusta (-)	Qld Kauri	T	Pi L Cones - brown
Araucaria bidwillii (-)	Bunya Pine	T	Pi Sp Large, heavy green cones
Araucaria cunninghamii	Hoop Pine	T Pi	Sp Small green cones
Cupressaceae			
Callitris macleayana	Scrub Cypress	T	Pi Cone - grey/brown
Callitris columellaris var. columellaris	Bribie Island Pine	T	Pi Cone - brown
Podocarpaceae			
Podocarpus elatus	Brown or Plum Pine	T	Pi L 'Fr' - blue/black Bi Bf
MONOCOTYLEDONS			
Flagellariaceae			
Flagellaria indica	Supplejack	V	Fl - white Fr - white Bf
Pandanaceae			
Freycinettia excelsa	Climbing Pandanus	V	Fl - pink & white Fr - red
Freycinettia scandens	Climbing Pandanus	V	Fl - red/white Fr -red
Smilacaceae			
Ripogonum album	White Supplejack	V	Sp Sc Fl - pink Fr - black
Ripogonum brevifolium	Supplejack	V	Sp Fr - black
Ripogonum discolor	Prickly Supplejack	V	Sp Fl - white Fr - black
Ripogonum elseyanum	Hairy Supplejack	V	Sp Sc Fl - pink Fr - red

Scientific Name	Common Name	Form	Comments
DICOTYLEDONS			
Anacardiaceae			
Euroschinus falcata	Ribbonwood	T	Pi Fl
Rhodosphaera rhodanthema	Deep Yellowwood	T	Pi L Fl - red Fr - brown Bi
Annonaceae			
Melodorum leichhardtii (*Rauwenhoffia l.*)	Zig-Zag Vine	V	Pi Fl - yellow Fr - yellow
Apocynaceae			
Alstonia constricta	Quinine Tree	T	Fl - white Fr -brown
Melodinus acutiflorus	Merangarra	V	Fl - cream
Melodinus australis	Southern Melodinis	V	Sc Fl - yellow Fr - orange
Parsonsia eucalyptophylla	Gargaloo	V	Pi Sc Fl - cream Bf
Parsonsia fulva	Furry Silkpod	V	Fl - white Fr - brown Bf
Parsonsia lanceolata	Northern Silkpod	V	Sc Fl - white Bf
Parsonsia latifolia	Monkey Vine	V	Fl - white & yellow Bf
Parsonsia straminea	Monkey Rope	V	Pi L Sc Fl - cream Fr - green Bf
Parsonsia velutina	Velvet Silkpod	V	Pi Fl - cream Fr - russet Bf
Parsonsia ventricosa	Pointed Silkpod	V	Fl - white Bf
Araliaceae			
Polyscias elegans	Celerywood	T	Pi Fl - purple Fr - black Bi
Polyscias murrayi	Pencil Cedar	T	Pi Fl - cream Fr - blue Bi
Asclepiadaceae			
Marsdenia rostrata	Common Milk Vine	V	Sc Fl - cream
Atherospermataceae			
Daphnandra micrantha	Socketwood	T	Fl - white Fr -brown
Burseraceae			
Canarium australasicum	Carrotwood	T	Fl - red Fr - blue
Caesalpiniaceae			
Cassia marksiana (-)	Native Laburnum	T	Pi Fl - yellow Fr - brown Bf Rare
Caesalpinia bonduc	Caesalpinia	V	Sp L Fl - yellow Bi Bf
Caesalpinia scortechinii	Large Prickle Vine	V	Sp Fl - yellow Fr - green/brown
Caesalpinia subtropica	Corky Prickle Vine	V	Sp Fl - yellow Uncommon
Celastraceae			
Celastrus australis	Staff Climber	V	Sc Fl - cream Fr - orange
Celastrus subspicatus	Large Staff Vine	V	Fl - cream Fr - pink

Scientific Name	Common Name	Form	Comments
Loeseneriella barbata (Hippocratia b.)	Knot Vine	V	Fl - yellow Fr - green
Cunoniaceae			
Caldcluvia paniculosa	Rose-leaf Marara	T	L Fl - white Fr - red
Ceratopetalum apetalum (-)	Coachwood	T	Fl - green Fr - red
Geissois benthamii	Red Carabeen	T	L Fl - cream
Pseudoweinmannia lachnocarpa	Marara	T	Fl - silver Fr - russet
Schizomeria ovata	White Birch	T	L Fl - white Fr - white
Ebenaceae			
Diospyros fasciculosa	Grey Ebony	T	Fl - green Fr - yellow/ black Bi
Diospyros pentamera	Myrtle Ebony	T	Fl - white Fr - yellow/ red Bi
Ehretiaceae			
Cordia dichotoma (-)	Cordia	T	Sc Fl - cream Fr - yellow/pink
Ehretia acuminata	Koda	T	Pi Sc Fl - white Fr - orange Bi
Elaeocarpaceae			
Elaeocarpus eumundi	Eumundi Quandong	T	Sc Fl - cream Fr - blue
Elaeocarpus grandis	Blue Quandong	T	Pi L Fl - white Fr - blue
Elaeocarpus kirtonii	White Quandong	T	Sc Fl - white Fr - blue
Elaeocarpus obovatus	Hard Quandong	T	Pi Fl - white Fr - blue Bi
Sloanea australis	Maiden's Blush	T	L Fl - white Fr -brown
Sloanea woollsii	Yellow Carabeen	T	Fl - white Fr - yellow/ brown
Escalloniaceae			
Quintinia verdonii	Grey Possumwood	T	Fl - cream
Euphorbiaceae			
Austrobuxus swainii (-)	Pink Cherry	T	Fl - green Fr - brown
Baloghia inophylla (B. lucida)	Scrub Bloodwood	T	Sc Fl - white/pink Fr - brown
Bridelia exaltata	Scrub Ironbark	T	Pi Fl - green Fr - red/ black Bi
Bridelia leichhardtii	Leichhardt's Ironbark	T	Pi Fl - green Fr - red Bi
Dissiliaria baloghioides	Lancewood	T	L Fl - cream/brown Fr - brown
Drypetes australasica	Yellow Tulip	T	L Fl - yellow Fr - red/ orange
Petalostigma triloculare	Quinine Berry	T	Sc Fl-cream Fr-orange
Exocoecaria dallachyana	Scrub Poison Tree	T	Fl - yellow Fr - brown
Fontainea venosa	Fontainea	T	L Fl - white Fr -orange Rare
Glochidion ferdinandi	Cheese Tree	T	Pi Fl - green Fr - green/ red Bi
Glochidion sumatranum	Buttonwood	T	Pi Fl - green Fr - pink

Scientific Name	Common Name	Form	Comments
Mallotus discolor	Yellow Kamala	T	Pi L Fl - grey Fr - yellow Bi
Mallotus philippensis	Red Kamala	T	Pi Fl - brown Fr - red
Fabaceae (Leguminosae)			
Austrosteenisia blackii	Blood Vine	V	Pi Fl - red Fr - brown Bf
Castanospermum australe	Black Bean	T	Pi Fl - red & yellow Fr - brown Bf
Derris involuta	Native Derris	V	Fl - white/pink/mauve Fr - brown
Erythrina sp. Lacey's Creek	Corkwood	T	Pi Sp Fl - pink/red/ orange Fr - brown
Erythrina vespertilio	Batswing Coral Tree	T	Pi Sp Fl - pink/red/ orange Fr - brown
Milletia (Callerya) megasperma	Native Wisteria	V	Fl - purple Bf
Mucuna gigantea	Burny Bean	V	Fl - green Fr - black Bi
Flacourtiaceae			
Scolopia braunii	Flintwood	T	Pi L Sc Fl - cream Fr - red/black
Flindersiaceae			
Flindersia australis	Crows Ash	T	Pi Fl - white Fr -brown Bf
Flindersia bennettiana	Bennett's Ash	T	Pi Sc - unpleasant Fl - cream Fr - brown
Flindersia collina	Leopard Ash	T	Pi Fl - white Fr brown Bf
Flindersia schottiana	Cudgerie or Bumpy Ash	T	Pi Fl - white Fr -brown Bf
Flindersia xanthoxyla	Yellowwood	T	Pi Fl - yellow Fr - brown Bf
Icacinaceae			
Citronella moorei	Churnwood	T	Fl - cream Fr - black Bi
Pennantia cunninghamii	Brown Beech	T	L Fl - white Fr - black Bi
Lauraceae			
Beilschmiedia elliptica	Grey Walnut	T	Pi Fl - cream Fr - black
Beilschmiedia obtusifolia	Blush Walnut	T	Sc - offensive Fl - cream Fr - black Bi
Cinnamomum oliveri	Camphorwood	T	L Fl - cream Bi Bf
Cryptocarya erythroxylon	Pigeonberry Ash	T	Fl - green Fr - red Bi
Cryptocarya foetida (-)	Stinking Cryptocarya	S/T	Sc - foul Fl - cream Fr - black Rare
Cryptocarya glaucescens	Silver Sycamore	T	Pi Fl - white Fr - black Bi
Cryptocarya hypospodia	Rib-fruit Pepperberry	T	Fl - white Fr - black Bf
Cryptocarya macdonaldii	Cooloola Laurel	T	Sc - unpleasant Fl - yellow Fr - black

Scientific Name	Common Name	Form	Comments
Cryptocarya microneura	Murrogun	T	L Fl -white Fr - black
Cryptocarya obovata	Pepperberry Tree	T	Pi L Fl - cream Fr - black Bi
Endiandra discolor	Rose Walnut	T	L Fl - green Fr - black
Endiandra globosa (-)	Black Walnut	T	L Fl - white Fr - black
Endiandra muelleri	Mueller's Walnut	T	Fl - green Fr - black
Endiandra pubens	Hairy Walnut	T	L Fl - white Fr - red
Endiandra sieberi (-)	Hard Corkwood	T	Fl - white Fr - black Bi Bf
Litsea leefeana	Brown Bolly Gum	T	L Fl - green Fr - black Bi
Litsea reticulata	Bolly Gum	T	Fl - green Fr - black Bi
Neolitsea australiensis	Grey Bolly Gum	T	L Sc Fl - yellow Fr - black Bi
Neolitsea dealbata	White Bolly Gum	T	L Fl - yellow Fr - black Bi Bf
Malvaceae			
Hibiscus tiliaceus	Cotton Tree	T	Pi Fl - yellow & red Fr - brown
Lagunaria patersonii (-)	Norfolk Is Hibiscus	T	Pi Fl - pink
Meliaceae			
Anthocarapa nitidula (*Pseudocarapa nitidula*)	Incense Cedar	T	Fl - cream Fr - brown Bf
Dysoxylum fraseranum	Rosewood	T	Fl - cream Fr - red
Dysoxylum mollissimum ssp. molle (*D. muelleri*)	Red Bean	T	Fl - cream Fr - brown & red
Dysoxylum rufum	Hairy Rosewood	T	Fl - white Fr - yellow/ brown
Melia azedarach	White Cedar	T	Pi Sc Fl - purple/mauve Fr - brown
Owenia cepiodora (-)	Onion Cedar	T	L Fl - white Fr - red
Toona ciliata (T. australis)	Red Cedar	T	Pi Sc Fl - white Fr - brown
Menispermaceae			
Legnephora moorei	Wild Grape	V	Pi Fl - white Fr - black
Sarcopetalum harveyanum	Pearl Vine	V	
Stephania aculeata	Prickly Snake Vine	V	
Tinospora smilacina	Snake Vine	V	Fl - green Fr - yellow/ red
Tinospora tinosporoides	Arrow-head Vine	V	Uncommon
Mimosaceae			
Acacia aulacocarpa var. aulacocarpa	Hickory Wattle	T	Pi Sc Fl - yellow Fr - brown Bi Bf
Acacia bakeri	Marblewood	T	Pi L Fl - cream Fr - brown Bf Rare
Acacia melanoxylon	Blackwood	T	Pi Sc Fl - cream Fr - brown Bf

Scientific Name	Common Name	Form	Comments
Archidendron grandiflorum	Lace Flower	T	Sc Fl - white & pink Fr - brown Bf
Archidendron hendersonii (-)	White Lace Flower	T	Sc Fl - cream Fr - orange/red
Archidendron muellerianam (-)		T	Fl - green Fr - red & black
Monimiaceae			
Palmeria scandens	Anchor Vine	V	Fl - white Fr - pink & black Bi
Moraceae			
Ficus macrophylla	Moreton Bay Fig	T	Pi L Fr - orange/purple Bi Bf
Ficus obliqua	Small-leafed Fig	T	Pi Fr - yellow/orange Bi Bf
Ficus platypoda	Rock Fig	T	Pi Fr - yellow/red Bi Bf
Ficus superba var. henneana	Deciduous Fig	T	Pi Fr - purple & cream/ pink Bi Bf
Ficus virens var. sublanceolata	White Fig	T	Pi Fr - white & pink Bi Bf
Ficus watkinsiana	Nipple Fig	T	Pi Fr - purple & yellow Bi Bf
Maclura cochinchinensis (*Cudrania c.*)	Cockspur Thorn	V	Pi Sp Fr - yellow Bi
Malaisia scandens	Burny Vine	V	Fl - cream Fr- red & cream Bi Bf
Myrtaceae			
Acmena hemilampra	Blush Satinash	T	L Fl - cream Fr -white
Acmena ingens (*A. brachyandra*)	Red Apple	T	L Fl - white Fr -pink/red Bi
Acmena smithii	Creek Lilly Pilly	T	Pi Fl - white Fr - white/ pink/mauve
Austromyrtus bidwillii	Python Tree	T	Sc Fl - white Fr - black Bi
Austromyrtus gonoclada		T	Sc Fl - white Fr - black Bi Rare
Backhousia anisata (-)	Aniseed Tree	T	Pi Fl - white Aniseed leaves
Backhousia sciadophora (-)	Shatterwood	T	Fl - white
Choricarpia subargentea	Giant Ironwood	T	L Fl - white Uncommon
Rhodamnia argentea	Malletwood	T	Pi L Fl - white Fr - black
Rhodamnia rubescens	Brown Malletwood	T	Sc Fl - white Fr - black Bi
Syncarpia glomulifera	Turpentine	T	Pi Fl - white Fr - brown
Syncarpia hillii (-)	Satinay	T	Pi Fl - white Fr - brown Uncommon
Syzygium australe	Scrub Cherry	T	Pi L Fl - white Fr - pink/red Bi
Syzygium corynanthum	Sour cherry	T	Fl - white Fr - red Bi

Scientific Name	Common Name	Form	Comments
Syzygium crebrinerve	Purple Cherry	T	L Fl - white Fr - purple/violet Bi
Syzygium francisii	Giant Water Gum	T	Pi L Fl - white Fr - mauve/purple Bi
Syzygium leuhmannii (-)	Small-leaf Water Gum	T	Pi L Fl - white Fr -red Bi
Syzygium moorei (-)	Durobby	T	Fl - pink Fr - white Bi
Syzygium oleosum	Blue Lilly Pilly	T	Pi L Fl -white Fr - blue
Tristaniopsis collina	Hill Kanuka	T	Pi Fl - yellow
Tristaniopsis laurina	Water Gum	T	Pi Fl - yellow
Waterhousia floribunda	Weeping Myrtle	T	Pi L Fl - cream Fr - green/pink
Xanthostemon oppositifolius(-)	Southern Penda	T	Fl -white Rare

Nyctaginaceae

Pisonia aculeata	Native Bougainvillea	V	Sc Fl - cream/brown

Oleaceae

Olea paniculata	Native Olive	T	Pi Fl - white Fr - black Bi

Piperaceae

Piper novae-hollandiae	Native Pepper Vine	V	L Sc Fl - cream Fr -red

Pittosporaceae

Pittosporum rhombifolium	Hollywood	T	Pi Fl - white Fr - orange

Proteaceae

Alloxylon flammeum (-) (*Oreocallis wickhamii*)	Satin Oak	T	Pi Fl - red Fr - brown Bi
Alloxylon pinnatum (-)	Pink Silky Oak	T	Fl - pink Fr - brown Bi
Floydia praealta	Ball Nut	T	Fl - cream Fr - brown Uncommon
Grevillea hilliana (-)	Hill's Silky Oak	T	Pi Fl - white
Grevillea robusta	Silky Oak	T	Pi Fl - orange Bi
Helicia glabriflora	Smooth Helicia	T	Fl - yellow Fr -purple
Macadamia integrifolia	Queensland Nut	T	Pi Sc Fl - white Fr - brown
Macadamia ternifolia	Maroochy Nut	T	L Fl - pink Uncommon
Macadamia tetraphylla (-)	Rough-shell Bush Nut	T	Pi L Sc Fl - pink/purple Fr - brown
Stenocarpus salignus (-)	Scrub Beefwood	T	Pi Sc Fl - white Fr - brown Bi
Stenocarpus sinuatus	Wheel of Fire Tree	T	Pi L Fl - red Fr - brown Bi

Ranunculaceae

Clematis aristata	Old Man's Beard	V	Fl - white

Rhamnaceae

Alphitonia excelsa	Red Ash	T	Pi Sc Fl - white Fr - black Bi Bf

Scientific Name	Common Name	Form	Comments
Alphitonia petrei (-)	Pink Ash	T	Pi L Sc Fl - white Fr - black Bi Bf
Emmenosperma alphito-nioides	Yellow Ash	T	Fl - white Fr - yellow & red Bi
Rosaceae			
Rubus moluccanus	Molucca Bramble	V	Sp Fl - white Fr - red Bi
Rubiaceae			
Canthium odoratum (-)	Native Coffee	T	Sc Fl - cream Fr - black
Timonius timon (-)		T	Fl - white
Rutaceae			
Acronychia acidula (-)	Lemon Aspen	T	Pi Sc Fl - yellow Fr - white
Acronychia laevis (-)	Hard Aspen	T	Fl - cream Fr - pink/purple
Acronychia oblongifolia	White Lilly Pilly	S/T	L Fl - cream Fr - white
Acronychia pubescens (-)	Hairy Acronychia	T	Fl - cream Fr - yellow/pink
Acronychia suberosa	Corky Acronychia	T	Fl - white Fr - white
Bosistoa selwynii	Heart-leaf Bonewood	T	L Fl - white Uncommon
Bouchardatia neurococca	Union Nut	S/T	Fl - white
Geijera salicifolia	Scrub Wilga	T	Fl - white Fr - brown Bf
Halfordia kendack	Safron Heart	T	Fl - cream Fr - black
Melicope elleryana (Euodia e.)	Pink Evodia	T	Pi Fl - pink/mauve Fr - black Bi Bf
Melicope erythrococca (-)	Tingle Tongue	T	Fl - white Fr - red
Melicope melanophloia (-)	Black-bark Doughwood	T	Fl - white
Melicope micrococca (Euodia m.)	Doughwood	T	Pi Fl - white Fr - black
Melicope octandra (-)	Doughwood	T	Fl - white Fr - brown
Pentaceras australis	Bastard Crow's Ash	T	Pi Sc Fl - cream Fr - brown
Sarcomelicope simplicifolia	Bauerella	T	Pi Fl - cream Fr - brown
Zanthoxylum brachyacanthum	Thorny Yellowwood	T	Sp Fl - yellow & red Fr - red
Sapindaceae			
Alectryon reticulatus	Alectryon	T	Bi Uncommon
Arytera lautererana	Corduroy Tamarind	T	L Fl - white fr - red & yellow
Atalaya multiflora	Broad-leaf Whitewood	T	Fl - white Fr - brown Rare
Atalaya salicifolia (A. virens)	Scrub Whitewood	T	Fl - white Fr - brown
Castanospora aphanandi (-)	Brown Tamarind	T	Pi L Sc Fl - white Fr - brown/red
Cupaniopsis anacardioides	Tuckeroo	T	Pi L Fl - yellow Fr - orange Bi Bf
Cupaniopsis flagelliformis (-)	Brown Tuckeroo	S/T	Pi L Fl - pink Fr - brown

Scientific Name	Common Name	Form	Comments
Diploglottis campbellii	Small-leaf Tamarind	T	Pi Fl - cream Fr - brown Rare
Diploglottis cunninghamii	Native Tamarind	T	L Fl - white Fr - orange Bf
Guioa semiglauca	Wild Quince	T	Pi L Fl - white Fr - purple
Harpullia hilli	Blunt-leaf Tulip	T	Pi Fl - white Fr - yellow Bi
Harpullia pendula	Tulipwood	T	Pi Fl - white Fr - orange Bi Bf
Jagera pseudorhus	Foam Bark Tree	T	L Fl - brown Fr - red
Mischocarpus anodontus	Veiny Pear-fruit	T	L Fl - green Fr - orange & red
Mischocarpus pyriformis	Yellow Pear-fruit	T	L Sc Fl - cream Fr - yellow Bi
Rhysotoechia bifoliolata (-)	Twin-leaf Tuckeroo	T	Fl - orange Fr - orange
Sarcopteryx stipata	Corduroy	T	Fl - white Fr - red
Toechima dasyrrhache	Blunt-leaf Steelwood	T	Fl - brown Fr - orange/ red Bi
Sapotaceae			
Amorphospermum antilogum	Brown Pearwood	T	L Fl - cream Fr - black
Amorphospermum whitei (-)	Rusty Plum	T	L Fl - green Fr - black
Planchonella (Pouteria) australis	Black Apple	T	Fl - white Fr - black
Planchonella (Pouteria) laurifolia (-)	Blush Coondoo	T	L Sc Fl - white Fr - black
Planchonella laurifolia pohlmaniana	Yellow Boxwood	T	L Fl - cream Fr -green/ black
Simaroubaceae			
Ailanthus triphysa	White Siris	T	L Fl -cream Fr - brown
Siphonodontaceae			
Siphonodon australis	Ivorywood	T	Fl - yellow Fr - yellow
Sterculiaceae			
Commersonia bartramia	Brown Kurrajong	T	Pi Fl - white
Argyrodendron actinophyllum	Black Booyong	T	Fl - cream
Argyrodendron trifoliolatum	Brown Tulip Oak	T	L Fl - cream
Brachychiton acerifolius	Flame Tree	T	Pi Fl - red Fr - brown Bf
Brachychiton discolor	Lace Bark	T	Pi Fl - pink Fr - brown
Brachychiton populneus	Kurrajong	T	Pi L Fl - cream Fr - black Bf
Sterculia quadrifida	Peanut Tree	T	Pi Fl - yellow Fr - red & black
Symplocaceae			
Symplocos stawelli	White Hazelwood	T	Fl - white Fr - black
Ulmaceae			
Aphananthe philippinensis	Native Elm	T	Pi Fl - green Fr - yellow/ black Bi

Scientific Name	Common Name	Form	Comments
Celtis paniculata	Investigator Tree	T	Pi Fl - green Fr - black Bi Bf
Urticaceae			
Dendrocnide excelsa	Giant Stinging Tree	T	Pi Fl - green Fr - pink Stings
Dendrocnide photinophylla	Mulberry Stinger	T	Pi Fl - green Fr - green Bf Stings
Verbenaceae			
Gmelina leichhardtii	White Beech	T	Pi Fl - purple/white Fr - blue
Premna lignum-vitae	Lignum-vitae	T	L Fl - pink Fr - red Bi
Vitaceae			
Cissus antarctica	Kangaroo Vine	V	Pi Fl - green/brown Fr - black Bi
Cissus hypoglauca	Five-leaf Watervine	V	Pi Fl - yellow Fr - black
Cissus sterculiifolia	Long-leaf Watervine	V	Fl - white Fr - black
Cayratia eurynema	Soft Water Vine	V	Fl - white Fr - black
Tetrastigma nitens	Shining Grape	V	Pi L Fl - Fr - black

Annual Bridge to Bridge Raft Race - Pine River (PRSC)

2

Planting List for Open Areas

Form: S = Shrub; T = Tree; P = Palm; V = Vine; G = Grass; Se = Sedge; H = Herb; eH = epiphytic Herb; aH = aquatic Herb; eO = epiphytic Orchid; tO = terrestrial Orchid; eF = epiphytic Fern; tF = terrestrial Fern; Gc = Ground cover

Comments: L = colourful new leaves; Fl = Flowers; Fr = 'Fruit'; Sc = scented flowers; Sp = spiny; Bi = Birds attracted; Bf = Butterfly larvae food; Pi = Pioneer species or can be used as such.

(-) = may not occur naturally in Pine Rivers Valley but has not proved invasive.

Small Plants for Low Shrubbery, Heath-land Gardens and Rockeries

The following are suitable for growing as low shrubbery, rockery plants and as under-storey plants among larger trees and shrubs where there is still plenty of sunlight. They naturally grow to about 2 metres or less. Many are much smaller. Many can be pruned after flowering to increase future flower production.

Scientific Name	Common Name	Form	Comments
GYMNOSPERMS			
Podocarpaceae			
Podocarpus spinulosus (-)	Spiny Plum	S	Sp 'Fr' - black
Zamiaceae			
Macrozamia miquelii	Zamia Palm	S	Orange Seeds
Macrozamia pauli-guiliemi (-)	Zamia	S	L red seeds
MONOCOTYLEDONS			
Amaryllidaceae			
Crinum angustifolium	Narrow-leaf Crinum Lily	H	Fl - white
Crinum pedunculatum	River Lily	H	Fl - white
Commelinaceae			
Commelina cyanea	Scurvy Plant	H	Gc Fl - blue
Murdannia graminea	Grass Lily	H	Fl - mauve
Convolulaceae			
Convolvulus erubescens	Australian Bindweed	V	Fl - pink/white
Polymeria calycina	Swamp Bindweed	V	Fl - pink/mauve
Iridaceae			
Patersonia glabrata	Purple Flag Iris	H	Fl - purple
Patersonia sericea	Silky Flag Iris	H	Fl - purple

Scientific Name	Common Name	Form	Comments
Lillaceae			
Bulbine bulbosa (-)	Bulbine Lily	H	Fl - yellow
Dianella brevipedunculata	Flax Lily	H	Fr - blue
Dianella caerulea	Blue Flax Lily	H	Fr - blue
Dianella revoluta	Flax Lily	H	Fr - blue
Drymophila moorei (-)	Orange Berry	H	Fr - orange
Sowerbaea juncea	Vanilla Lily	H	Fl - pink
Tripladenia cunninghamii	Bush Lily	H	Fl - pink Semi-shade
Thysanotus tuberosus	Fringed Lily	H	Fl - purple
Orchidaceae			
Geodorum neocaledonicum	Nodding Orchid	tO	Fl - pink Semi-shade
Philesiaceae			
Eustrephus latifolius	Wombat Berry	V	Fr - orange Bi
Geitonoplesium cymosum	Scrambling Lily	V	Fr - black Bi
Philydracaceae			
Philydrum lanuginosum	Frogsmouth	aH	Fl - yellow Wet areas
Poaceae			
Cymbopogon refractus	Barbwire Grass	G	
Danthonia induta	Wallaby Grass	G	
Danthonia tenuior	Wallaby Grass	G	
Entolasia stricta	Wiry Panic	G	
Erogrostis brownii	Brown's Love Grass	G	Fl - white
Micraira subulifolia (-)	Mountain Couch	G	
Oplismenus aemulus	Creeping Beard Grass	G	Gc Semi-shade
Oplismenus imbecillus	Pademelon Grass	G	Gc Semi-shade
Panicum pygmaeum	Dwarf Panic	G	Semi-shade
Pennisetum alopecuroides	Swamp Foxtail	G	Fl - white
Poa labillardieri	Tussock Grass	G	Bf
Themeda triandra	Kangaroo Grass	G	Bf
Smilacaceae			
Smilax australis	Barbwire Vine	V	Sp L Fl - cream Fr - black/red Bf
Smilax glycophylla	Sweet Sarsparilla	V	Fl - white Fr - black Bi
Stylideaceae			
Stylidium graminifolium	Grass Trigger Plant	H	Fl - pink
Stylidium ornatum	Ornate Trigger Plant	H	Fl - pink
Xanthorrhoeaceae			
Lomandra confertifolia	Mat Rush	H	Bf
Lomandra filiformis	Fine-leaf Mat Rush	H	Bf
Lomandra hystrix	Creek Mat Rush	H	Bf Sc - sweet spicy
Lomandra longifolia	Long-leaf Mat Rush	H	Bf Sc - sweet spicy
Lomandra multiflora	Many-flower Mat Rush	H	Bf
Xanthorrhoea johnsonii	Forest Grass Tree	S	Fl - cream

Scientific Name	Common Name	Form	Comments
Xanthorrhoea fulva	Swamp Grass Tree	S	Fl - cream Wet areas
Xanthorrhoea latifolia	Grass Tree	S	Fl - cream

DICOTYLEDONS

Aizoaceae
Carpobrotus glaucescens	Pig Face	H	Gc Fl -purple Fr - pink

Baueraceae
Bauera rubioides (-)	Wiry Dog Rose	S	Fl - white/pink

Acanthaceae
Pseuderanthemum tenellum	Pseuderanthemum	H	Fl - white Bf Semi-shade
Pseuderanthemum variabile	Love Flower	H	Fl - pink/lilac Bf Semi-shade

Apiaceae
Centella australis	Pennywort	H	Gc

Asteraceae
Brachycome multifida (-)	Hawkesbury River Daisy	H	Fl - mauve/pink
Bracteantha bracteata	Golden Everlasting	H	Fl - yellow; & other colours Bf
Chrysocephalum apiculatum	Yellow Buttons	H	Gc Fl - yellow
Epaltes australis	Nut Heads	H	Fl - green/white Bf
Helichrysum diosmofolium	Sago Flower	S	Fl - white
Helichrysum elatum	White Paper Daisy	H	Fl - white
Helichrysum lanuginosum	White Paper Daisy	H	Fl - white
Helichrysum semipapposum (-)		H	Fl - yellow

Caesalpineaceae
Cassia artemisioides (-)	Silver Cassia	S	L Fl -yellow

Campanulaceae
Lobelia trigonocaulis	Forest Lobelia	H	Gc Fl - blue
Wahlenbergia gracilis	Bluebells	H	Fl - blue

Convolulaceae
Convolulus erubescens	Blushing Bindweed	V	Fl - white/pink
Dichondra repens	Kidney Weed	H	Gc
Polymeria calycina	Swamp Bindweed	V	Fl - pink

Dilleniaceae
Hibbertia aspera	Rough Guinea Flower	S	Fl - yellow
Hibbertia dentata	Toothed Guinea Flower	V	Fl - yellow
Hibbertia linearis	Showy Guinea Flower	S	Fl - yellow
Hibbertia obtusifolia	Hoary Guinea Flower	S	Fl - yellow
Hibbertia stricta	Erect Guinea Flower	S	Fl - yellow
Hibbertia scandens	Twining Guinea Flower	V	Fl - yellow Fr - red
Hibbertia vestita	Hairy Guinea Flower	S	Fl - yellow

Scientific Name	Common Name	Form	Comments
Fabaceae			
Abrus precatorius	Crab's Eye Vine	V	'Fr' - red & black Seeds poisonous
Aotus lanigera	Pointed Aotis	S	Fl - yellow Semi-shade
Glycine clandestina	Twining Glycine	V	Fl - purple
Glycine tomentella	Wooly Glycine	V	Fl - mauve
Hardenbergia violacea	False Sarsparilla	V	Fl - purple
Hovea linearis	Common Hovea	S	Fl - purple
Indigophora australis	Australian Indigo	S	Fl - pink
Kennedia rubicunda	Dusky Coral Pea	V	Fl - red
Oxylobium ilicifolium (-)	Holly Pea	S	Sp Fl - yellow
Oxylobium scandens (-)	Netted Shaggy Pea	S	Gc Fl - yellow
Pultenaea retusa	Blunt-leaf Bush Pea	S	Fl - yellow
Pultenaea spinulosa (-)	Prickly Pea	S	Gc Fl - yellow
Pultenaea villosa (-)	Hairy Bush Pea	S	Fl - yellow
Swainsona galegifolia	Darling Pea	S	Fl - white/pink/red Bf
Vigna vexillata	Native Cow Pea	V	Fl - blue
Geraniaceae			
Geranium homeanum	Native Geranium	H	Fl -pink
Geranium solanderi	Native Geranium	H	Fl - pink
Gesneriaceae			
Boea hygroscopica (-)	Rock Violet	H	Fl - purple
Goodeniaceae			
Goodenia rotundifolia	Star Goodenia	H	Gc Fl - yellow
Scaevola aemula (-)	Fairy Fan Flower	H	Gc Fl - blue
Scaevola albida (-)	Fan Flower	H	Fl - white/mauve
Scaevola calendulacea (-)	Scented Fan Flower	H	Gc Sc Fl - blue
Scaevola ramosissima (-)	A Fan Flower	H	Gc Sc Fl - blue
Lamiaceae			
Ajuga australis	Southern Bugle	H	Fl - blue/pink/purple
Plectranthus argentatus (-)	Silver Native Coleus	H	L Fl -blue Semi-shade
Plectranthus graveolens	Native Coleus	H	Fl - blue
Plectranthus parviflorus	Cockspur Flower	H	Fl - blue
Prostanthera phylicifolia (-)	Mint Bush	S	Fl - mauve
Westringia fruiticosa (-)	Coast Rosemary	S	Fl - white Bf
Westringia Wynyabbie Gem (-)	W. 'Wynyabbie Gem'	S	Fl - mauve
Malvaceae			
Pavonia hastata (-)	Pavonia	S	Fl - pink
Hibiscus diversifolius	Swamp Hibiscus	S	Fl - yellow/purple
Hibiscus geranioides (-)		S	Fl - pink Semi-shade
Melastomaceae			
Melastoma affine	Pink Lasiandra	S	Fl - pink/mauve
Mimosaceae			
Acacia amblygona (-)		S	Sc Fl - yellow Bf

Scientific Name	Common Name	Form	Comments
Acacia baueri (-)		S	Sc Fl - yellow Bf
Acacia complanata	Flat-stem Wattle	S	Sc Fl - yellow Bf
Acacia hubbardiana	Yellow Prickly Moses	S	Sc Sp Fl - yellow Bf
Acacia myrtifolia	Myrtle Wattle	S	L Sc Fl - yellow Bf
Acacia suaveolens	Sweet Wattle	S	Sc Fl - cream Bf
Acacia ulicifolia	Prickly Moses	S	Sp Fl - cream Bf
Myrtaceae			
Austromyrtus dulcis	Midyim Berry	S	Fl - white Fr - white
Baeckea (Babingtonia)	Twiggy Heath Myrtle	S	Fl - white Dwarf &
virgata			prostrate forms
Calytrix tetragona (-)	Common Fringe Myrtle	S	Fl - pink/white 'Fr' - red
Callistemon citrinus Anzac (-)	C. 'Anzac'	S	Fl - white Bi
Callistemon 'Little John' (-)	C. 'Little John'	S	Fl - red Bi
Callistemon pachyphyllus	Wallum Bottlebrush	S	Fl - red/white/green/pink Bi
Callistemon sp. Blackdown			
Tableland (-)	C. Blackdown	S	Fl - red Bi
Callistemon viminalis			
'Running River' (-)	C. Running River	S	Fl - red Bi
Kunzia capitata (-)	Pink Buttons	S	Fl - mauve
Kunzea opposita (-)		S	Fl - pink
Leptospermum liversidgei	Swamp May	S	Fl - white/pink
Leptospermum polygalifolia			
'Pacific Beauty'	L. Pacific Beauty	S	Fl - white Prostrate form
Melaleuca bracteata			
'Golden Gem'	M. 'Golden Gem'	S	L Fl - white Dwarf form Bi
Melaleuca erubescens	Pink Paperbark	S	Fl - mauve Bi
Melaleuca thymifolia (-)	Thyme Honey Myrtle	S	Fl - mauve, pink, white forms Bi
Thryptomene saxifolia (-)	Payne's Hybrid	S	Fl - pink
Myoporaceae			
Eremophila debilis	Winter Apple	S	Gc Fl - white/mauve Fr - pink
Myoporum boninense			
(M. ellipticum)	Boobialla	S	Gc Fl - white Fr - purple
Myoporum montanum	Mountain Boobialla	S	Gc Fl - mauve Fr - red
Portulacaeae			
Portulaca oleracea	Pig Weed	H	Gc Fl -yellow Bf
Passifloraceae			
Passiflora aurantia	Red Passion Flower	V	Fl - gold to red Bf
Pittosporaceae			
Billardiera scandens	Sweet Apple Berry	V	Fl - yellow Fr - green
Proteaceae			
Banksia oblongifolia	Dwarf Banksia	S	Fl - lemon Bf Bi

Scientific Name	Common Name	Form	Comments
Banksia robur	Swamp Banksia	S	Fl - green to brown Bf Bi
Grevillea leiophylla	Wallum Grevillea	S	Fl - pink Bi
Grevillea 'Robyn Gordon'	G. 'Robyn Gordon'	S	Fl - pink Bi
Grevillea sericea	Pink Spider Flower	S	Fl - pink Bi
Grevillea 'Shirley Howie'	G. 'Shirley Howie'	S	Fl - pink Bi
Grevillea 'Superb'	G. 'Superb'	S	Fl - salmon-pink & yellow Bi
Hakea actites (-)	Bushy Needlewood	S	Sp Fl - white Bi
Hakea florulenta	Hakea	S	Fl - white Bi
Hakea purpurea		S	Sp Fl - red Bi
Lambertia formosa (-)	Mountain Devil	S	Sp Fl - red & green Bi
Lomatia silaifolia	Crinkle Bush	S	Fl - cream Bi
Stenocarpus angustifolius (-)		S	Fl - cream Bi

Rosaceae

Rubus parvifolia	Pink Raspberry	S	Fl - white Fr - red

Rutaceae

Phebalium woombye (-)	Phebalium	S	L Fl - white/pink

Scrophulariaceae

Artanema fimbriatum	Koala Bells	H	Fl - blue

Sterculiaceae

Keraudrenia hillii (-)		S	Fl - mauve
Lasiopetalum macrophyllum (-)		S	L Fl - white/pink & black
Rulingia hermanniifolia (-)	Rulingia	S Gc	Fl - white/pink Fr - brown
Rulingia dasyphylla	Rulingia	S	Fl - white

Tetragoniaceae

Tetragonia tetragonioides	Native Spinach	H	Gc

Thymeliaceae

Pimelea linifolia	Slender Rice Flower	S	Fl -white/pink Bf
Wikstroemia indica	Tie Bush	S	Fr - red

Tremandraceae

Tetratheca thymifolia	Black-eyed Susan	S	Fl - pink/mauve

Verbenaceae

Callicarpa pedunculata	Velvet Bush	S	Fr - white/mauve Fr - purple Bi
Phyla nodiflora (-)	Condamine Couch	H	Gc Fl - white Slope binder
Vitex ovata (-)	Vitex	S	Gc Fl -white Slope binder

Violaceae

Viola betonicifolia	Purple Violet	H	Fl - purple
Viola hederacea	Native Violet	H	Gc Fl - white & purple

Vitaceae

Cayratia clematidea	Slender Grape	V	Fl - white Fr - black
Cissus opaca	Small-leaf Water Vine	V	Fl - white Fr - black

Scientific Name	Common Name	Form	Comments
PTERIDOPHYTES			
Adiantaceae			
Adianthum hispidulum	Rough Maidenhair	tF	Gc Semi-shade
Blechnaceae			
Doodia aspera	Prickly Rasp Fern	tF	L Semi-shade
Doodia caudata	Small Rasp Fern	tF	Semi-shade
Doodia media	Common Rasp Fern	tF	Gc L Semi-shade
Polypodiaceae			
Drynaria rigidula	Basket Fern	eF/tF	

Medium Plants for Open Areas in the Pine Rivers Area

The following plants are suitable for growing as medium shrubs and as under-storey plants among larger trees where there is still plenty of sunlight. They naturally grow to about 5 metres or less. Many are much smaller. Many can be pruned after flowering to increase future flower production. These plants may be used with the smaller plants from the previous list but care must be taken not to shade out the smaller ones by planting too closely.

Form: S = Shrub; V = Vine

Comments: L = colourful new leaves; Fl = Flowers; Fr = Fruit; Sc = scented flowers; Sp = spiny; Bi = Birds attracted; Bf = Butterfly larvae food

(-) = may not occur naturally in Pine Rivers Valley but has not proved invasive.

Scientific Name	Common Name	Form	Comments
MONOCOTYLEDONS			
Agavaceae			
Doryanthes palmeri (-)	Spear Lily	S	Fl - red
Doryanthes excelsa (-)	Gymea Lily	S	Fl - red
DICOTYLEDONS			
Convolulaceae			
Ipomoea pes caprae	Goat's Foot	V	Fl - pink & red Coastal
Fabaceae			
Canavalia maritima	Coastal Jack Bean	V	Fl - pink Coastal Bf
Dillwynia retorta	Bacon and Eggs	S	Fl - yellow & red
Hovea acutifolia	Pointed-leaf Hovea	S	Fl - purple
Hovea longifolia (-)	Long-leaf Hovea	S	Fl - purple
Jacksonia scoparia	Dogwood	S	Fl - yellow Bf
Kennedia retrorsa (-)		V	Fl - purple/pink Fr - brown Rare
Vigna marina	Dune bean	V	Fl - yellow Bf Coastal

Scientific Name	Common Name	Form	Comments
Lamiaceae			
Prostanthera ovalifolia (-)	Oval-leaf Mint Bush	S	Fl - violet
Malvaceae			
Hibiscus heterophyllus	Native Rosella	S	Fl - pink/yellow & white
Hibiscus 'Pink Ice' (-)	H. 'Pink Ice'	S	Fl - pink/red
Hibiscus splendens (-)	Native Hibiscus	S	Fl - pink/red
Mimosaceae			
Acacia baeuerlenii	Baeuerlin's Wattle	S	Fl - cream Bf
Acacia conferta (-)	Crowded-leaf Wattle	S	Fl - yellow Bf
Acacia falcata	Sickle-leaf Wattle	S	Fl - cream Bf
Acacia farnesiana (-)	Perfume Wattle	S	Sp Sc Fl - orange Fr - brown Bf
Myrtaceae			
Baeckea camphorata (-)	Camphor Heath Myrtle	S	Fl - white
Baeckea sp.Clarence River (-)	B. 'Clarence River'	S	Fl -white
Baeckea stenophylla (-)	Weeping Heath Myrtle	S	Fl - white
Baeckea (Babingtonia) virgata	Twiggy Heath Myrtle	S	Fl - white
Callistemon citrinus 'Endeavour'	C. 'Endeavour'	S	Fl -crimson Bi
Callistemon citrinus 'Mauve Mist' (-)	C. 'Mauve Mist'	S	Fl - mauve Bi
Callistemon citrinus 'Reeves Pink' (-)	C. 'Reeves Pink'	S	Fl - pink Bi
Callistemon citrinus 'Starlight' (-)	C. 'Starlight'	S	Fl - white Bi
Callistemon citrinus 'Violet Clusters' (-)	C. 'Violet Clusters'	S	Fl - violet Bi
Callistemon montanus (-)	Mountain Bottlebrush	S	Fl - red Bi
Callistemon polandii (-)	Gold-tip Bottlebrush	S	Fl - red & gold Bi
Callistemon rigidus (-)	Stiff Botttlebrush	S	Fl - red Likes damp Bi
Callistemon sp. 'Baroondah Station' (-)	C. 'Baroondah Station'	S	Fl - pink Bi
Callistemon sp. 'Bluff' (-)	C. 'Bluff'	S	Fl - cream Bi
Callistemon sp. 'Injune' (-)	C. 'Injune'	S	Fl - pink/red Bi
Callistemon sp. 'Tinaroo Falls' (-)	C. 'Tinaroo Falls'	S	Fl - red & gold Bi
Callistemon viminalis 'Captain Cook'	C. 'Captain Cook'	S	Fl - red Bi
Callistemon viminalis 'Hannah Ray'	C. 'Hannah Ray'	S	Fl - red Weeping Bi
Callistemon viminalis 'Rose Opal'	C. 'Rose Opal'	S	Fl - red Bi
Callistemon viminalis 'Wild River'	C. 'Wild River'	S	Fl - red Bi
Kunzia flavescens (-)		S	Fl - cream
Leptospermum brachyandrum	Creek Tea-tree	S	Fl - white Some weeping forms
Leptospermun juniperimum	Juniper Tea-tree	S	Fl - white
Leptospermum leuhmannii	Hillside May	S	Fl - white

Scientific Name	Common Name	Form	Comments
Leptospermum microcarpum	Small-fruit May	S	Fl - white
Leptospermum petersonii	Lemon Scented Tea-tree	S	Fl - white
Leptospermum polygalifolia	Native May	S	Fl - white
Leptospermum speciosum	Showy Tea-tree	S	Fl - white
Leptospermum trinervium		S	Fl - white
Melaleuca cheelii (-)	Burrum River Paperbark	S	Fl - cream Bi
Melaleuca groveana (-)		S	Fl - cream Bi
Melaleuca nodosa	Ball Honey Myrtle	S	Fl - cream Bi
Melaleuca sieberi		S	Sc Fl - white Bi Uncommon
Melaleuca 'Snowstorm' (-)	M. 'Snowstorm'	S	L Fl - white Bi
Neofabricia myrtifolia	(Leptospermum fabricia)	S	Fl - yellow
Myoporaceae			
Myoporum acuminatum	Coast Boobialla	S	Fl - white Fr - purple Coastal
Myoporum montanum	Mountain Boobialla	S	Fl - mauve/white Fr- red
Pittosporaceae			
Bursaria spinosa	Blackthorn	S	Sp Sc Fl - white Fr - brown Bi Bf
Proteaceae			
Banksia conferta (-)		S	Fl - cream Bi
Banksia 'Giant Candles' (-)	B. 'Giant Candles'	S	Fl - orange Bi
Banksia spinulosa	Hill Banksia	S	Fl - gold & red/ yellow/black Bi
Grevillea banksii (-)	Red Silky Oak	S	Fl - red/cream/pink Shrub form Bi
Grevillea 'Boongala Spinebill' (-)	G. 'Boongala Spinebill'	S	Fl - crimson Bi
Grevillea 'Honey Gem' (-)	G. 'Honey Gem'	S	Fl - apricot and yellow Bi
Grevillea 'Majestic' (-)	G. 'Majestic'	S	Fl - red & cream Bi
Grevillea 'Misty Pink' (-)	G. 'Misty Pink'	S	Fl - pink & cream Bi
Grevillea sp.Coochin Hills (-)	G. 'Honeycomb'	S	Fl - yellow Bi
Grevillea venusta (-)		S	Fl - green,yellow & blue Bi
Hakea plurinervia	Hakea	S	Sp Fl - white/pink Bi
Hakea gibbosa	Needle Hakea	S	Sp Fl - white Bi
Xylomelum pyriforme (-)	Woody Pear	S	Fl - cream Fr - grey
Rhamnaceae			
Pomaderris lanigera	Woolly Pomaderris	S	L Fl - yellow
Rutaceae			
Zieria smithii	Sandy Zieria	S	Fl - white - pink
Sapindaceae			
Dodonaea triquetra	Large-leaf Hop Bush	S	Fr - brown
Dodonaea viscosa	Sticky Hop Bush	S	Fr - brown/yellow/red/ purple
Verbenaceae			
Vitex purpurea	Purple Vitex	S	L Fl - lavender
Vitex trifolia (-)	Vitex	S	L Fl - lavender Fr - black

Large Shrubs and Small Trees for open areas

The following plants are suitable for growing as large shrubs and small trees in open areas and among larger trees where there is still plenty of sunlight. They naturally grow to about 8 metres or less. Many are much smaller. Many can be pruned after flowering to increase future flower production. These plants may be used with the smaller plants from the previous lists, but care must be taken not to shade out the smaller ones, that may need strong sunlight to promote flowering, by planting too closely.

Form: S = Shrub; T = Tree

Comments: L = colourful new leaves; Fl = Flowers; Fr = Fruit; Sc = scented flowers; Sp = spiny; Bi = Birds attracted; Bf = Butterfly larvae food

(-) = may not occur naturally in Pine Rivers Valley but has not proved invasive.

Scientific Name	Common Name	Form	Comments
DICOTYLEDONS			
Casuarinaceae			
Allocasuarina littoralis	Black She-oak	T	Fr - black cockatoo food
Mimosaceae			
Acacia fimbriata	Brisbane Wattle	S	Fl - yellow Bf
Acacia irrorata	Blue Skin	S/T	Fl - yellow Bf
Acacia leptoloba (-)		S	Fl - cream Bf
Acacia podalyriifolia (-)	Qld Silver Wattle	S	Fl - golden Bf
Acacia spectabilis (-)	Mudgee Wattle	S	Fl - golden Bf
Myrtaceae			
Angophora hispida (-)	Dwarf Apple	S/T	Fl - white Bi
Callistemon formosus (-)	Kingaroy Bottlebrush	S/T	Fl - lemon/red Bi
Callistemon salignus	White Bottlebrush	S/T	L Fl - white Bi
Callistemon viminalis	Weeping Bottlebrush	S/T	Fl - red Bi
Callistemon viminalis '*Dawson River*' (-)	C. 'Dawson River'	S/T	Fl - red Bi
Eucalyptus bakeri (-)	Baker's Mallee	T	Fl - white Bi
Eucalyptus bancroftii	Tumbledown Gum	T	Fl - white Bi
Eucalyptus conglomerata (-)	Swamp Stringybark	S/T	Fl - white Bi Rare
Eucaluptus curtisii (-)	Plunket Mallee	T	Fl - white Bi
Eucalyptus shirleyi (-)	Shirley's Silver-leaf Ironbark	T	Fl - cream Bi
Eucalyptus ptychocarpa (-) (*Corymbia p.*)	Swamp Bloodwood	T	Fl - red/pink/white Bi
Eucalyptus kabiana (-)	E. 'Mt. Beerwah'	T	Fl - white/pink Bi Rare
Melaleuca irbyana (-)	Swamp Tea Tree		Fl - white Bi
Melaleuca symphocarpa (-)		S/T	Fl - orange Bi
Tristaniopsis laurina	Water Gum	T	Fl - yellow Bf
Proteaceae			
Banksia aemula (-)	Wallum Banksia	T	Fl - cream Bi Bf
Banksia integrifolia	Coast Banksia	T	Fl - yellow Bi Bf
Grevillea banksii (-)	Red Silky Oak	S/T	Fl - red/cream/pink Bi
Grevillea 'Pink Surprise' (-)	G. 'Pink Surprise'	S/T	Fl - pink & cream Bi

Scientific Name	Common Name	Form	Comments
Grevillea pteridifolia (-)	Golden Grevillea	S/T	Fl - golden Bi
Hakea trineura (-)		S/T	Fl - green Bi Uncommon
Sterculaceae			
Commersonia bartramia	Brown Kurrijong	T	Fl - cream

Medium Trees for Open Areas

These plants of the open forests and woodlands are mostly locally occurring. Some hardy rainforest plants are also included in this list. As well, some other rainforest species can be grown in open areas - use those marked Pi (= Pioneer) from the rainforest plant lists Many of the following, including even the largest, still occur in developed residential, industrial and rural areas. Some of these trees may become large with old age.

Form: S = Shrub; T = Tree
Size: M = Medium L = Large
Comments: L = colourful new leaves; Fl = Flowers; Fr = Fruit; Sc = scented flowers; Sp = spiny; Bi = Birds attracted; Bf = Butterfly larval food.

(-) = may not occur naturally in Pine Rivers Valley but has not proved invasive.

For planting, these medium-sized trees (to about 20 metres) are suitable for large blocks, acreage, parks and rural properties.

Scientific Name	Common Name	Form	Comments
GYMNOSPERMS			
Cupressaceae			
Callitris macleayeana	Scrub Cypress	T	
Callitris columellaris	Bribie Island Pine	T M/L	
DICOTYLEDONS			
Casuarinaceae			
Allocasuarina torulosa	Forest She Oak	T	Bi - Black cockatoos
Casuarina cunninghamiana	River She Oak	T M/L	
Casuarina equisetifolia	Coast She Oak	T	Bi
Casuarina glauca	Swamp She Oak	T M/L	Salty soils
Elaeocarpaceae			
Elaeocarpus grandis	Blue Quandong	T M/L	Fl - white Fr - blue
Elaeocarpus obovatus	Hard Quandong	T M/L	Bi Slow Bf
Fabaceae			
Erythrina vespertilio	Bat's Wing Coral Tree	T	Fl - red Bi
Flindersiaceae			
Flindersia australis	Crow's Ash	T	Fl - white Fr - brown
Flindersia collina	Leopard Ash	T	Fl - white Slow Bf
Flindersia schottiana	Bumpie Ash	T	Sc Fl - white
Flindersia xanthoxyla	Yellowwood	T	Fl - yellow Fr

Scientific Name	Common Name	Form	Comments
Mimosaceae			
Acacia aulacocarpa	Hickory Wattle	T	Sc Fl - yellow Bi Bf
Acacia harpophylla	Brigalow Wattle	T	Sc Fl - yellow Bi Bf
Acacia implexa	Light Wood	T	Sc Fl - cream Bi Bf
Acacia melanoxylon	Blackwood	T	Sc Fl - cream Bi Bf
Acacia oshanesii	O'Shanesy's Wattle	T	Sc Fl - yellow Bi Bf
Myrtaceae (Those marked (C.) are now classified as Corymbia, not Eucalyptus)			
Angophora leiocarpa	Rusty Apple Gum	T	Fl - white Bi Bf
Angophora subvelutina	Broad-leaf Apple	T	Fl - white Bi
Angophora woodsiana	Smudgee	T	Fl - white Bi
Callistemon salignus	White Bottlebrush	S/T	L Fl - white/cream Bi
Callistemon viminalis	Weeping Bottlebrush	T	Fl - red Bi
Eucalyptus (C.) *gummifera*	Red Bloodwood	T	Fl - white Bi Bf
Eucalyptus (C.) *intermedia*	Pink Bloodwood	T	Fl - white Bi Bf
Eucalyptus melanophloia	Silver-leaf Ironbark	T M/L	Fl - white Bi Bf
Eucalyptus racemosa	Scribbly Gum	T M/L	Fl - white Bi Bf
Eucalyptus seena	Narrow-leaf Red Gum	T	Fl - white Bi Bf
Eucalyptus (C.) *tessellaris*	Moreton Bay Ash	T	Fl - white Bi Bf
Eucalyptus (C.) *trachyphloia*	Brown Bloodwood	T	Fl - white Bi Bf
Lophostemon suaveolens	Swamp Box	T	Fl - white Bi
Melaleuca bracteata	River Tea Tree	T	Fl - white Bi
Melaleuca quinquenervia	Swamp Paperbark	T	Fl - white Bi
Syncarpia glomulifera	Turpentine	T	Fl - white Bi
Syncarpia hillii	Satinay	T	Fl - white Bi
Proteaceae			
Macadamia integrifolia	Queensland Nut	T	Sc Fl -cream Bf
Macadamia ternifolia	Maroochy Nut	T	Fl - pink Bf Inedible
Macadamia tetraphylla	Rough Shell Bush Nut	T	Sc Fl - cream Bf
Rhamnaceae			
Alphitonia excelsa	Red Ash	T	Fl - white Fr - black Bi Bf
Alphitonia petriei	Pink Ash	T	L Fl - white Fr -black Bf
Sterculiaceae			
Brachychiton populneus	Kurrajong	T	Fl - white Bi Bf
Sterculia quadrifida	Peanut Tree	T	Fl - white 'Fr' - red & black
Commersonia bartramia	Brown Kurrajong	T	Fl - white
Ulmaceae			
Aphananthe philippinensis	Native Elm	T	Fr - green Bi Bf

Large Trees for Acreage, Parks and Rural Properties

The following large plants are best planted on acreage, parks and in rural areas. Here they can be grown in addition to the medium ones listed for large gardens and the small plants suitable for the open areas of small gardens. Pioneer rainforest plants are also suitable.

Scientific Name	Common Name	Form	Comments
GYMNOSPERMS			
Aracariaceae			
Agathis robusta (-)	Queensland Kauri	T	Slow
Araucaria bidwilli (-)	Bunya Pine	T	Sp Slow. Heavy cones
Araucaria cunninghamii	Hoop Pine	T	Sp Slow growing
Podocarpus elatus	Brown Pine	T	'Fr' - black Bf
DICOTYLEDONS			
Myrtaceae (Those marked (C.) are now classified as Corymbia, not Eucalyptus)			
Eucalyptus acmenoides	White Mahogany	T	Fl - white Bi Bf
Eucalyptus biturbinata	Grey Gum	T	Fl - white Bi Bf
Eucalyptus carnea	White Mahogany	T	Fl - white Bi Bf
Eucalyptus crebra	Narrow-leaf Ironbark	T	Fl - white Bi Bf
Eucalyptus fibrosa	Broad-leaf Ironbark	T	Fl - white Bi Bf
Eucalyptus grandis	Flooded Gum	T	Fl - white Bi Bf
Eucalyptus (C.) *henryi*	Large-leaf Spotted Gum	T	Fl - white Bi Bf
Eucalyptus (C.) *maculata*	Spotted Gum	T	Fl - white Bi Bf
Eucalyptus major	Grey Gum	T	Fl - white Bi Bf
Eucalyptus microcorys	Tallowwood	T	Fl - white Bi Bf
Eucalyptus moluccana	Gum-topped Box	T	Fl - white Bi Bf
Eucalyptus pilularis	Blackbutt	T	Fl - white Bi Bf
Eucalyptus propinqua	Grey Gum	T	Fl - white Bi Bf
Eucalyptus resinifera	Red Stringybark	T	Fl - white Bi Bf
Eucalyptus robusta	Swamp Mahogany	T	Fl - white Bi Bf
Eucalyptus saligna	Sydney Blue Gum	T	Fl - white Bi Bf
Eucalyptus siderophloia	Grey Ironbark	T	Fl - white Bi Bf
Eucalyptus tereticornis	Qld Blue Gum	T	Fl - white/pink Bi Bf
Eucalyptus tindaliae	White Stringy Bark	T	Fl - white Bi Bf
Lophostemon confertus	Brush Box	T	Fl - white Bi Bf
Proteaceae			
Grevillea robusta	Silky Oak	T	Fl - orange Bi

Great Egret - Pine River (JB)

APPENDIX **3**

Plants for Ponds and Bog Gardens

* = plants that need controlling by growing in submerged pots so that roots and shoots can be trimmed periodically.

Emergent Plants :
Bulrushes - Broad-leaf Cumbungi *Typha orientalis* *, Narrow-leaf Cumbungi *Typha domingensis* *

Water 'Lilies' - Giant 'Water Lily' *Nymphia gigantea* *; Native 'Waterlily' *N. violacea* *; Wavy Marshwort *Nymphoides crenata* *; *N. exiliflora*; Star Fringe *N. geminata*; Water Snowflake *N. indica*; Swamp Lily *Ottelia ovalifolia*; Erect Marsh Flower *Villarsia exaltata*; Water Shield *Brasenia schreberi*.

Sedges - Jointed Twigrush *Baumea articulata* *; *B. rubiginosa* *; Twigrush *Baumea juncea*; *Lepironia articulata* *; Water Chestnut *Elaeocharis dulcis* *; Tall Spike Rush *E. sphacelata* *; Grey Rush *Lepironia articulata* *; River Clubrush *Schoenoplectus validus (Scirpus validus)* *; Water Ribbons *Triglochin procerum*; Streaked Arrow Grass *T. striata*.

Grasses - Common Reed *Phragmites australis* *.

Ferns - Nardoo *Marsilea mutica* ; *M. drummondii*.

Floating Plants:
Ferns - *Azolla filiculoides*; *A. pinnata*.

Duckweeds - *Lemna trisulca*; *L. minor*; *Spirodella punctata*; *Wolffia angusta*.

Some emergent plants (eg water lilies) and those of nearby bog plants (eg water primrose) will also have floating parts.

Submerged plants:
Pond Lily *Aponogeton elongatus* *; Water Thyme *Hydrilla verticillata*; *Ottelia alismoides*; Curley Pondweed *Potamogeton crispus*; Blunt Pondweed *Potamogeton ochreatus*; Water Milfoil *Myriophyllum papillosum (M. propinquum)*; Ribbon Weed *Vallisneria spiralis*.

Bog Plants:
Austral Bugle *Ajuga australis*; Koala Bells *Artanema fimbriata*; Bare Twig-rush *Baumea juncea*; Fishbone Waterfern *Blechnum nudum*; Swamp Fern *Blechnum indicum*; Tall Sedge *Carex appressa*; Sedge *C. declinata*; *C. polyantha*; *Caustis blakei*; *C. flexuosa*; *Bacopa monieri*; Galloon *Curculigo ensifolia*; Bunchy Sedge *Cyperus polystachyos*; Sedge *C. tetraphyllus*; Pale Flax Lily *Dianella longifolia D. brevipedunculata*; Flax Lily *D. revoluta*; Spoon-leaf Sundew *Drosera spathulata*; Fringe Rush *Fimbristylis dichotoma*; *F. polytrichoides*; Saw Sedge *Gahnia aspera*; Star Goodenia *Goodenia bellidifolia*; Native Geranium *Geranium homeanum*; Wallum Grevillea *Grevillea leiophylla*; Tussock Rush *Juncus polyanthemus*; Common Rush *J. usitatus*; *J. continuus*; Variable Sword Sedge *Lepidosperma laterale*; Purple Loosestrife *Lythrum saliearia*; Water Primrose *Ludwigia peploides*; Willow Primrose *L. octavalvis*; Grass Lily *Murdannia graminea*; Frogsmouth *Philydrum lanuginosum*; Fog-fruit *Phylla nodiflora*; Pomax *Pomax umbellata*; Platted Pratia *Pratia pedunculata;* Australian Buttercup *Ranunculus lappaceus*; Foxtails *Restio tetraphyllus*; Swamp Clubrush *Schoenoplectus inundatus*; *Thelionema caespirosum*; Ladies Tresses *Spiranthes sinensis*; Common Fringe Lily *Thysanotus tuberosus*; Yellow Rush Lily *Tricoryne elatior*; Purple Violet *Viola betonicifolia*; Native Violet *Viola hederacea*; Bluebells *Wahlenbergia gracilis*; Hat Pins *Xyris complanata*; *X. juncus*; Wild Pansy *Velleia spathulata*.

Low shrubs (less than 2 m) and plants for near ponds and bog gardens:
(These plants can also be used as heath garden plants)
Yellow Prickly Mosses *Acacia hubbardiana*, Flat-stem Wattle *A. complanata*; Dune Wattle *Acacia sophorae;* Prickly Mosses *Acacia ulicifolia*; Midyim *Austromyrtus dulcis*; Twiggy Heath Myrtle (dwarf forms) *Baeckea virgata*; Dwarf Banksia *Banksia oblongifolia*; Wallum Banksia *B. robur*; Wallum Bottlebrush *Callistemon pachyphyllus*; Callistemon 'Little John'; River Lily *Crinum pedunculata*; Barbwire Grass *Cymbopogon refractus*; Hairy Bush Pea *Daviesia villosa*; *Grevillea 'Robyn Gordon'*; Needle Hakea *Hakea gibbosa*; Swamp Hibiscus *Hibiscus diversifolius*; Swamp May *Leptospermum liversidgei*; Creek Mat Rush *Lomandra hystrix*; Long-leaf Mat Rush *L. longifolia*; Many-flower Mat Rush *L. multiflora*; Swamp Mazus *Mazus pumilio*; small Monkey Flower *Mimulus prostratus*; Melaleuca 'Golden Gem' *Melaleuca bracteata*, Thyme Honey-myrtle *M. thymifolia*, Blue Tongue *Melastoma affine*; Boobialla *Myoporum boninense*; Winter Apple *M. debile (Eremophila debilis)*; Swamp Foxtail *Pennisetum alopecuroides*; Slender Rice Flower *Pimelia linifolia*; Tussock Grass *Poa labillardieri*; Kangaroo Grass *Themeda triandra*; Swamp Grasstree *Xanthorrhoea fulva*; Forest Grasstree *X. johnsonii*; Wide-leaf Grasstree *X. latifolia*.

Shrubs and small trees for planting near ponds and bog gardens:
In the vicinity of ponds and bog gardens taller shrubs and trees, appropriate to these aquatic habitats, can also be planted.

Green Wattle *Acacia irrorata*; Early Black Wattle *Acacia leiocalyx*; Black She Oak *Allocasuarina littoralis*; Coast Banksia *Banksia integrifolia*; Hill Banksia *Banksia spinulosa*; Pink Tips *Callistemon salignus*; Weeping Bottlebrush *Callistemon viminalis*; Lolly Bush *Clerodendrum floribundum*; Large-leaf Hop Bush *Dodonaea triquetra*;

Blueberry Ash *Elaeocarpus reticulatus*; Creek Tea Tree *Leptospermum brachyandrum*; Lemon Tea Tree *Leptospermum petersonii*; Wild May *Leptospermum polygalifolium*; Showy Tea Tree *Leptospermum speciosum*; River Tea Tree *Melaleuca bracteata (Revolution Green, Revolution Gold)*; Snow in Summer *Melaleuca linariifolia*; Ball Honey Myrtle *Melaleuca nodosa*; Prickly Broom Heath *Monotoca scoparia*; Water Box *Tristaniopsis laurina*; Forest Grasstree *Xanthorrhoea johnsonii*.

Boardwalk - John Oxley Reserve (PRSC)

A P P E N D I X 4

Trees and Shrubs for Street Planting

Where there are no overhead lines and no close (less than 5 metres) underground water and sewerage pipes, height of tree growth may not be so important and large trees may be grown. The only other factors to consider then are whether the roots may damage kerbing, channelling and road surfaces, and the effects on sunlight and shade for nearby houses. The following trees and shrubs are suitable for planting where there are overhead service lines. Pruning may be needed to keep plants below the required height, especially under low wires. Trees that may become large if not pruned but which are amenable to and disciplined by pruning are indicated.

Form: S = Shrub; T = Tree; Pr = may become too high if not pruned.

Comments: L = colourful new leaves; Fl = Flowers; Fr = Fruit; Sc = scented flowers; Bi = Birds attracted; Bf = Butterfly larvae food; Rf = Rainforest natural habitat; Of = open forest or woodland. (-) = may not occur naturally in Pine Rivers Valley but has not proved invasive.

Scientific Name	Common Name	Form	Comments
Acanthaceae			
Graptophyllum excelsum (-)	Scarlet Fuchia	S	Rf Fl - red Bi
Caesalpineaceae			
Barklya syringifolia	Crown of Gold	T Pr	Rf Fl - yellow Slow
Casuarinaceae			
Allocasuarina littoralis	Black She Oak	T Pr	Of Bi - black cockatoos
Celastraceae			
Cassine australis	Red Olive Berry	S/T	Rf Fr - red
Elaeocarpaceae			
Elaeocarpus reticulatus	Blueberry Ash	S/T	Rf Of Sc Fl - white Fr - blue Bi
Euphorbiaceae			
Alchornea ilicifolia	Native Holly	S/T	Rf L Slow
Mallotus philippensis	Red Kamala	T Pr	Rf Of L Fr - red
Moraceae			
Ficus coronata	Creek Sandpaper Fig	T Pr	Rf Of Fr Bi Bf
Myrtaceae			
Acmena smithii	Creek Lilly Pilly	T Pr	Rf Fl - white Fr - pink Bi
Backhousia citriodora	Lemon Myrtle	T Pr	Rf Fl - white
Backhousia myrtifolia	Carrol	T	Rf Of Fl - white
Callistemon polandii (-)	Gold-tip Bottlebrush	S/T	Of Fl - red & yellow Bi

Scientific Name	Common Name	Form	Comments
Callistemon sp. Baroonda Station (-)	C. 'Baroondah Station'	S	Of Fl - pink/white Bi
Callistemon sp. Injune (-)	C. 'Injune'	S	Of Fl - pink/white Bi
Callistemon sp. Tinaroo (-)	C. 'Tinaroo'	S	Of Fl - red & yellow Bi
Callistemon salignus	White Bottlebrush	S/T Pr	Of Fl - white Bi
Callistemon viminalis	Weeping Bottlebrush	S/T	Of Fl - red Bi
Eucalyptus bakeri (-)	Baker's Mallee	T Pr	Of Fl - white Bi
Eucalyptus bancroftii	Tumbledown Gum	T Pr	Of Fl - white Bi
Eucalyptus conglomerata (-)	Swamp Stringybark	T Pr	Of Fl - white Bi
Eucalyptus curtissii (-)	Plunkett Mallee	T Pr	Of Fl - white Bi
Eucalyptus ptychocarpa (-)	Swamp Bloodwood	T Pr	Of Fl - red/pink Fr Bi
Eucalyptus shirleyi (-)	Shirley's Silver-leafed Ironbark	T	Of Fl - lemon Bi
Eucalyptus sp.Mt Beerwah (-)	Mt Beerwah Red Gum	T Pr	Of Fl - white Bi
Leptospermum brachyandrum	Creek Tea Tree	S	Of Fl - white
Leptospermum leuhmannii	Hillside May	S	Of Fl - white
Leptospermum petersonii	Lemon-scented Tea Tree	S	Of Fl - white
Lophostemon confertus	Brush Box	T Pr	Rf Of Fl - white Bi
Melaleuca bracteata	River Tea Tree	T Pr	Of Fl - white Bi
Melaleuca linariifolia	Snow in Summer	T Pr	Of Fl - white Bi
Melaleuca nodosa	Ball Honey Myrtle	S/T	Of Fl - cream Bi
Melaleuca stypheloides (-)	Prickly Paperbark	T Pr	Of Fl - cream Bi
Syzygium australe	Scrub Cherry	T Pr	Rf Fl - white Fr -pink Bi
Syzygium luehmannii (-)	Small-leaf Lilly Pilly	T Pr	Rf L Fl - white Fr -red Bi
Syzygium oleosum	Purple Cherry	T Pr	Rf Fl - white Fr -purple Bi
Tristaniopsis laurina	Water Gum	T Pr	Rf Fl - yellow Bi
Xanthostemon chrysanthus (-)	Golden Penda	T Pr	Rf Fl - yellow Bi

Pittosporaceae

Scientific Name	Common Name	Form	Comments
Pittosporum rhombifolium	Hollywood	T Pr	Rf Fl - white Fr - orange Bi
Pittosporum undulatum	Mock Orange	T Pr	Rf Fl - cream Fr - orange Bi

Proteaceae

Scientific Name	Common Name	Form	Comments
Banksia integrifolia	Coast Banksia	T Pr	Of Fl - lemon Bi
Macadamia integrifolia	Queensland Nut	T Pr	Rf Sc Fl - cream Fr
Macadamia tetraphylla (-)	Rough Macadamia	T Pr	Rf L Sc Fl - pink Fr

Sapindaceae

Scientific Name	Common Name	Form	Comments
Alectryon coriaceus (-)	Beach Bird's Eye	T	Rf L Fr - red Bi
Alectryon subdentalis (-)	Holly-leaf Bird's Eye	T	Rf L Fr - red Bi
Alectryon tomentosus	Hairy Bird's Eye	T Pr	Rf L Fr - red Bi
Cupaniopsis anacardioides	Tuckeroo	T Pr	Rf Of L Fr - yellow Bi
Cupaniopsis parvifolia	Small-leaf Tuckeroo	T Pr	Rf Of L Fr - orange Bi
Cupaniopsis serrata	Rusty Tuckeroo	T Pr	Rf L Fr - orange Bi
Cupaniopsis tomentella (-)	Boonah Tuckeroo	T Pr	Rf Of L Fr - yellow Bi
Elattostachys xylocarpa	White Tamarind	T Pr	Rf L Fr - pink & brown Bi
Harpullia hillii	Blunt-leaf Tulip	T Pr	Rf Fr - yellow Bi
Harpullia pendula	Tulipwood	T Pr	Rf Fr - yellow Bi

Scientific Name	Common Name	Form	Comments
Lepiderima pulchella (-)	Fine-leaf Tuckeroo	T Pr	Rf Fl - orange Fr - brown Bi
Toechima tenax	Brush Teak	T Pr	Rf L Fr - yellow Bi
Sterculaceae			
Brachychiton bidwilli	Little Kurrajong	S	Rf Of Fl - pink
Commersonia bartramia	Brown Kurrajong	T Pr	Rf Of Fl - cream
Ulmaceae			
Aphananthe philippinensis	Native Elm	T Pr	Rf L Fr - green Bi Bf

Fishing at sundown on one of the Shire's lakes (PRSC)

Slope-binding Plants

Many of these plants have adventitious roots (roots that form along stems where these touch the ground), are low growing plants (mostly with fibrous roots) that grow well on slopes, or are trailing vines that cover and protect the surface.

Form: S = Shrub; V = Vine; G = Grass; Se = Sedge; H = Herb; eF = epiphytic Fern; tF = terrestrial Fern

Comments: L = colourful new leaves; Fl = Flowers; Fr = 'Fruit'; Sc = scented flowers; Sp = spiny; Bi = Birds attracted; Bf = Butterfly larvae food; Gc = Ground cover; S = south.

(-) = may not occur naturally in Pine Rivers Valley but has not proved invasive.

Scientific Name	Common Name	Form	Comments
MONOCOTYLEDONS			
Amaryllidaceae			
Crinum pedunculatum	River Lily	H	Fl - white
Commelinaceae			
Commelina cyanea	Scurvy Plant	H Gc	Fl - blue
Convolulaceae			
Convolvulus erubescens	Australian Bindweed	V	Fl - pink/white
Polymeria calycina	Swamp Bindweed	V	Fl - pink/mauve
Lillaceae			
Dianella brevipedunculata	Flax Lily	H	Fr - blue
Dianella caerulea	Blue Flax Lily	H	Fr - blue
Dianella revoluta	Flax Lily	H	Fr - blue
Philesiaceae			
Eustrephus latifolius	Wombat Berry	V	Fr - orange Bi
Poaceae			
Cymbopogon refractus	Barbwire Grass	G	
Danthonia induta	Wallaby Grass	G	
Danthonia tenuior	Wallaby Grass	G	
Entolasia stricta	Wiry Panic	G	
Erogrostis brownii	Brown's Love Grass	G	Fl - white
Micraira subulifolia (-)	Mountain Couch	G	
Oplismenus aemulus	Creeping Beard Grass	G	Gc Semi-shade - S slopes
Oplismenus imbecillus	Pademelon Grass	G	Gc Semi-shade - S slopes

Scientific Name	Common Name	Form	Comments
Panicum pygmaeum	Dwarf Panic	G	Semi-shade - S slopes
Pennisetum alopecuroides	Swamp Foxtail	G	Fl - white
Poa labillardieri	Tussock Grass	G	
Themeda triandra	Kangaroo Grass	G	
Xanthorrhoeaceae			
Lomandra confertifolia	Mat Rush	H	Bf
Lomandra filiformis	Fine-leaf Mat Rush	H	Bf
Lomandra hystrix	Creek Mat Rush	H	Bf Sc - sweet spicy
Lomandra longifolia	Long-leaf Mat Rush	H	Bf Sc - sweet spicy
Lomandra multiflora	Many-flower Mat Rush	H	Bf
DICOTYLEDONS			
Agavaceae			
Doryanthes palmeri (-)	Spear Lily	S	Fl - red
Doryanthes excelsa (-)	Gymea Lily	S	Fl - red
Aizoaceae			
Carpobrotus glaucescens	Pig Face H	Gc	Fl - purple Fr - pink
Baueraceae			
Bauera rubioides (-)	Wiry Dog Rose	S	Fl - white/pink
Acanthaceae			
Pseuderanthemum variabile	Love Flower	H	Fl - pink/lilac Semi-shade - S slopes
Apiaceae			
Centella australis	Pennywort	H	Gc
Asteraceae			
Bracteantha bracteata	Golden Everlasting	H	Fl - yellow; & other colour forms
Chrysocephalum apiculatum	Yellow Buttons	H	Gc Fl - yellow
Dilleniaceae			
Hibbertia scandens	Twining Guinea Flower	V	Fl - yellow Fr - red
Fabaceae			
Abrus precatorius	Crabs Eye Vine	V	'Fr' - red & black Seeds - poisonous
Glycine clandestina	Twining Glycine	V	Fl - purple
Glycine tomentella	Wooly Glycine	V	Fl - mauve
Hardenbergia violacea	False Sarsparilla	V	Fl - purple
Kennedia rubicunda	Dusky Coral Pea	V	Fl - red
Oxylobium ilicifolium (-)	Holly Pea	S	Sp Fl - yellow
Pultenaea villosa (-)	Hairy Bush Pea	S	Fl - yellow
Goodeniaceae			
Goodenia rotundifolia	Star Goodenia	H	Gc Fl - yellow
Scaevola calendulacea (-)	Scented Fan Flower	H	Gc Sc Fl - blue Sandy soil

Scientific Name	Common Name	Form	Comments
Lamiaceae			
Ajuga australis	Southern Bugle	H	Fl - blue/pink/purple
Plectranthus argentatus (-)	Silver Native Coleus	H	L Fl -blue Semi-shade - S slope
Plectranthus graveolens	Native Coleus	H	Fl - blue
Plectranthus parviflorus	Cockspur Flower	H	Fl - blue
Mimosaceae			
Acacia sophorae	Dune Wattle	S	Sc Gc Fl - yellow Sandy soil
Acacia ulicifolia	Prickly Moses	S	Sp Fl - cream
Myrtaceae			
Austromyrtus dulcis	Midyim Berry	S	Gc Fl - white Fr - white
Baeckea virgata (Dwarf forms)	Twiggy Heath Myrtle	S	Fl - white
Callistemon 'Little John' (-)	C. 'Little John'	S	Fl - red Bi
Leptospermum polygalifolia 'Pacific Beauty'	L. 'Pacific Beauty'	S	Fl -white Prostrate form
Melaleuca bracteata 'Golden Gem'	M. 'Golden Gem'	S	L Fl - white Dwarf form
Myoporaceae			
Eremophila debilis (Myoporum debile)	Winter Apple	S	Gc Fl -white/mauve Fr - pink
Myoporum boninense (M. ellipticum)	Boobialla	S	Gc Fr - purple
Rosaceae			
Rubus parvifolia	Pink Raspberry	S	Fl - white Fr - red
Tetragoniaceae			
Tetragonia tetragonioides	Native Spinach	H	Gc
Thymeliaceae			
Pimelea linifolia	Slender Rice Flower	S	Fl - white/pink
Wikstroemia indica	Tie Bush	S	Fr - red
Verbenaceae			
Phyla nodiflora (-)	Condamine Couch	H	Gc Fl - white
Vitex ovata (-)	Vitex	S	Gc Fl -white
Violaceae			
Viola hederacea	Native Violet	H	Gc Fl - white & purple S. slopes
PTERIDOPHYTES			
Adiantaceae			
Adianthum hispidulum	Rough Maidenhair	tF	Gc Semi-shade S slopes
Polypodiaceae			
Drynaria rigidula	Basket Fern	eF/tF	

Annual Lowlands Festival - Osprey House (PRSC)

APPENDIX 6

Colourful Native Plants to Replace Exotic Annuals in Flower Beds

The following list includes plants that are perennial as well as ones that are annuals or can be used as such. All are small plants (1 metre or less, or can be pruned to this height or less. Pruning after flowering will usually increase subsequent flower or fruit production). Some of these plants require good drainage and do best in raised beds with a good percentage of sand. Mulch is of great benefit. It is best not to use any fertilizers.

Colour: B = Blue; G = Green; M = Mauve; O = Orange; Cr = Cream; Pk = Pink; Pu = Purple; R = Red; W = White; Y = Yellow. (-) = may not occur naturally in Pine Rivers Valley but has not proved invasive.

Pr = Prune; Per = Perennial; Fr = Fruit; Fl = Flowers; Sh = Shade.

Scientific Name	Common Name	Colour	Comments
Amaryllidaceae			
Calostemma luteum (-)	Native Daffodil	YR	
Crinum angustifolium	Field Lily	W	
Crinum pedunculatum	River Lily	W	Dormant in winter
Proiphys cunninghamii	Brisbane Lily	W	
Commelinaceae			
Murdannia graminea	Grass Lily	M	
Haemodoraceae			
Anigozanthos flavidus	Giant Kangaroo Paw	Y R O	Disease resistant hybrids
Iridaceae			
Patersonia species	Flag Irises	Pu	
Liliaceae			
Bulbine bulbosa (-)	Native Leek	Y	
Dianella species	Flax Lilies	B (Fr)	
Stypandra species	Blue Lilies	B/M	
Thysanotus tuberosus	Fringe Lily	Pu	
Tricoryne elatior	Rush Lily	Y	
Tripladenia cunninghamii	Bush Lily	B	
Philydraceae			
Philydrum lanuginosum	Frogsmouth	Y	Wet areas
Zingiberaceae			
Curcuma australasica (-)	Curcuma	Pk	

Scientific Name	Common Name	Colour	Comments
Aizoaceae			
Carpobrotus glaucescens	Pig Face	Pk	
Acanthaceae			
Pseuderanthemum species	Love Flowers	Pk	Semi Shade
Apiaceae			
Trachymene species	Trachymenes	W	
Asclepidaceae			
Hoya australis	Hoya	W & Pk	
Asteraceae			
Brachyscome species	Forest Daisies	W Pk M	
Bracteantha bracteata	Everlastings	W Y O Pk R	Many colours
Camptacra barbata (-)	A Daisy	W & Y	
Cassinia subtropica	Bushy Rosemary	W	
Chrysocephalum apiculatum	Yellow Buttons	Y	
Helichrysum (Rhodanthe) species	Paper Daisies	W/Pk	Pr
Olearia species	Daisy Bush	W Y	Pr
Oxothamnus diosmifolius	Sago Bush	W	Pr
Baueraceae			
Bauera rubioides (-)	Dog Rose	Pk/W	
Campanulaceae			
Lobelia membranacea		B/Pu	Sh
Lobelia trigonocaulis	Forest Lobelia	W Pk	Sh
Wahlenbergia species	Bluebells	B	
Dilleniaceae			
Hibbertia species	Guinea Flowers	Y Pr	Vines/Shrubs
Epacridaceae			
Acrotriche aggregata	Ground Berry	R (Fr)	
Epacris species	Heath	W Pk	
Fabaceae			
Aotis ericoides (-)	Common Aotus	Y Pr	
Aotis lanigera	Pointed Aotis	Y Pr	
Cassia artemisioides	Silver Cassia	Y Pr	
Cassia pumila	Dwarf Cassia	Y	
Daviesia species	Bitter Peas	Y & Red Pr	
Dillwynia species	Bush Peas	Y & R	
Hardenbergia violacea	False sarsparilla	Pu	
Hovea species	Hoveas	Pu Pr	
Indigofera australis	Australian Indigo	Pk Pr	
Pultenaea species	Bush Peas	Y Pr	
Swainsona species	Darling Peas	Pk/Pu	
Goodeniaceae			
Dampiera species	Dampiera	Pu	
Goodenia species	Goodenias	Y	

Scientific Name	Common Name	Colour	Comments
Scaevola species	Fan Flowers	W/M/B/Pu/Pk	
Velleia spathulata	Wild Pansy	Y	
Lamiaceae			
Ajuga australis	Southern Bugle	Pu/B Pr	
Orthosiphon aristatus (-)	Cat's Whiskers	W/M	
Plectranthus species	Native Coleus	B/Pu	
Westringia species	Westringias	W/P/M Pr	
Malvaceae			
Hibiscus diversifolius	Swamp Hibiscus	Y Pr	
Hibiscus geranioides (-)	Geranium Hibiscus	Pk	
Melastoma affine	Pink Lasiandra	Pk/M Pr	
Mimosaceae			
Acacia complanata	Flat-stem Wattle	Y Pr	
Acacia hubbardiana	Yellow Prickly Moses	Y Pr	
Acacia juncifolia	Rush-leaf wattle	Cr Pr	
Acacia suaveolens	Sweet Wattle	Cr Pr	
Acacia ulicifolia	Prickly Moses	Cr Pr	
Myoporaceae			
Eremophila species (-)	Emu/Turkey/Fuchsia Bushes	W/Y/Pk/R/M/Pu	
Myrtaceae			
Baeckea (Babingtonia) virgata			
(dwarf forms)	Twiggy Heath Myrtle	W Pr	
Callistemon 'Little John' (-)	Little John Bottlebrush	R	
Callistemon pachyphyllus	Wallum Bottlebrush	R/G/Pk Pr	
Callistemon sieberi	Marsh Bottlebrush	Y Pr	
Leptospermum species	(Dwarf/prostrate forms)	W/Pk Pr	
Melaleuca thymifolia	Thyme Honey Myrtle	W/Pk/M Pr	
Thryptomene species	Thryptomene	W/Pk Pr	
Onagraceae			
Ludwigia peploides	Water Primrose	Y	Wet areas
Proteaceae			
Banksia oblongifolia	Dwarf Banksia	Cr Pr	
Banksia robur	Swamp Banksia	G/Cr Pr	
Grevillia (hybrids)	(Dwarf & prostrate forms)	W/P/R/Y/O etc	
Grevillia leiophylla	Wallum Grevillia	Pk	
Hakea florulenta	Hakea	W Pr	
Hakea plurinervia	Many-vein Hakea	W Pr	
Persoonia species (small)	Geebungs	Y Pr	
Sapindaceae			
Dodonaea rupicola	Velvet Hop Bush	Fr - R	Wet areas
Ranunculaceae			
Ranunculus inundatus	River Buttercup	Y	Wet areas
Ranunculus lappaceus	Common Buttercup	Y	Wet areas

Scientific Name	Common Name	Colour	Comments
Rutaceae			
Boronia species	Boronias	Pk/M/W	
Zieria species	Zierias	W Pk Pr	
Scrophulariaceae			
Artanema fimbriatum	Koala Bells	Pu	
Stylidiaceae			
Stylidium species	Trigger Plants	Pk/M	
Thymeliaceae			
Pimelea species	Riceflower	W/Pk	
Verbenaceae			
Callicarpa pedunculata	Velvet Leaf	Fl - Pk/M Fr - Pu	
Violaceae			
Viola betonicifolia	Purple Violet	Pu	
Viola hederacea	Native Violet	W & B	

Fishing at Dohles Rocks (PRSC)

7

Bushland Weeds

Many of these plants are also common weeds of the garden and should be removed and disposed of by composting thoroughly. They should not be dumped in bushland areas.

Form: S = Shrub; T = Tree; P = Palm; V = Vine; G = Grass; Se = Sedge; H = Herb; eH = epiphytic Herb; aH = aquatic Herb; eO = epiphytic Orchid; tO = terrestrial Orchid; eF = epiphytic Fern; tF = terrestrial Fern; aF = aquatic Fern

Control Method: Cp = Cut and paint; Sp = Scrape stem and paint; Cd = Chip and dab; Sf = spray foliage; Hp = Hand pull; D = Dig out; Lc = Lift and cut; C = Cut. CSf = cut, allow regrowth and then spray foliage. See pages 117 &118.
Weed Potential: + = weed; ++ = serious weed; +++ = very serious weed; ++++ = diabolical

(-) = may not occur in the Pine Rivers Valley.

Scientific Name	Common Name	Form	Comments
Pinaceae			
Pinus elliotii	Slash Pine	T	Cp Cd ++
Agavaceae			
Agave species	Yucca/Century Plant	H	Cp ++
Araceae			
Pistia stratiotes	Water Lettuce	aH	Hp +++
Arecaceae			
Archontophoenix alexandrae	Alexandra Palm	P	C ++
Arecastrum romanzoffianum	Queen Palm	P	C +
Commelinaceae			
Tradescantia albiflora	Wandering Jew	H	Lc +++
Zebrina pendula	Purple Wandering Jew	H	Lc ++
Cyperaceae			
Cyperus eragrostis	Umbrella Sedge	Se	Hp D ++
Cyperus papyrus	Papyrus	Se	D CSf ++
Cyperus rotundus	Nut Grass	Se	Hp D +
Cyperus sesquiflorus	Kyllinga Weed	Se	Hp D +
Lilaceae			
Protasparagus americanus	Asparagus Vine	V	D +++
Protasparagus densiflorus	Asparagus Fern	V	D +++
Protasparagus plumosa	Asparagus Vine	V	D +++

Scientific Name	Common Name	Form	Comments
Nymphaeceae			
Nymphaea capensis	Blue Waterlily	aH	Hp D +
Poaceae			
Brachyaria mutica	Para Grass	G	D +++
Chloris gayana	Rhodes Grass	G	D ++
Cortaderia sellowiana	Pampas Grass	G	D CSf ++
Digitaria sanguinalis	Summer Grass	G	D +
Eleusine indica	Crowsfoot Grass	G	Hp D +
Leptochloa digitata	Cane Grass	G	D CSf +
Melinus minutiflora	Molasses Grass	G	D ++
Panicum maximum	Guinea Grass	G	D CSf ++
Paspalum dilatatum	Paspalum	G	D CSf ++
Pennisetum clandestinum	Kikuya Grass	G	Sf +
Pennisetum purpureum	Elephant Grass	G	D CSf +
Rhynchelytrum repens	Red Natal Grass	G	Sf +
Setaria species	Pigeon Grass	G	D CSf ++
Sorghum halepense	Johnson Grass	G	D CSf ++
Acanthaceae			
Hypoestes phyllostachya	Polka Dot Plant	H	Lc ++
Thunbergia alata	Black-eyed Susan	V	Hp Sp +
Amaranthaceae			
Amaranthus spinosus	Needle Burr	H	D +
Anacardiaceae			
Mangifera indica	Mango	T	Cp Cd +
Schinus terebinthifolius	Broad-leafed Pepper	S	Cp Cd +++
Apiaceae			
Apium leptophyllum	Slender Celery	H	D +
Apocynaceae			
Vinca rosea	Madagascar Periwinkle	H	Hp D ++
Araliaceae			
Schefflera actinophylla	Umbrella Tree	T	Cp +++
Asclepiadaceae			
Araujia hortorum	Moth Vine	V	Hp D ++
Asclepias curvassavica	Red Cotton Bush	S	Hp D +
Gomphocarpus physocarpus	Balloon Cotton Bush	S	Hp D ++
Asteraceae			
Ageratum houstonianum	Billy Goat Weed	H	Hp D +++
Baccharis halimifolia	Groundel	S	Cp Cd +++
Bidens pilosa	Cobbler's Pegs	H	Hp D +
Circium vulgare	Scotch Thistle	H	D ++
Crassocephalum crepidioides	Thickhead	H	Hp D ++
Eupatorium adenophorum	Croften Weed	H	Hp D ++

Scientific Name	Common Name	Form	Comments	
Eupatorium riparium	Mist Weed	H	Hp D	++
Gnaphalium	Cudweed	H	Hp D	+
Gymnocoronis spilanthoides	Senegal Tea	H	Hp D	+++
Hypochoeris radicata	Flatweed	H	Hp D	+
Sonchus oleraceus	Common Sow Thislte	H	Hp D	+
Tagetes minuta	Stinking Roger	H	Hp D	++
Wedelia trilobata	Singapore Daisy	H	Lc	++++
Basalaceae				
Anredera cordifolia	Madiera Vine	V	Sp	+++
Bignoniaceae				
Jacaranda mimosaefolia	Jacaranda	T	Cp Cd	++
Macfadyena unguis-cati	Cat's Claw Creeper	V	Cp D	++++
Spathodea campanulata	African Tulip Tree	T	Cp Cd	++
Cactaceae				
Hylocerius undatus	Climbing Cactus	V	Cp D	+
Opuntia spp.	Prickly Pear	S	Cp D	+
Caesalpiniaceae				
Caesalpinia decapetala	Wait-a-while	V	Cp Cd	+
Cassia didymobotrya	Ethiopian Cassia	S	Cp Cd	+
Cassia floribunda	Arsenic Bush	S	Cp Cd	+
Senna pendula	Easter Cassia	S	Cp Cd	++
Cannaceae				
Canna indica	Canna	H	D	++
Caprifoliaceae				
Lonicera japonica	Honeysuckle Vine	V	Lc	++
Convolvulaceae				
Ipomoea cairica	Mile-a-minute	V	Cp D	++
Ipomoea purpurea	Common Morning Glory	V	Cp D	++
Crassulaceae				
Bryophyllum spp.	Mother-of-millions	H	Hp Lc	+++
Cucurbitaceae				
Lagenaria siceraria	Bottle Gourd	V	Cp	+
Ebenaceae				
Diospyros kaki	Persimmon	T	Cp Cd	+
Euphorbiaceae				
Euphorbia hirta	Asthma Plant	H	Hp	+
Ricinus communis	Castor Oil Plant	S	Cp Cd	+++
Sapium sebiferum	Chinese Tallow Tree	T	Cp Cd	+

Scientific Name	Common Name	Form	Comments
Fabaceae			
Crotalaria grahamiana	Graham's Rattlepod	S	Hp Cp +
Crotalaria spectabilis	Showy Rattlepod	H	Hp +
Desmodium tortuosum	Florida Beggar Weed	H	D +
Desmodium uncinatum	Silverleaf Desmodium	H	D ++
Erythrina crista-galli	Cockscomb Coral	S	Cp Cd ++
Erythrina x sykesii	Coral Tree	T	Cp Cd ++
Indigofera suffruticosa	American Indigo	S	Hp Cp +
Leucaena leucocephala	Leucaena	S	Cp Cd ++
Macroptilium atropurpureum	Siratro	V	Cp D ++
Macroptilium lathyroides	Phasey Bean	H/V	Hp +
Neonotonia wightii	GlycineVine	V	Cp Lc ++++
Tephrosia glomulifera	Pink Tephrosia	S	Hp Cp ++
Tipuana tipu	Pride of Bolivia	T	Cp Cd +
Vicia monantha	Spurred Vetch	H	Hp +
Flacourtiaceae			
Flacourtia catafracta	Madagascar Plum	T	Cp Cd ++
Haloragaceae			
Myriophyllum aquaticum	Parrot's Feathers	aH	Hp +++
Lamiaceae			
Salvia coccinea	Red Salvia	H	Hp +
Lauraceae			
Cinnamomum camphoratum	Camphor Laurel	T	Cp Cd ++++
Lythraceae			
Lagerstroemia indica	Pride of India	T	Cp Cd +
Moraceae			
Ficus benjamninii	Weeping Fig	T	Cp Cd ++
Ficus elastica	Indian Rubber Tree	T	Cp Cd ++
Morus alba	White Mulberry	S/T	Cp Cd ++
Morus nigra	Mulberry	S/T	Cp Cd ++
Myrsinaceae			
Ardisia crispa	Ardisia	S	Cp Cd +
Myrtaceae			
Eucalyptus torelliana	Cadaga	T	Cp Cd +++
Eugenia uniflora	Brazilian Cherry	S/T	Cp Cd ++
Psidium guajava	Common Guava	S	Cp Cd +++
Nymphaceaceae			
Nymphaea caerulea (N. capensis)	Cape Waterlily	aH	Hp +
Ochnaceae			
Ochna serrulata	Ochna	S	Cp Cd +++

Scientific Name	Common Name	Form	Comments
Oleaceae			
Ligustrum lucidum	Broad-leafed Privot	S/T	Cp Cd +++
Ligustrum sinense	Small-leafed Privot	S/T	Cp Cd +++
Onagraceae			
Oenothera affinis	Evening Primrose	H	D +
Oxalidaceae			
Oxalis corymbosa	Pink Shamrock	H	D +
Papaveraceae			
Argemone ochraleuca	Prickly Poppy	H	Hp D +
Passifloraceae			
Passiflora edulis	Common Passionfruit	V	Hp Cp +
Passiflora foetida	Stinking Passionfruit	V	Hp Cp +
Passiflora suberosa	Corky Passionfruit	V	Hp Cp ++
Passiflora subpeltata	White Passionfruit	V	Hp Cp ++
Phytolaccaceae			
Phytolacca octandra	Ink Weed	H	Hp Cp +
Rivina humilus	Coral Berry	H	Hp +++
Polygonaceae			
Polygonum spp.	Smart Weeds	H	Hp CSf ++
Rumex crispus	Curled Dock	H	Hp D +
Pontederiaceae			
Eichornia crassipes	Water Hyacinth	aH	Hp +++
Portulacaceae			
Solanaceae			
Cestrum parqui	Green Cestrum	S	Cp +++
Solanum americanum	Glossy Nightshade	H	Hp Cp +
Solanum capsicastrum	False Jerusalem Cherry	S	Hp Cp +
Solanum capsicoides	Devil's Apple	S	Cp +
Solanum hermannii	Apple of Sodom	S	Cp +
Solanum hispidum	Giant Devil's Fig	S	Cp Cd +++
Solanum mauritianum	Wild Tobacca	S	Cp ++
Solanum pseudocapsicum	Jerusalem Cherry	S	Hp Cp ++
Solanum seaforthianum	Brazilian Nightshade	V	Cp Sp ++
Ulmaceae			
Celtis sinensis	Chinese Elm	T	Cp Cd +++
Urticaceae			
Urtica urens	Stinging Nettle	H	D +
Verbenaceae			
Duranta repens	Pigeon Berry	S	Cp +

Scientific Name	Common Name	Form	Comments
Lantana camera	Lantana	S	Cp CSf D +++
Lantana montevidensis	Creeping Lantana	S	Ls ++
Stachytarpheta jamaicensis	Snakeweed	H	Hp Lc ++
Verbena bonariensis	Purple Top	H	Hp D +
Verbena littoralis	Wild Verbena	H	Hp D +
Nephrolepidaceae			
Nephrolepis sp.	Fishbone Fern	tF	Hp D Lc +++
Salviniaceae			
Salvinia molesta	Salvinia	aF	Hp +++

Bush Track - Cedar Creek Falls (KH)

Exotic Garden Plants/Weeds, and Replacement Native Plants

Exotic/Weeds	Native Plants To Replace These
Pinaceae	
Exotic Pine Spp.	Brown Pine, Hoop Pine, Bribie Is Pine, Bailey's Cypress, Scrub Cypress, Bunya Pine, Kauri Pine
Agavaceae	
Agave or Yukka	River Lily, Spear Lily
Arecaceae	
Alexandra Palm	Picabean Palm, Walking Stick Palm,
Queen Palm	Picabean Palm, Cabbage Tree Palm, Pandanus Palm
Commeliniaceae	
Wandering Jew &	Scurvey Plant (Native Wandering Jew), Aneilema, Pollia, Oplismenus,
Purple Wandering Jew	Ottochloa, Native Violet
Cyperaceae	
Umbrella Sedge &	Swamp Foxtail, Lomandra, Carex species, Gahnia, Lomandra
Papyrus	
Liliaceae	
Asparagus Vine	Wombat Berry, Scrambling Lily, Sweet Sarsparilla, Barbed-wire Vine, Wonga Vine
Asparagus Fern	Rough Maidenhair, Cartilage Fern, Basket Fern, Wombat Berry, Scrambling Lily
Lilies	River Lily, Brisbane Lily, Dianellas
Nymphaeceae	
Blue Waterlily	Giant Water Lily, Native Water Lily, Water Snowflake, Wavy Marshwort, Star Fringe, Swamp Lily
Poaceae	
Pampas Grass	Swamp Foxtail, Lomandra, Gahnia, Common Reeds
Grasses - Rhodes,	Grasses - Kangaroo, Wallaby, Barbwire, Black Spear, Swamp Foxtail,
Paspalum, Guinea,	Cockatoo, Wiry Panic, Love, Tussock, & Blady
Red Natal, Para,	
Crowsfoot, Pigeon,	
& Johnson	
Lawn Grasses	For sunny areas - Green Couch (native), Creeping Beard Grass.
(exotic)	For shady areas - Creeping Beard Grass, Pademelon Grass, Ottochloa, Native Violet, Centella, Condamine 'Couch'.

Exotic/Weeds	Native Plants To Replace These

Zingiberaceae
Ginger — Native Ginger, Wild Ginger, Palm Lilies, Dianella, Walking Stick Palm

Acacanthaceae
Black-eyed Susan — Twining Guinea Flower

Anacardiaceae
Broad-leaf Pepper — Brisbane Laurel, Native Mock Orange, Koda

Apocynaceae
Periwinkle — Everlasting Daisies, Forest Daisies, Native Peperomia

Araceae
Water Lettuce — Azolla, Duckweed

Araliaceae
Umbrella Tree — Rock Fig, Sandpaper Fig, Tuckeroo, Davidson's Plum, Native Tamarind, Macaranga

Aristolocaeae
Dutchman's Pipe — Richmond Birdwing Vine, Pipe Vine (native)

Asclepidadaceae
Moth Vine — Hoya australis, Bower-of-Beauty, Wonga Vine

Asteraceae
Billy Goat Weed, Crofton Weed & Mist Weed — Native Coleus, Native Cockspur Flower, Southern Bugle, Soft Bracken, Cat's Whiskers, Binung, Midyim

Groundsel Bush — Ball Honey Myrtle, Snow in Summer, Threadbark Myrtle, Twiggy Heath Myrtle, Wild May

Singapore Daisy — Twining Guinea Flower, Yellow Buttons, Prostrate Grevilleas, Midyim, Boobiala, Pollia

Basalaceae
Madiera Vine — Hoya australis, Slender Grape, Small-leaf Water Vine, Native Wisteria, Milk Vines

Bignoniaceae
Jacaranda — White Cedar, Red Cedar, Koda
Cat's Claw Creeper — Bower of Beauty, Wonga Vine, Monkey Rope,
African Tulip Tree — Black Bean, Flame Tree, Wheel-of-Fire, Oreocallis (Alloxylon),Tulipwood, Pyramid Tree

Caesalpiniaceae
Cassia spp — Silver Cassia, Native Laburnum, Velvet Bean, Sophora

Cannaceae
Canna — River Lily, Native Ginger, Kangaroo Paws, Flax Lilies, Palm Lily, Spear Lily

Exotic/Weeds	Native Plants To Replace These
Caprifoliaceae	
Japanese Honeysuckle	Golden Guinea Flower, Bower of Beauty, Hoya australis
Convolvulaceae	
Morning Glory &	Native Wisteria, Bower-of-beauty, Swamp Bindweed, Forest Bindweed,
Mile-a-minute	Dusky Coral Pea
Crassulaceae	
Mother-of-Millions	Native Coleus, Native Cockspur Flower, Pig Face, Cartilage Fern
Ebenaceae	
Persimmon	Native Ebonies, Lilly Pilly, Water Gum
Euphorbiaceae	
Castor Oil Plant	Macaranga, Qld Bleeding Heart
Fabaceae	
Cockscomb Coral	Bat's Wing Coral, Little Kurrajong
Coral Tree	Bat's Wing Coral, Flame Tree, Wheel of Fire, Oreocallis (Alloxylon)
Leucaena	
Pink Tephrosia	Acacia spp, Lace Flowers, Thyme Honey Myrtle, Hovea spp, Little Kurrajong
Pride of Bolivia	Acacia species, Snow Wood
Lamiaceae	
Red Salvia	Bottlebrush 'Little John', Golden Everlastings
Lauraceae	
Camphor Laurel	Native Laurels, Hard Quondong
Lythraceae	
Pride of India	Lagerstroemia archeriana, Bottlebrushes, Grevilleas, Melastoma
Malvaceae	
Hibiscus species	Native Hibiscus, Native Rosella
Mimosacee	
Zig-zag Wattle	Brisbane Wattle, Eprepah Wattle, Flat-stem Wattle
Moraceae	
Mulberry	Native Mulberry, Peanut Tree, Koda
Rubber Tree	Moreton Bay Fig, Watkins's Fig
Weeping Fig	Small-leaf Fig, White Fig
Myrsinaceae	
Ardisia	Palm Lilies, Native Ginger
Myrtaceae	
Brazilian Cherry	Blue Lilly Pilly, Small-leaf Water Gum
Cadaga	Moreton Bay Ash, Grey Gum, Bloodwoods
Common Guava	Native Guava, Bolwarra, Scaly Myrtle, Thread-bark Myrtle

Exotic/Weeds	Native Plants To Replace These
Ochnaceae	
Ochna (Mickey-Mouse Plant)	Native Coffee (Breynia), Graptophyllum
Oleaceae	
Privet	Mock Olives, Native Olive, Graptophyllum
Passifloraceae	
Passionfruits	Red Passion Flower, Yellow Passion Flower
Phytolaccaceae	
Ink Weed &	Velvet leaf, Tie Bush, Native
Coral Berry	Coffee(Breynia), Palm Lilies
Rosaceae	
Loquat	Cudgerie (Grease Nut), Brown Kurrajong
Indian Hawthorn	Smooth Psychotria, Graptophyllum
Rutaceae	
Mock Orange	Murraya ovatifoliolata (Native Mock Orange), Brisbane Laurel, Lilly Pilly
(Murraya)	(small forms).
Salicaceae	
Weeping Willow	Weeping Bottlebrush, Weeping Lilly Pilly
Pencil Willow	River She Oak, Lilly Pilly, Sand-paper Figs, Rock Fig
Verbenaceae	
Lantana	Velvet Leaf, Peach Leaf, Chain Fruit, Orange Thorn, Currant Bush, Round Lime, Blackthorn, Black-fruit Thornbush
Creeping Lantana	Vitex ovata, Condamine Couch, Native Violet, Purple Violet, Hardenbergia, Dog Rose
Nephrolepidaceae	
Fishbone Fern	Basket Fern, Rough Maidenhair, Mulga Fern, Rock Fern, Cartilage Fern

NORTHSIDE TRUSSES
& FRAMES • 8812000

Landscaping of industrial premises (PRSC)

Some Butterflies and Larval Food Plants of Pine Rivers

Butterflies		Some Plant Foods
Hesperidae (Skippers)		
Cephrenes augiades	Orange Palmdart	Palm species
Ocybadiastes walkeri	Yellow-banded Dart	Grass species
Papilionidae (Swallowtails)		
Cressida cressida	Big Greasy	Aristolochia species
Graphium euryplus	Pale-green Triangle	Custard apple; zigzag vine
Graphium sarpedon	Blue Triangle	Camphor laurel and some other Lauraceae; Macaranga; custard apple
Papilio aegeus	Orchard Butterfly	Citrus; Microcitrus
Papilio anactus	Dingy Swallowtail	Flindersia; Achronychia
Papilio demoleus	Chequered Swallowtail	Citrus; some Papilionaceae
Pieridae (Whites and Yellows)		
Anapheus java	Caper White	Capparis species
Catopsilia pomona	Lemon Migrant	Cassia species
Delius argenthona	Northern Jezabel	Mistletoe species
Delius nigrina	Common Jezabel	Mistletoe species
Eurema hecabe	Common Grass Yellow	Phyllanthus; Sesbania; Breynia
Eurema smilax	Small Grass Yellow	Cassia species
Pieris rapae	Cabbage White	Cabbage; cauliflower etc
Lycaenidae (Blues and Coppers)		
Candalides absimilis	Pencilled Blue	Macadamia; Millettia; black bean; tuckeroo; flame tree
Danis hymetus	Small Green-banded Blue	Alphitonia excelsa
Hypochrysops delicia	Blue Jewel	Wattles
Hypochrysops ignita	Feiry Jewel	Banksias
Ogris amaryllis	Amaryllis Azure	Mistletoe (eg *Amyema cambagei*)
Neolucia sulpitius	Saltpan Blue	Various Chenopodiaceae
Zizina labradus	Common Grass Blue	Clover
Nymphalidae (Nymphs and Browns)		
Acraea andromacha	Glasswing	Passiflora species

Butterflies		Some Plant Foods
Danaus affinus	Black and White Tiger	A few Asclepiadaceae
Danaus chrysippus	Lesser Wanderer	Red cotton bush; balloon cotton bush
Danaus hamatus	Blue Tiger	Parsonsia
Danaus plexippus	Wanderer	Red cotton bush; balloon cotton bush
Euploea core	Common Crow	Ficus species; Parsonsia; Oleander
Hypolimnas bolina	Common Eggfly	Portulaca; Sida species
Junonia villida	Meadow Argus	Centarium; plantains; Portulaca
Phaedyma shepherdi	Common Aeroplane	Pongamia; burny bean; native elm; Flame Tree; Chinese elm
Polyura pyrrhus	Tailed Emperor	Acacia; Cassia; camphor laurel; Brachychiton; Celtis; Poinsiana
Melanitis leda	Evening Brown	Blady grass; other grasses

Note: This list contains some plant food species that are introduced invasive weeds. Do not plant these.

Old Scribbly Gum - a wildlife habitat tree (PRSC)

APPENDIX **10**

Fire Retardant Native Plants

<u>Form</u>: S = Shrub; T = Tree; V = Vine; H = Herb; Gc = Ground cover; eO = epyphytic Orchid; eF = epyphytic Fern; tF = terrestrial Fern.

<u>Fire-retardance</u>: Lm = due to leaf water contents; St = due to salt content; Sl = succulent leaves

<u>Comments</u>: Wb = suitable for windbreak/fire barrier; Ad = suitable as addition to windbreak/fire barrier but not as main species; Us = suitable for understory of windbreak/fire barrier; Oa = suitable for open areas near house; Sa = suitable for sheltered areas near house; Pf = suitable if protected from direct flames; De = Deciduous in winter, in flower or in dry periods

(-) = may not occur naturally in Pine Rivers Valley but has not proved invasive.

Fire-Retardant Plants for Small Gardens

Scientific Name	Common Name	Form	Fire Retardance	Comments
GYMNOSPERMS				
Zamaceae				
Lepidozamia peroffskyana	Shining Burrawang	S	Lm	Us Sa
Macrozamia lucida	Pineapple Zamia	S	Lm	Us Sa
Macrozamia miquelii	Wild Pineapple	S	Lm	Us Oa Sa
Agavaceae				
Cordyline petiolaris	Broad-leaf Palm Lily	S	Lm	Us Sa
Cordyline rubra	Red-fruit Palm Lily	S	Lm	Us Sa
Cordyline strica	Slender Palm Lily	S	Lm	Us Sa
MONOCOTYLEDONS				
Amaryllidaceae				
Crinum pedunculatum	River Lily	H	Lm Sl	Us Oa Sa
Doryanthes palmeri (-)	Spear Lily	H	Lm Sl	Us Oa Sa
Proiphys cunninghamii	Brisbane Lily	H	Lm Sl	Us Sa
Araceae				
Alocasia brisbanensis	Cunjevoi	H	Lm	Us Sa
Gymnostachys anceps	Settlers Flax	H	Lm	Us Sa
Pothos longipes	Pothos	V	Lm	Us Sa
Typhonium brownii	Stinking Lily	H	Lm	Us Sa
Arecaceae				
Linospadix monostachya	Walking Stick Palm	P	Lm	Us Sa

Scientific Name	Common Name	Form	Fire Retardance	Comments
Commelinaceae				
Aneilema acuminatum	Aneilema	H Gc	Lm	Us Sa
Aneilema biflorum (-)	Aneilema	H Gc	Lm	Us Sa
Commelina cyanea	Scurvy Plant	H Gc	Lm	Us Op Sa
Pollia crispata	Snake Weed	H Gc	Lm	Us Sa
Pollia macrophylla	Large Snake Weed	H Gc	Lm	Us Sa
Dioscoraceae				
Dioscorea transversa	Native Yam	V	Lm	Us Sa
Lillaceae				
Bulbine bulbosa (-)	Bulbine Lily	H	Lm Sl	Oa
Dianella brevipedunculata	Blue Flax Lily	H	Lm	Us Oa Sa
Dianella caerulea	Blue Flax Lily	H	Lm	Us Oa Sa
Dianella revoluta	Flax Lily	H	Lm	Us Oa Sa
Drymophila moorei (-)	Orange Berry	H	Lm	Us Sa
Tripladenia cunninghamii	Bush Lily	H	Lm	Us Sa
Orchidaceae				
Dendrobium gracilicaule	Spotted Orchid	eO	Lm	Sa
Dendrobium X gracillimum	Natural Hybrid	eO	Lm	Sa
Dendrobium monophyllum	Lily of the Valley Orchid	eO	Lm	Sa
Dendrobium schoeninim (D. beckleri)	Pencil Orchid	eO	Lm	Sa
Dendrobium speciosum	King Orchid	eO	Lm	Sa
Dendrobium teretifolium	Bridal Veil Orchid	eO	Lm	Sa
Dendrobium tetragonum	Spider Orchid	eO	Lm	Sa
Philesiaceae				
Eustrephus latifolius	Wombat Berry	V	Lm	Us Oa Sa
Geitonoplesium cymosum	Scrambling Lily	V	Lm	Us Sa
Philydraceae				
Philydrum lanuginosum	Frogsmouth	aH	Lm Sl	Oa Wet areas
Smilacaceae				
Smilax glycophylla	Sweet Sarsparilla	V	Lm	Us Sa
Xanthorrhoeaceae				
Lomandra confertifolia	Mat Rush	H	Lm	Oa
Lomandra hystrix	Creek Mat Rush	H	Lm	Us Sa
Lomandra longifolia	Long-leaf Mat Rush	H	Lm	Us Oa Sa
Lomandra filiformis	Fine-leaf Mat Rush	H	Lm	Oa
Lomandra multiflora	Many-flower Mat Rush	H	Lm	Oa
Lomandra spicata	Mountain Mat Rush	H	Lm	Us Oa Sa
Zingiberaceae				
Alpinia arundeliana	Wild Ginger	H	Lm	Us Sa
Alpinia coerulea	Native Ginger	H	Lm	Us Sa

Scientific Name	Common Name	Form	Fire Retardance	Comments
DICOTYLEDONS				
Aizoaceae				
Carpobrotus glaucescens	Pig Face	H Gc	Lm Sl	Oa
Acanthaceae				
Graptophyllum excelsum (-)	Scarlet Fuchsia	S	Lm	Us Sa
Graptophyllum spinigerum	Samford Holly	S	Lm	Us Sa
Pseuderanthemum tenellum	Pseuderanthemum	H	Lm	Us Sa
Pseuderanthemum variabile	Love Flower	H	Lm	Us Sa
Apiaceae				
Centella australis	Pennywort	H Gc	Lm	Oa
Hydrocotyle acutiloba	Pennywort	H Gc	Lm	Us Sa
Hydrocotyle pedicellosa	Pennywort	H Gc	Lm	Us Sa
Apocynaceae				
Alyxia ruscifolia	Chain fruit	S	Lm	Us Sa
Carissa ovata	Current Bush	S	Lm	Us Oa Sa
Neisosperma poweri (-)	Milkbush	S	Lm	Us Sa
Ochrosia moorei (-)	Southern Ochrosia	S	Lm	Us Sa
Parsonsia lenticellata	Narrow-leaf Silkpod	V	Lm	Us Sa
Parsonsia lilacina	Delicate Silkpod	V	Lm	Us Sa
Tabernaemontana pandacaqui	Banana Bush	S	Lm	Us Sa
Aristolochiaceae				
Aristolochia sp. aff. pubera	Pipe Vine	V	Lm	Us Sa
Aristolochia praevenosa	Richmond Birdwing Vine	V	Lm	Us Sa
Asclepiadaceae				
Hoya australis	Wax Flower	V	Lm	Us Sa
Marsdenia longiloba	Slender Milk Vine	V	Lm	Us Sa
Secamone elliptica	Corky Milk Vine	V	Lm	Us Sa
Tylophora paniculata	Thin-leaf Tylophora	V	Lm	Us Sa
Bignoniaceae				
Pandorea floribunda	New sp. Pine R	V	Lm	Us Oa Sa
Pandorea jasminoides	Bower of Beauty	V	Lm	Us Oa Sa
Caesalpineaceae				
Cassia artemisioides (-)	Silver Cassia	S		Oa
Campanulaceae				
Lobelia trigonocaulis	Forest Lobelia	H Gc	Lm	Us Oa
Wahlenbergia gracilis	Bluebells	H		Oa
Capparaceae				
Capparus arborea	Native Caper	S/T	Lm	Us Sa
Capparis sarmentosa	Scrambling Caper	V	Lm	Us Sa

Scientific Name	Common Name	Form	Fire Retardance	Comments
Celastraceae				
Cassine australis	Red Olive Berry	S/T	Lm	Us Sa
Denhamia celastroides	Orange Boxwood	S/T	Lm	Us Sa
Denhamia pittosporoides	Orange Boxwood	S/T	Lm	Us Sa
Maytenus bilocularis	Orangebark	S/T	Lm	Us Sa
Chenopodiaceae				
Einadia hastata	Berry Salt Bush	S Gc	St	Oa
Enchylaena tomentosa	Ruby Salt Bush	S Gc	St Sl	Oa
Halosarcia indica	Samphire	S Gc	St Sl	Oa Salty soil
Sarcocornia quinqueflora	Samphire	S Gc	St Sl	Oa Salty soil
Suaeda australis	Seablite	S Gc	St Sl	Oa Salty soil
Suaeda arbusculoides	Jellybean Plant	S Gc	St Sl	Oa Salty soil
Convolulaceae				
Convolulus erubescens	Australian Bindweed	V	Lm	Oa
Dichondra repens	Kidney Weed	H Gc	Lm	Us Sa
Polymeria calycina	Swamp Bindweed	V	Lm	Oa
Cunoniaceae				
Aphanopetalum resinosum	Gum Vine	V Gc	Lm	Us Sa
Vesselowskya rubifolia (-)	Southern Marara	S/T	Lm	Us Sa
Davidsoniaceae				
Davidsonia pruriens (-)	Davidson's Plum	T	Lm	Us Sa
Dilleniaceae				
Hibbertia aspera	Rough Guinea Flower	S	Lm	Oa
Hibbertia dentata	Toothed Guinea Flower	V	Lm	Us Oa Sa
Hibbertia linearis	Showy Guinea Flower	S	Lm	Oa
Hibbertia obtusifolia	Hoary Guinea Flower	S	Lm	Oa
Hibertia stricta	Erect Guinea Flower	S	Lm	Oa
Hibbertia scandens	Twining Guinea Flower	V	Lm	Us Oa Sa
Elaeocarpaceae				
Elaeocarpus reticulatus	Blueberry Ash	S/T	Lm	Us Oa Sa
Epacridaceae				
Trochocarpa laurina	Tree Heath	S/T	Lm	Us Sa
Escalloniaceae				
Abrophyllum ornans	Native Hydrangea	S	Lm	Us Sa
Polyosma cunninghamii	Featherwood	S/T	Lm	Us Sa
Euphorbiaceae				
Acalypha capillipes	Small-leaf Acalypha	S	Lm	Us Sa
Acalypha eremorum	Native Acalypha	S	Lm	Us Sa
Acalypha nemorum	Southern Acalypha	S	Lm	Us Sa
Actephila lindleyi	Actephila	S/T	Lm	Us Sa
Alchornea ilicifolia	Native Holly	S	Lm	Us Sa
Breynia oblongifolia	Native Coffee Bush	S	Lm	Us Oa Sa
Cleistanthes cunninghamii	Cleistanthes	S/T	Lm	Us Sa

Scientific Name	Common Name	Form	Fire Retardance	Comments
Croton phlebaliodes	Narrow-leaf Croton	S	Lm	Us Sa
Croton verreauxii	Native Cascarilla	S/T	Lm	Us Sa
Macaranga tanarius	Macaranga	S/T	Lm	Us
Mallotus claoxyloides	Scrub Odour Bush	S/T	Lm	Us Sa
Omalanthus nutans				
(O. populifolius)	Qld Bleeding Heart	S/T	Lm	Us Sa
Eupomatiaceae				
Eupomatia bennettii	Small Bolwarra	S	Lm	Us Sa
Eupomatia laurina	Bolwarra	S	Lm	Us Sa
Escaloneaceae				
Cuttsia viburnea (-)	Native Elderberry	T	Lm	Us Sa
Fabaceae				
Abrus precatorius	Crabs Eye Vine	V	Lm	Us Oa Sa
Aotus lanigera	Pointed Aotis	S	Lm	Oa Sa
Glycine clandestina	Twining Glycine	V	Lm	Oa
Glycine tomentella	Wooly Glycine	V	Lm	Oa
Hardenbergia violacea	False Sarsparilla	V	Lm	Oa
Hovea linearis	Common Hovea	S	Lm	Oa
Hovea longipes (-)	Brush Hovea	S	Lm	Sa
Indigophora australis	Australian Indigo	S	Lm	Oa
Kennedia rubicunda	Dusky Coral Pea	V	Lm	Oa
Oxylobium ilicifolium (-)	Holly Pea	S	Lm	Oa
Oxylobium scandens (-)	Netted Shaggy Pea	S	Lm	Oa
Pultenaea retusa	Blunt-leaf Bush Pea	S	Lm	Oa
Pultenaea spinulosa (-)	Prickly Pea	S	Lm	Oa
Pultenaea villosa (-)	Hairy Bush Pea	S	Lm	Oa
Swainsona galegifolia	Darling Pea	S	Lm	Oa
Goodeniaceae				
Goodenia rotundifolia	Star Goodenia	H Gc	Lm	Oa
Scaevola aemula (-)	Fairy Fan Flower	H Gc	Lm	Oa
Scaevola albida (-)	Fan Flower	H	Lm	Oa
Scaevola calendulacea (-)	Scented Fan Flower	H Gc	Lm	Oa
Scaevola ramosissima (-)	A Fan Flower	H Gc	Lm	Oa
Lamiaceae				
Ajuga australis	Southern Bugle	H	Lm	Oa
Plectranthus argentatus (-)	Silver Native Coleus	H	Lm	Us Sa
Plectranthus graveolens	Native Coleus	H	Lm	Us Sa
Plectranthus parviflorus	Cockspur Flower	H	Lm	Us Sa
Prostanthera ovalifolia	Oval-leaf Mint Bush	S	Lm	Os Sa
Lauraceae				
Cryptocarya laevigata	Glossy Laurel	S/T	Lm	Us Sa
Cryptocarya meisneriana	Thick-leaf Laurel	S/T	Lm	Us Sa
Leeaceae				
Leea indica (-)	Bandicoot Berry	S	Lm	Us Sa

Scientific Name	Common Name	Form	Fire Retardance	Comments
Lythraceae				
Lagerstroemia archeriana (-)	Native Crepe Myrtle	S/T	Lm	Us Oa Sa De
Malvaceae				
Pavonia hastata (-)	Pavonia	S	Lm	Oa Sa
Hibiscus heterophyllus	Native Rosella	S/T	Lm	Us Sa
Hibiscus geranioides (-)		S	Lm	Oa
Melastomaceae				
Melastoma affine	Pink Lasiandra	S	Lm	Us Sa Oa
Meliaceae				
Turraea pubescens (brownii)	Native Witch-Hazel	S/T	Lm	Us Sa
Menispermaceae				
Pleogyne australis	Pleogyne	V	Lm	Us Sa
Mimosaceae				
Acacia complanata	Flat-stem Wattle	S		Oa Pf
Acacia hubbardiana	Yellow Prickly Moses	S		Oa Pf
Acacia irrorata	Blue Skin	S		Oa Pf
Acacia myrtifolia	Myrtle Wattle	S		Oa Pf
Acacia suaveolens	Sweet Wattle	S		Oa Pf
Acacia ulicifolia	Prickly Moses	S		Oa Pf
Archidendron lovelliae (-)	Baconwood	S/T	Lm	Us Sa
Monimiaceae				
Wilkiea huegeliana	Tetra Beech	S/T	Lm	Us Sa
Wilkiea macrophylla	Large-leaf Wilkiea	S/T	Lm	Us Sa
Myoporaceae				
Eremophila debilis	Winter Apple	S Gc	Lm	Os
Myoporum boninense				
(M. ellipticum)	Boobialla	S Gc	Lm	Os
Myoporum montanum	Mountain Boobialla	S	Lm	Os
Myrsinaceae				
Aegiceras corniculatum	Milky Mangrove	S/T	Lm St	Oa Coastal
Rapanea howittiana	Scrub Muttonwood	S/T	Lm	Us Sa
Rapanea subsessilis	Red Muttonwood	S/T	Lm	Us Sa
Myrtaceae				
Archirhodomyrtus beckleri (-)	Rose Myrtle	S	Lm	Us Sa
Austromyrtus fragrantissima (-)	Sweet Myrtle	T	Lm	Us Sa
Austromyrtus hillii	Scaly Myrtle	S/T	Lm	Us Sa
Austromyrtus inophloia	Thread-bark Myrtle	S/T	Lm	Us Sa
Austromyrtus aff. lasioclada (-)	Velvet Myrtle	T	Lm	Us Sa
Austromyrtus metrosideros (-)		S	Lm	Us Sa
Pilidiostigma glabrum (-)	Plum Myrtle	S	Lm	Us Sa
Pilidiostigma rhytisperma	Small-leaf Plum Myrtle	S	Lm	Us Sa
Rhodamnia acuminata (-)	Cooloola Ironwood	S	Lm	Us Sa

Scientific Name	Common Name	Form	Fire Retardance	Comments
Rhodamnia dumicola	Rib-fruit Malletwood	S/T	Lm	Us Sa
Rhodamnia maidenii (-)	Smooth Scrub Turpentine	S	Lm	Us Sa
Rhodomyrtus psidioides	Native Guava	S	Lm	Us Sa
Syzygium wilsoni (-)	Powder-puff Lilly Pilly	S	Lm	Us Sa
Nyctaginaceae				
Pisonia aculeata	Native Bougainvillia	V	Lm	Us Sa
Oleaceae				
Jasminum simplicifolium	Slender Jasmine	V	Lm	Us Sa
Notelaea ovata	Netted Mock Olive	S	Lm	Us Sa
Notelaea venosa	Veined Mock Olive	S	Lm	Us Sa
Passifloraceae				
Passiflora aurantia	Red Passion Flower	V	Lm	Us Oa Sa
Passiflora herbertiana	Yellow Passion Flower	V	Lm	Us Oa Sa
Peperomiaceae				
Peperomia blanda				
(leptostachya)	Native Peperomia	H	Lm	Us Sa
Peperomia tetraphylla	Native Peperomia	H	Lm	Us Sa
Pittosporaceae				
Citriobatus linearis	Black-fruit Thornbush	S	Lm	Us Sa
Citriobatus paucifloris	Orange Thornbush	S	Lm	Us Sa
Pittosporum revolutum	Brisbane Laurel	S	Lm	Us/Wb Sa/Oa
Proteaceae				
Banksia oblongifolia	Dwarf Banksia	S		Oa Pf
Banksia robur	Swamp Banksia	S		Oa Pf
Grevillea leiophylla	Wallum Grevillea	S		Oa Pf
Grevillea 'Robyn Gordon'	G. 'Robyn Gordon'	S		Oa Pf
Grevillea sericea	Pink Spider Flower	S		Oa Pf
Grevillea 'Shirley Howie'	G. 'Shirley Howie'	S		Oa Pf
Grevillea 'Superb'	G. 'Superb'	S		Oa Pf
Hakea florulenta	Hakea	S		Oa Pf
Hakea purpurea	Purple Hakea	S		Oa Pf
Lambertia formosa (-)	Mountain Devil	S		Oa Pf
Lomatia silaifolia	Crinkle Bush	S		Oa Pf
Stenocarpus angusifolia (-)		S		Oa Pf
Rhizophoraceae				
Bruguiera gymnorrhiza	Orange Mangrove	S/T	Lm St	Oa Coastal
Ceriops tagal	Yellow Mangrove	S/T	Lm St	Oa Coastal
Rhizophora stylosa	Stilted Mangrove	S/T	Lm St	Oa Coastal
Rosaceae				
Rubus parvifolia	Pink Raspberry	S	Lm	Oa
Rubus rosifolius	Native Raspberry	S	Lm	Us Sa
Rubiaceae				
Canthium coprosmoides	Coast Canthium	S/T	Lm	Us Oa Sa
Canthium lamprophyllum	Large-leaf Canthium	S/T	Lm	Us Sa

Scientific Name	Common Name	Form	Fire Retardance	Comments
Canthium microphyllum	Small-leaf Canthium	S	Lm	Us Sa
Ixora bleckleri	Brown Coffeewood	S/T	Lm	Us Sa
Morinda acutifolia	Veiny Morinda	V	Lm	Us Sa
Morinda jasminoides	Sweet Morinda	V	Lm	Us Sa
Pavetta australiensis	Pavetta	S	Lm	Us Sa
Psychotria daphnoides	Smooth Psychotria	S	Lm	Us Sa
Psychotria loniceroides	Hairy Psychotria	S	Lm	Us Sa
Psychotria simmondsiana	Small Psychotria	S	Lm	Us Sa
Randia benthamiana	Native Gardenia	S	Lm	Us Sa
Randia chartacea	Narrow-leaf Gardenia	S	Lm	Us Sa
Rutaceae				
Clausena brevistyla (-)	Clausena	S	Lm	Us Sa
Microcitrus australasica (-)	Finger Lime	S	Lm	Us Sa
Murraya ovatifoliolata (-)	Native Murraya	S/T	Lm	Us Sa
Phebalium woombye (-)	Phebalium	S	Lm	Oa
Sambucaceae				
Sambucus australasica	Yellow Elderberry	S	Lm	Us Sa
Sapindaceae				
Alectryon coriaceus (-)	Beach Bird's Eye	S/T	Lm	Wb Oa
Arytera microphylla (-)	Dwarf Coogara	S	Lm	Us Sa
Cupaniopsis newmanii (-)	Long-leaf Tuckeroo	T	Lm	Us Sa Oa
Cupaniopsis serrata	Rusty Tuckeroo	S/T	Lm	Us Sa Oa
Cupaniopsis wadsworthii (-)	Dwarf Tuckeroo	S	Lm	Us Sa
Harpullia alata (-)	Wing-leaf Tulip	S	Lm	Us Sa
Mischocarpus sundaicus	Red Pear-fruit	T	Lm	Us Sa
Sapotaceae				
Planchonella myrsinoides	Yellow Plumwood	S/T	Lm	Us Sa
Scrophulariaceae				
Artenema fimbriatum	Koala bells	H	Lm	Oa
Tetragoniaceae				
Tetragonia tetragonioides	Native Spinach	H Gc	St Sc	Oa
Solanaceae				
Duboisia myoporoides	Corkwood	S/T	Lm	Us Sa
Solanum aviculare	Kangaroo Apple	S	Lm	Us Sa Oa
Solanum densevestitum (-)	Furry Nightshade	S	Lm	Us Sa
Solanum stelligerum (-)	Star Nightshade	S	Lm	Us Sa
Sterculiaceae				
Brachychiton bidwillii	Little Kurrajong	S	Lm	Us Sa Oa
Commersonia fraserii	Scrub Kurrajong	S	Lm	Us Sa Oa
Symplocaceae				
Symplocus baeuerlenii (-)	Shrubby Hazelwood	S	Lm	Us Sa

Scientific Name	Common Name	Form	Fire Retardance	Comments
Thymeliaceae				
Phaleria clerodendron (-)		S	Lm	Us Sa
Phaleria chermsideana	Scrub Daphne	S/T	Lm	Us Sa
Pimelea linifolia	Slender Rice Flower	S		Oa
Wikstroemia indica	Tie Bush	S	Lm	Us Oa Sa
Tiliaceae				
Corchorus cunninghamii	Corchorus	S	Lm	Us Sa
Urticaceae				
Elatostema reticulatum	Rainforest Spinach	H	Lm	Us Sa
Elatostema stipitatum (-)	Small Soft Nettle	H	Lm	Us Sa
Pipturus argenteus	Native Mulberry	S/T	Lm	Us Sa
Verbenaceae				
Callicarpa pedunculata	Velvet-leaf	S	Lm	Us Sa
Clerodendrum floribundum	Lolly Bush	S/T	Lm	Us Oa Sa
Clerodendrum tomentosum	Hairy Lolly Bush	S/T	Lm	Us Oa Sa
Phyla nodiflora (-)	Condamine Couch	H Gc	Lm	Oa
Vitex ovata (-)	Vitex	S Gc	Lm	Oa
Violaceae				
Viola betonicifolia	Purple Violet	H	Lm	Us Sa
Viola hederacea	Native Violet	H	Lm	Us Sa
Vitaceae				
Cayratia acris	Hairy Water Vine	V	Lm	Us Sa
Cayratia clematidea	Slender Grape	V	Lm	Us Oa Sa
Cayratia eurynema	Soft Water Vine	V	Lm	Us Sa
Cissus opaca	Small-leaf Water Vine	V	Lm	Us Oa Sa
Winteraceae				
Tasmannia insipida	Pepper Bush	S	Lm	Us Sa

PTERIDOPHYTES

Scientific Name	Common Name	Form	Fire Retardance	Comments
Aspleniaceae				
Asplenium attenuatum	A Spleenwort	F	Lm	Sa
Asplenium australasicum	Crow's Nest Fern	eF	Lm	Sa
Osmondaceae				
Todea barbara	King Fern	tF	Lm	Us Sa
Polypodiaceae				
Drynaria rigidula	Basket Fern	eF	Lm	Sa
Phymatodes scandens	Scented Climbing Fern	tF	Lm	Sa
Platycerium bifurcatum	Elkhorn	eF	Lm	Sa
Platycerium superbum	Staghorn	F	Lm	Sa
Pyrrosia confluens	Felt Fern	eF	Lm	Sa
Pyrrosia rupestris	Rock Felt Fern	eF	Lm	Sa

Fire-Retardant Plants for Medium Gardens

The following plants can be used in addition to the list of plants for small gardens.

Scientific Name	Common Name	Form	Fire Retardance	Comments
MONOCOTYLEDONS				
Arecaceae				
Archontophoenix cunninghamii	Picabeen Palm	P	Lm	Ad
Calamus muelleri	Lawyer Cane Vine	P	Lm	Ad
Livistona australis	Cabbage Palm	P	Lm	Ad
Smilacaceae				
Ripogonum fawcettianum	Small Supplejack	V	Lm	Sa
Smilax australis	Barb-wire Vine	V	Lm	Sa Oa
DICOTYLEDONS				
Akaniaceae				
Akania lucens	Turnipwood	T	Lm	Us
Alangiaceae				
Alangium villosum polyosmoides	Muskwood	T	Lm	Us
Alangium villosum tomentosum	Muskwood	T	Lm	Us
Annonaceae				
Polyalthia nitidissima	Canary Beech	T	Lm	Us
Apocynaceae				
Alstonia constricta	Quinine Tree	T	Lm	Us
Melodinus acutiflorus	Merangarra	V	Lm	Sa
Melodinus australis	Southern Melodinus	V	Lm	Sa
Araliaceae				
Cephalaralia cephalobotrys	Climbing Panax	V	Lm	Sa
Bignoniaceae				
Pandorea pandorana	Wonga Vine	V	Lm	Oa Sa
Caesalpiniaceae				
Barklya syringifolia	Crown of Gold Tree	T	Lm	Us Sa Oa
Cassia tomentella (-)	Velvet Bean	S/T	Lm	Us Oa
Cunoniaceae				
Callicoma serratifolia (-)	White Alder	S/T	Lm	Us
Dilleniaceae				
Tecomanthe hillii (-)	Fraser Island Climber	V	Lm	Sa

Scientific Name	Common Name	Form	Fire Retardance	Comments
Ebenaceae				
Diospyros australis	Black Plum	T	Lm	Us/Wb
Diospyros geminata	Scaly Ebony	T	Lm	Us/Wb
Diospyros mabacea (-)	Red-fruited Ebony	T	Lm	Us
Escalloniaceae				
Anopterus macleayanus (-)	Queensland Laurel	T	Lm	Us
Polyalthia nitidissima	Canary Beech	T	Lm	Us
Euphorbiaceae				
Claoxylon australe	Brittlewood	S/T	Lm	Us
Croton achronychioides	Thick-leaved Croton	S/T	Lm	Us
Croton insularis	Queensland Cascarilla	S/T	Lm	Us
Croton stigmatosus	White Croton	T	Lm	Us
Fabaceae				
Erythrina vespertilio	Bat's Wing Coral Tree	T	Lm	Ad De
Hernandiaceae				
Hernandia bivalvis	Cudgerie	T	Lm	Wb
Lauraceae				
Cryptocarya bidwilli	Yellow Laurel	T	Lm	Wb
Cryptocarya meisneriana	Thick-leaf Laurel	T	Lm	Wb
Cryptocarya sclerophylla	Boonah Laurel	T	Lm	Wb
Cryptocarya triplinervis	Brown Laurel	T	Lm	Wb
Cryptocarya triplinervis var. pubens	Hairy Brown Laurel	T	Lm	Wb
Meliaceae				
Owenia venosa	Crow's Apple	T	Lm	Us/Wb
Synoum glandulosum	Scentless Rosewood	S/T	Lm	Us
Turraea pubescens (*T. brownii*)	Native Witch-Hazel	T	Lm	Us
Menispermaceae				
Stephania japonica var. discolor	Tape Vine	V	Lm	Sa Oa
Mimosaceae				
Acacia aulacocarpa	Hickory Wattle	T	Lm	Wb/Pf
Acacia implexa	Light Wood	T	Lm	Wb/Pf
Acacia melanoxylon	Blackwood	T	Lm	Wb/Pf
Acacia cincinnata	Wattle	S/T	Lm	Wb/Pf
Pararchidendron pruinosum	Snowwood	T	Lm	Us/Wb
Moraceae				
Ficus coronata	Creek Sandpaper Fig	T	Lm	Us/Wb
Ficus fraseri	A Sandpaper Fig	T	Lm	Us/Wb
Ficus opposita	A Sandpaper Fig	T	Lm	Us/Wb
Streblus brunonianus (*S. pendulinus*)	Whalebone Tree	T	Lm	Us/Wb

Scientific Name	Common Name	Form	Fire Retardance	Comments
Myoporaceae				
Myoporum acuminatum	Coast Boobialla	S/T	Lm	Wb Oa
Myrsinaceae				
Rapanea variabilis	Muttonwood	T	Lm	Us
Myrtaceae				
Acmena smithii				
(small varieties)	Creek Lilly Pilly	T	Lm	Us/Wb
Decaspermum humile	Silky Myrtle	S/T	Lm	Us
Metrosideros queenslandica (-)	Pink Myrtle	T	Lm	Us
Rhodamnia rubescens	Brown Malletwood	T	Lm	Us/Wb
Syzygium hodgkinsonia (-)	Smooth-bark Rose Apple	T	Lm	Us
Oleaceae				
Notelaea johnsonii	Veinless Mock Olive	S/T	Lm	Us
Notelaea longifolia	Large Mock Olive	S/T	Lm	Us/Wb
Notelaea microcarpa	Velvet Mock Olive	S/T	Lm	Us/Wb
Pittosporaceae				
Hymenosporum flavum	Native Frangipani	T	Lm	Us Ad
Pittosporum undulatum	Mock Orange	T	Lm	Us/Wb
Proteaceae				
Buckinghamia celsissima (-)	Ivory Curl Flower	T	Lm	Wb
Grevillea helmsiae (-)		T	Lm	Us Pf
Hicksbeachia pinnatifolia (-)	Red Boppel Nut	T	Lm	Us Ad Pf
Lomatia arborescens (-)	Tree Lomatia	S/T	Lm	Us Pf
Macadamia integrifolia	Queensland Nut	T	Lm	Wb
Macadamia ternifolia	Maroochy Nut	T	Lm	Wb
Macadamia tetraphylla	Rough Shell Bush Nut	T	Lm	Wb
Triunia youngiana	Spice Bush	T	Lm	Us
Rubiaceae				
Coelospermum paniculatum	Coelospermum	V	Lm	Sa
Hodgkinsonia ovatiflora	Golden Ash	T	Lm	Us/Wb
Rununculaceae				
Clematis glycinoides	Headache Vine	V	Lm	Sa
Rutaceae				
Acronychia imperforata	Coast Aspen	S/T	Lm	Us/Wb
Acronychia pauciflora	Soft Acronychia	S/T	Lm	Us
Microcitrus australis	Round Lime	S	Lm	Us
Sapindaceae				
Alectryon connatus	Alectryon	T	Lm	Wb Slow at first
Alectryon subcinereus	Wild Quince	T	Lm	Wb
Alectryon subdentalus	Holly-leaf Bird's Eye	T	Lm	Wb
Alectryon tomentosus	Hairy Bird's Eye	T	Lm	Wb
Arytera distylis	Twin-leaf Coogera	T	Lm	Wb

Scientific Name	Common Name	Form	Fire Retardance	Comments
Arytera divaricata	Rose Tamarind	T	Lm	Wb
Arytera foveolata	Pitted Coogera	T	Lm	Wb
Cupaniopsis parvifolia	Small-leaf Tuckeroo	T	Lm	Wb
Cupaniopsis shirleyana (-)	Wedge-leaf Tuckeroo	T	Lm	Us/Wb
Cupaniopsis tomentella (-)	Boonah Tuckeroo	T	Lm	Wb
Elattostachys nervosa	Beetroot	T	Lm	Us/Wb
Elattostachys xylocarpa	White Tamarind	T	Lm	Wb
Guioa semiglauca	Wild Quince	T	Lm	Wb
Lepiderema pulchella (-)	Fine-leaf Tuckeroo	T	Lm	Wb
Mischocarpus australis	Red Pear-fruit	T	Lm	Wb
Toechima tenax	Scrub Teak	T	Lm	Wb
Sapotaceae				
Planchonella chartacea	Thin-leaf Plum	S/T	Lm	Us Sa
Planchonella cotinifolia	Small-leaf Plum	S/T	Lm	Us Sa
Simaroubaceae				
Guilfoylia monostylis	Native Plum	T	Lm	Us
Symplocaceae				
Symplocus thwaitesii	Buff Hazelwood	S/T	Lm	Us
PTERIDOPHYTES				
Cyatheaceae				
Cyathea australis	Rough Tree Fern	tF	Lm	Us
Cyathea cooperi	CommonTree Fern	tF	Lm	Us
Cyathea leichhardtiana	Prickly Tree Fern	tF	Lm	Us

Fire-Retardant Plants for Large Gardens, Acreage Blocks, Parks and Farms

The following plants can be used in addition to the lists of plants for small and medium gardens.

Scientific Name	Common Name	Form	Fire Retardance	Comments
GYMNOSPERMS				
Araucariaceae				
Agathis robusta (-)	Qld Kauri	T	Lm	Pf - resin
Araucaria bidwillii (-)	Bunya Pine	T	Lm	Pf - resin
Araucaria cunninghamii	Hoop Pine	T	Lm	Pf - resin
Podocarpaceae				
Podocarpus elatus	Brown or Plum Pine	T	Lm	Pf - resin
MONOCOTYLEDONS				
Arecaceae (Palmae)				
Calamus muelleri	Lawyer Cane Vine	V	Lm	Sa Oa

Scientific Name	Common Name	Form	Fire Retardance	Comments
Flagellariaceae				
Flagellaria indica	Supplejack	V	Lm	Sa
Pandanaceae				
Freycinettia excelsa	Climbing Pandanus	V	Lm	Sa
Freycinettia scandens	Climbing Pandanus	V	Lm	Sa
Smilacaceae				
Ripogonum album	White Supplejack	V	Lm	Sa
Ripogonum brevifolium	Supplejack	V	Lm	Sa
Ripogonum discolor	Prickly Supplejack	V	Lm	Sa
Ripogonum elseyanum	Hairy Supplejack	V	Lm	Sa
DICOTYLEDONS				
Anacardiaceae				
Euroschinus falcata	Ribbonwood	T	Lm	Wb
Rhodosphaera rhodanthema	Deep Yellowwood	T	Lm	Wb
Annonaceae				
Melodorum leichhardtii				
(Rauwenhoffia l.)	Zig-Zag Vine	V	Lm	Sa
Apocynaceae				
Alstonia constricta	Quinine Tree	T	Lm	Wb
Melodinus acutiflorus	Merangarra	V	Lm	Sa
Melodinus australis	Southern Melodinus	V	Lm	Sa
Parsonsia eucalyptophylla	Gargaloo	V	Lm	Sa Oa
Parsonsia fulva	Furry Silkpod	V	Lm	Sa
Parsonsia lanceolata	Northern Silkpod	V	Lm	Sa
Parsonsia latifolia	Monkey Vine	V	Lm	Sa
Parsonsia straminea	Monkey Rope	V	Lm	Sa Oa
Parsonsia velutina	Velvet Silkood	V	Lm	Sa Oa
Parsonsia ventricosa	Pointed Silkpod	V	Lm	Sa
Arecaceae				
Calamus muelleri	Lawyer Cane	V	Lm	Sa
Araliaceae				
Cephalaralia cephalobotrys	Climbing Panax	V	Lm	Sa
Polyscias elegans	Celerywood	T	Lm	Wb/Ad Oa Sa
Polyscias murrayi	Pencil Cedar	T	Lm	Ad Oa Sa
Asclepiadaceae				
Marsdenia rostrata	Common Milk Vine	V	Lm	Sa
Atherospermataceae				
Daphnandra micrantha	Socketwood	T	Lm	Wb

Scientific Name	Common Name	Form	Fire Retardance	Comments
Avicenniaceae				
Avicennia marina	Grey Mangrove	T	Lm St	Oa Coastal
Burseraceae				
Canarium australasicum	Carrotwood	T	Lm	W b
Caesalpiniaceae				
Cassia marksiana (-)	Native Laburnum	T	Lm	W b
Caesalpinia bonduc	Caesalpinia	V	Lm	Sa
Caesalpinia scortechinii	Large Prickle Vine	V	Lm	Sa
Caesalpinia subtropica	Corky Prickle Vine	V	Lm	Sa
Celastraceae				
Celastrus australis	Staff Climber	V	Lm	Sa
Celastrus subspicatus	Large Staff Vine	V	Lm	Sa
Loeseneriella barbata				
(Hippocratea b.)	Knot Vine	V	Lm	Sa
Cunoniaceae				
Caldcluvia paniculosa	Rose-leaf Marara	T	Lm	W b
Ceratopetalum apetalum (-)	Coachwood	T	Lm	W b
Geissois benthamii	Red Carabeen	T	Lm	W b
Pseudoweinmannia				
lachnocarpa	Marara	T	Lm	W b
Schizomeria ovata	White Birch	T	Lm	Us/Wb
Ebenaceae				
Diospyros fasciculosa	Grey Ebony	T	Lm	W b
Diospyros pentamera	Myrtle Ebony	T	Lm	W b
Ehretiaceae				
Cordia dichotoma (-)	Cordia	T	Lm	W b
Ehretia acuminata	Koda	T	Lm	Ad De
Elaeocarpaceae				
Elaeocarpus eumundi	Eumundi Quandong	T	Lm	W b
Elaeocarpus grandis	Blue Quandong	T	Lm	W b
Elaeocarpus kirtonii	White Quandong	T	Lm	W b
Elaeocarpus obovatus	Hard Quandong	T	Lm	W b
Sloanea australis	Maiden's Blush	T	Lm	W b
Sloanea woollsii	Yellow Carabeen	T	Lm	W b
Escalloniaceae				
Quintinia verdonii	Grey Possumwood	T	Lm	W b
Euphorbiaceae				
Austrobuxus swainii (-)	Pink Cherry	T	Lm	W b
Baloghia inophylla (*B. lucida*)	Scrub Bloodwood	T	Lm	W b
Bridelia exaltata	Scrub Ironbark	T	Lm	W b
Bridelia leichhardtii	Leichhardt's Ironbark	T	Lm	W b
Claoxylon australe	Brittlewood	T	Lm	W b

Scientific Name	Common Name	Form	Fire Retardance	Comments
Dissiliaria baloghioides	Lancewood	T	Lm	Wb
Drypetes australasica	Yellow Tulip	T	Lm	Wb
Exocoecaria agallocha	Milky Mangrove	T	Lm St	Ad Coastal
Exocoecaria dallachyana	Scrub Poison Tree	T	Lm	Wb
Glochidion ferdinandi	Cheese Tree	T	Lm	Wb
Glochidion sumatranum	Buttonwood	T	Lm	Wb
Mallotus discolor	Yellow Kamala	T	Lm	Wb
Mallotus philippensis	Red Kamala	T	Lm	Wb
Fabaceae				
Austrosteenisia blackii	Blood Vine	V	Lm	Sa Oa
Castanospermum australe	Black Bean	T	Lm	Wb
Derris involuta	Native Derris	V	Lm	Sa
Erythrina sp. Lacey's Creek	Corkwood	T	Lm	Ad De
Erythrina vespertilio	Batswing Coral Tree	T	Lm	Ad De
Mucuna gigantea	Burny Bean	V	Lm	Sa
Flacourtiaceae				
Scolopia braunii	Flintwood	T	Lm	Wb
Flindersiaceae				
Flindersia australis	Crows Ash	T	Lm	Wb
Flindersia bennettiana	Bennett's Ash	T	Lm	Wb
Flindersia collina	Leopard Ash	T	Lm	Wb
Flindersia schottiana	Cudgerie or Bumpy Ash	T	Lm	Wb
Flindersia xanthoxyla	Yellowwood	T	Lm	Wb
Icacinaceae				
Citronella moorei	Churnwood	T	Lm	Wb
Pennantia cunninghamii	Brown Beech	T	Lm	Wb
Lauraceae				
Cryptocarya erythroxylon	Pigeonberry Ash	T	Lm	Wb
Cryptocarya hypospodia	Rib-fruit Pepperberry	T	Lm	Wb
Cryptocarya macdonaldii	Cooloola Laurel	T	Lm	Wb
Cryptocarya microneura	Murrogun	T	Lm	Wb
Cryptocarya obovata	Pepperberry Tree	T	Lm	Wb
Endiandra muelleri	Mueller's Walnut	T	Lm	Wb
Endiandra pubens	Hairy Walnut	T	Lm	Wb
Endiandra sieberi (-)	Hard Corkwood	T	Lm	Wb
Neolitsea australiensis	Grey Bolly Gum	T	Lm	Wb
Neolitsea dealbata	White Bolly Gum	T	Lm	Us/Wb
Malvaceae				
Hibiscus tiliaceus	Cotton Tree	T	Lm	Wb
Lagunaria patersonii (-)	Norfolk Is Hibiscus	T	Lm	Wb
Meliaceae				
Anthocarapa nitidula				
(Pseudocarapa nitidula)	Incense Cedar	T	Lm	Wb
Dysoxylum fraseranum	Rosewood	T	Lm	Wb

Scientific Name	Common Name	Form	Fire Retardance	Comments
Dysoxylum mollissimum				
ssp. molle (*D. muelleri*)	Red Bean	T	Lm	Wb
Dysoxylum rufum	Hairy Rosewood	T	Lm	Wb
Melia azedarach	White Cedar	T	Lm	Wb/Ad De
Owenia cepiodora	Onion Cedar	T	Lm	Wb
Toona australis	Red Cedar	T	Lm	Wb/Ad De
Menispermaceae				
Legnephora moorei	Wild Grape	V	Lm	Sa
Sarcopetalum harveyanum	Pearl Vine	V	Lm	Sa
Stephania aculeata	Prickly Snake Vine	V	Lm	Sa
Tinospora smilacina	Snake Vine	V	Lm	Sa
Tinospora tinosporoides	Arrow-head Vine	V	Lm	Sa
Mimosaceae				
Acacia aulacocarpa var.				
aulacocarpa	Hickory Wattle	T	Lm	Wb Pf
Acacia bakeri	Marblewood	T	Lm	Wb Pf
Acacia harpophylla (-)	Brigalow Wattle	T	Lm	Wb
Acacia melanoxylon	Blackwood	T	Lm	Wb Pf
Archidendron grandiflorum	Lace Flower	T	Lm	Wb
Monimiaceae				
Palmeria scandens	Anchor Vine	V	Lm	Sa
Moraceae				
Ficus macrophylla	Moreton Bay Fig	T	Lm	Wb
Ficus obliqua	Small-leafed Fig	T	Lm	Wb
Ficus platypoda	Rock Fig	T	Lm	Wb
Ficus superba var. henneana	Deciduous Fig	T	Lm	Ad De
Ficus virens var. sublanceolata	White Fig	T	Lm	Wb
Ficus watkinsiana	Nipple Fig	T	Lm	Wb
Maclura cochinchinensis				
(*Cudrania c.*)	Cockspur Thorn	V	Lm	Oa Sa
Malaisia scandens	Burny Vine	V	Lm	Sa
Myrtaceae				
Acmena hemilampra	Blush Satinash	V	Lm	Wb
Acmena ingens				
(*A. brachyandra*)	Red Apple	V	Lm	Wb
Acmena smithii	Creek Lilly Pilly	T	Lm	Wb
Lophostemon confertus	Brush Box	T	Lm	Wb
Syncarpia glomulifera	Turpentine	T	Lm	Wb
Syzygium australe	Scrub Cherry	T	Lm	Wb
Syzygium corynanthum	Sour cherry	T	Lm	Wb
Syzygium crebrinerve	Purple Cherry	T	Lm	Wb
Syzygium moorei (-)	Durobby	T	Lm	Wb
Nyctaginaceae				
Pisonia aculeata	Native Bougainvillea	V	Lm	Sa

Scientific Name	Common Name	Form	Fire Retardance	Comments
Oleaceae				
Olea paniculata	Native Olive	T	Lm	W b
Piperaceae				
Piper novae-hollandiae	Native Pepper Vine	V	Lm	Sa
Pittosporaceae				
Pittosporum rhombifolium	Hollywood	T	Lm	W b
Proteaceae				
Floydia praealta	Ball Nut	T	Lm	W b
Grevillea hilliana (-)	Hill's Silky Oak	T	Lm	Pf
Grevillea robusta	Silky Oak	T	Lm	Pf
Helicia glabriflora	Smooth Helicia	T	Lm	Pf
Macadamia integrifolia	Queensland Nut	T	Lm	W b
Macadamia ternifolia	Maroochy Nut	T	Lm	W b
Macadamia tetraphylla (-)	Rough-shell Bush Nut	T	Lm	W b
Oriocallis pinnata (-)	Pink Silky Oak	T	Lm	Pf
Oriocallis wickhamii (-)	Satin Oak	T	Lm	Pf
(Alloxylon flammeum)				
Stenocarpus salignus (-)	Scrub Beefwood	T	Lm	Pf
Stenocarpus sinuatus	Wheel of Fire Tree	T	Lm	W b
Ranunculaceae				
Clematis aristata	Old Man's Beard	V	Lm	Sa
Rhamnaceae				
Alphitonia excelsa	Red Ash	T	Lm	W b
Alphitonia petrei	Pink Ash	T	Lm	W b
Emmenosperma				
alphitonioides	Yellow Ash	T	Lm	W b
Rosaceae				
Rubus moluccanus	Molucca Bramble	V	Lm	Sa
Rutaceae				
Acronychia oblongifolia	White Lilly Pilly	S/T	Lm	W b
Acronychia suberosa	Corky Acronychia	T	Lm	W b
Sarcomelicope simplicifolia	Bauerella	T	Lm	W b
Sapindaceae				
Alectryon reticulatus	Alectryon	T	Lm	W b
Arytera lautererana	Corduroy Tamarind	T	Lm	W b
Atalaya multiflora	Broad-leaf Whitewood	T	Lm	W b
Atalaya salicifolia (A. virens)	Scrub Whitewood	T	Lm	W b
Castanospora aphanandi (-)	Brown Tamarind	T	Lm	W b
Cupaniopsis anacardioides	Tuckeroo	T	Lm	W b
Cupaniopsis flagelliformis (-)	Brown Tuckeroo	S/T	Lm	W b
Diploglottis campbellii (-)	Small-leaf Tamarind	T	Lm	W b
Diploglottis cunninghamii	Native Tamarind	T	Lm	Wb/Ad
Harpullia hillii	Blunt-leaf Tulip	T	Lm	W b
Harpullia pendula	Tulipwood	T	Lm	W b

Scientific Name	Common Name	Form	Fire Retardance	Comments
Jagera pseudorhus	Foam Bark Tree	T	Lm	Wb
Mischocarpus anodontus	Veiny Pear-fruit	T	Lm	Wb
Mischocarpus pyriformis	Yellow Pear-fruit	T	Lm	Wb
Rhysotoechia bifoliolata (-)	Twin-leaf Tuckeroo	T	Lm	Wb
Sarcopteryx stipata	Corduroy	T	Lm	Wb
Toechima dasyrrhache	Blunt-leaf Steelwood	T	Lm	Wb
Sapotaceae				
Amorphospermum antilogum	Brown Pearwood	T	Lm	Wb
Amorphospermum whitei (-)	Rusty Plum	T	Lm	Wb
Planchonella australis	Black Apple	T	Lm	Wb
Planchonella laurifolia (-)	Blush Coondoo	T	Lm	Wb
Planchonella pohlmaniana	Yellow Boxwood	T	Lm	Wb
Simaroubaceae				
Ailanthus triphysa	White Siris	T	Lm	Wb
Guilfoylia monostylis	Native Plum	T	Lm	Wb
Siphonodontaceae				
Siphonodon australis	Ivorywood	T	Lm	Wb
Sterculiaceae				
Argyrodendron actinophyllum	Black Booyong	T	Lm	Wb
Argyrodendron trifoliolatum	Brown Tulip Oak	T	Lm	Wb
Brachychiton acerifolius	Flame Tree	T	Lm	Ad De
Brachychiton discolor	Lace Bark	T	Lm	Ad De
Brachychiton populneus	Kurrajong	T	Lm	Wb
Brachychiton rupestris (-)	Qld Bottletree	T	Lm	Ad De
Brachychiton sp. (-)	Ormeau Bottletree	T	Lm	Ad De
Commersonia bartramia	Brown Kurrajong	T	Lm	Us/Wb
Sterculia quadrifida	Peanut Tree	T	Lm	Ad De
Symplocaceae				
Symplocos stawelli	White Hazelwood	T	Lm	Wb
Ulmaceae				
Aphananthe philippinensis	Native Elm	T	Lm	Wb
Celtis paniculata	Investigator Tree	T	Lm	Wb
Urticaceae				
Dendrocnide excelsa	Giant Stinging Tree	T	Lm	Wb
Dendrocnide photinophylla	Mulberry Stinger	T	Lm	Wb
Verbenaceae				
Gmelina leichhardtii	White Beech	T	Lm	Wb
Premna lignum-vitae	Lignum-vitae	T	Lm	Wb
Vitaceae				
Cissus antarctica	Kangaroo Vine	V	Lm	Wb
Cissus hypoglauca	Five-leaf Watervine	V	Lm	Wb
Cissus sterculiifolia	Long-leaf Watervine	V	Lm	Wb
Tetrastigma nitens	Shining Grape	V	Lm	Wb

Mangroves - nurseries for our fisheries (JB)

APPENDIX **11**

Contacts for Environmental Problems

People to Contact for Help with Environmental Problems

People in the community are often involved with wildlife care. The list of animal carers changes from time to time but information as to whom to call locally can be obtained from the Department of Environment and Heritage (3202 0200) and from the Pine Rivers Shire Council's Environment Services (3205 0642).

PROBLEM	NAME	CONTACT NO.
All native animals	Dept of Environment	3202 0200 (D.E.H.)
Koalas	Moggill Koala Hospital	3202 0200 (D.E.H.)
Rubbish, Recycling	Waste Management	3205 0776 (Council)
EPA, Noise, Vermin, Vectors Noxious Weeds, Barking Dogs	Community Response	3205 0693 (Council)
Snakes etc.	Queensland Museum	3840 7635
Tree Preservation	Environmental Services	3205 0642 (Council)

The bush can be retained (PRSC)

APPENDIX **12**

Bibliography and Further Reading

Australian Plants

Australian Native Plants, J. Wrigley & M. Fagg; Reed Books, 35 Cotham Rd Few, Victoria 3101

Australian Rainforest Plants, Parts 1, 2, 3 & 4, N. & H. Nicholson; Terania Rainforest Nursery, The Channon, NSW 2480

Australian Ferns and Fern Allies, D Jones & S. Clemesha; A. H. & A. W. Reed Pty Ltd 53 Myoora Rd, Terrey Hills Sydney NSW 2084

Australian Climbing Plants, D. Jones & B. Gray; A. H. & A. W. Reed Pty Ltd 53 Myoora Rd, Terrey Hills Sydney NSW 2084

Bringing Back The Bush, J Bradley; Ure Smith Press 372 Eastern Valley Way, Willoughby, NSW 2068

Bush Regeneration, Recovering Australian Landscapes, R. Buchanan; TAFE Student Learning Publications. Level 14, McKell Building, Rawson Place, Sydney NSW 2000

Extinct and Endangered Plants of Australia, J. Leigh, R. Boden & J. Briggs; The Macmillan Company of Australia, 107 Moray St, Sth Melbourne

Fragments Of Green, An Identification Field Guide for Rainforest Plants of the Greater Brisbane Area, J. Hauser; Rainforest Conservation Society 19 Colorado Av Bardon, Q 4065

Grow What Wet, The Australian Plant Study Group; Thomas Nelson Publishing Group 480 Latrobe Street Melbourne V 3000

Mangroves Of Australia, R. Lear & T. Turner; University Of Qld Press; St. Lucia Q 4067

Planting A Native Garden, J. Sked; Pine Rivers Society For Growing Australian Plants. PO Box 41 Lawnton Q 4501

Planting A Native Garden, Jan Sked; Pine Rivers Branch of the Society for Growing Australian Plants. P.O. Box 41 Lawnton Q 4501.

Rainforest Plants In Australia, D. Jones; Reed Books Pty Ltd 2 Aquatic Drive Frenchs Forest NSW 2086

The Flora of the Pine Rivers Valley, Jan Sked; Pine Rivers Branch of the Society for Growing Australian Plants. P.O. Box 41 Lawnton Q 4501.

Think Trees Grow Trees, Dept of Arts, Heritage and Environment in association with the Institute of Foresters of Australia; Australian Government Publishing Service, Canberra

Wildflowers Of The Noosa - Cooloola Area, A. Harold; Noosa Parks Association, Environment Centre PO Box 836 Noosa Heads 4567

Wild Flowers Of Bribie Island, I. MacRae; Bribie Island Environmental Protection Society; PO Box 350 Bribie Island Q 4507

Water Plants in Australia, G. Sainty & S. Jacobs; Sainty and Associates, 2/1B Darley St Darlinghurst NSW 2010

Wildlife and Gardens

A Garden of Birds, Attracting Birds To Australian Gardens, G. Pizzey; Collins Angus & Robertson Publishers 4 Eden Park, 31 Waterloo Rd North Ryde NSW 2113

Birdscaping Your Garden, G. Adams; Rigby Publishers 372 Eastern Valley Way, Chatswood NSW 2067

Dinkum Gardening, T. Low; Greening Australia - Qld; PO Box 9868 Brisbane Q 4001

Earthworms For Gardeners and Fishermen, K. Handreck, & K. Lee; CSIRO

Geological History

Australia - Evolution of a Continent,

Rocks and Landscapes of Brisbane and Ipswich, W. Willmott & N. Stevens; Geological Society of Australia (Qld Division) PO Box 1820 Brisbane Q 4001

Aboriginal and Pioneer History

Aboriginal Pathways In South-east Queensland and The Richmond River, J. Steele; University of Qld Press, St Lucia 4067.

Archaeology of the Dreamtime, J Flood; Angus & Robertson, 25 Ryde Road, Pymble, Sydney NSW 2073

Brisbane's Back Door - The story of the D'Aguilar Range, H. Horton; Booralong Publications, 12 Brookes Street, Bowen Hills, Brisbane Qld 4006

Brisbane Town In Convict Days 1824 - 1842, J. Steele; University of Queensland Press Box 42, St Lucia Q 4067

From Spear & Musket 1879 - 1979, Caboolture Shire Council, Caboolture Q 4510

Historical Sketch of Queensland, W. Traill; (First Pub. 1886); Landsdowne Press, 176 South Creek Road, Dee Why West, NSW 2099

Murrumba Downs 1823 - 1991, J. Lewis; Booralong Publications, 12 Brookes Street, Bowen Hills, Brisbane Qld 4006

The Explorers of the Moreton Bay District 1770 - 1830, J Steele; University of Qld Press, St Lucia 4067

The History of Albany Creek, Bridgeman Downs and Eaton's Hill, D. Teague; Colonial Press, Brisbane

Through The Eyes of Thomas Pamphlett - Convict and Castaway, C. Pearce; Booralong Publications, 12 Brookes Street, Bowen Hills, Brisbane Qld 4006

Tom Petrie's Reminiscences of Early Queensland, C. Campbell Petrie; Lloyd O'Neil Pty Ltd 19 Hornby Street, Windsor, V 2756

Tracks and Times - A History of the Pine Rivers District, L. Smith (Ed); Pine Rivers Shire Council, Strathpine Q 4500

Enviroment

Water Quality, J. Simpson and P. Oliver; Australian Water & Wastewater Association Inc., PO Box 388 Artarmon, NSW 2064

Saving Australia - A Blueprint For Our Survival, V. Serventy; Child & Associates, 5 Skyline Pl., Frenchs Forest, NSW 2086

Save Our Earth, K. Smith; Christopher Beck Books, 40 George St., Brisbane 4000.

These beautiful sedimentary rocks were deposited in freshwater lakes and swamps about 50 million years ago. Warner/Cashmere   (PRSC)